ELECTORAL VIOLENCE, CORRUPTION, AND POLITICAL ORDER

Electoral Violence, Corruption, and Political Order

Sarah Birch

PRINCETON UNIVERSITY PRESS

PRINCETON AND OXFORD

Published by Princeton University Press
41 William Street, Princeton, New Jersey 08540
6 Oxford Street, Woodstock, Oxfordshire OX20 1TR

press.princeton.edu

ISBN 978-0-691-20363-8
ISBN (pbk.) 978-0-691-20362-1
ISBN (e-book) 978-0-691-20364-5

British Library Cataloging-in-Publication Data is available

Editorial: Hannah Paul and Josh Drake
Production Editorial: Jenny Wolkowicki
Cover design: Chris Ferrante
Production: Brigid Ackerman
Publicity: Kate Farquhar-Thomson and Kate Hensley
Copyeditor: Maia Vaswani

Cover image: iStock

This book has been composed in Adobe Text and Gotham

Printed on acid-free paper. ∞

Printed in the United States of America

10 9 8 7 6 5 4 3 2 1

CONTENTS

ILLUSTRATIONS

Figures

Tables

Violence is perhaps the worst thing that can happen in an election. Voting is meant to be a tool of democracy—a fair and above all peaceful means of resolving differences. When force intrudes into the electoral process, something has gone profoundly wrong. Yet a surprising number of elections around the world are marred by violent conflict of some kind. The challenge addressed in this study is how electoral violence is to be explained and how it might be prevented. Though not by any means intended as the last word on the topic, the analyses presented here go a considerable way toward conceptualizing the problem, synthesizing what we already know about it, and developing a novel theoretical approach to understanding where and under what circumstances the electoral peace is likely to be disturbed.

The book is the culmination of a four-year research project that began in 2015, but the origins of the project go back to the late 1990s, when I met Jeff Fischer in Bosnia while we were both involved in efforts to improve electoral administration. It was Jeff who focused my mind on the topic of electoral violence and cajoled me into undertaking research on it, and it is to him that I owe my principal intellectual obligation. My second main debt is to David Muchlinski, who provided me with research assistance between 2015 and 2017 and has been a close collaborator throughout the period during which this manuscript was drafted.

I am very grateful to Sead Alihodzic, Inken von Borzyskowski, Jeffrey Carlson, Jonas Claes, Ursula Daxecker, Kristine Höglund, Niall McCann, Vasu Mohan, Pippa Norris, Rubén Ruiz-Rufino, Emre Toros, and Michael Wahman for helping me to understand the problem of electoral violence and for providing feedback on portions of the analyses that came together to form this monograph. Hannah Paul at Princeton University Press has also been extremely helpful in offering encouragement and keeping the book on the right track, and the book's two anonymous reviewers are to be thanked for providing very useful comments on an earlier draft. I would also like to thank Maia Vaswani for superb copyediting. In addition my gratitude is due to the University of Glasgow and to King's College London for supporting me while I was working on this project, and to the Economic and Social Research Council for Research Grant ES/L016435, which funded the bulk of the research that contributed to this study. Needless to say, I retain full responsibility for any errors of fact and interpretation herein.

Sarah Birch
June 2019

1

Introduction

In 2001 the populist Thaksin Shinawatra came to power in Thailand, vowing to reform the country's corrupt political system. His period of rule was characterized by heightened political tension, repression, and human rights violations. During this time, elections changed from being opportunities for power brokering among provincial bosses to high-stakes contests between the ruthless president and his opponents (Kongkirati 2014). The 2001 and 2005 Thai elections resulted in 26 and 30 deaths respectively, a dramatic increase from the pre-2001 period when election-related fatalities were rare (Callahan 2000; Callahan and McCargo 1996; Kongkirati 2014; McCargo and Desatová 2016). The aim of this book is to develop an enhanced understanding of the causes of electoral violence such as that witnessed in Thailand, and to assess strategies best suited to preventing conflict from disrupting the vote. In recent decades, more countries have begun to hold elections, but many of these events have been beset by the use of force, which undermines states' core economic, social, and political functions. In some contexts elections have helped to move nascent democracies toward accountable participatory modes of governance, whereas in other settings the democratic potential of elections has been distorted by manipulation and the use of coercion. In the aftermath of the Kenyan polls of 2007, an estimated 1133 people died, 3561 were injured, and 350,000 were displaced (CIPEV 2008). The Côte d'Ivoire election of 2010 led to conflict that killed an estimated 3000 people and displaced a million in late 2010 and early 2011 (Bekoe 2012a). At least 400 people were killed during the 2014 elections in

Bangladesh, a figure which is not atypical for this country (Macdonald 2016; cf. Akhter 2001), and close to 200 died in a series of violent attacks that took place in the run-up to the Pakistani election of 2018 (EU 2018). A recent surge in studies of electoral misconduct has gone some way toward helping scholars and practitioners to understand many forms of electoral manipulation, but scholarship on electoral violence is somewhat more fragmentary, with the majority of existing studies focusing on individual states or regions.

There is reason to believe that electoral violence is a serious global problem. The available data suggest that globally approximately 88 percent of elections in the 1995–2013 period were afflicted by one or more politically motivated, violent attacks during the electoral cycle. Moreover, electoral violence is not confined to fragile democracies and authoritarian states. Even established democracies are not immune to conflictual elections, as evidenced by the clashes between far-right and antiracist groups that took place at campaign events in the run-up to the 2019 European Parliament elections in the United Kingdom, the pipe bombs posted to prominent political figures in advance of the 2018 US midterm election, and the violence that broke out during and after the controversial Catalan independence vote of 2017.

Why are elections in some places generally peaceful, whereas other societies regularly experience conflictual polls? Why is one election in a country peaceful and the next violent? This book aims to provide a comprehensive account of the use of force to manipulate competitive electoral processes, with a particular emphasis on national-level elections held during peacetime in the post–Second World War period. The focus of analysis is on the strategic behavior of incumbent and opposition actors—also referred to here as state and nonstate actors—with particular (but not exclusive) emphasis on electoral authoritarian and hybrid states.[1] Some previous analyses have argued that opposition groups and other actors outside the state are those

1. The terms "incumbent" and "state" actors will largely be used interchangeably throughout this study, as will "opposition" and "nonstate." In some cases it will be necessary to distinguish between state actors who are autonomous and partisan incumbents (for example, autonomous electoral administrators or courts), but in the political contexts assessed here, politicization of the state is common, so in most electoral contexts "state" actors are effectively coextensive with political "incumbents." Where this is not the case, attention will be drawn to relevant distinctions. Nonstate actors always include many groups and individuals who are not part of the formal opposition, and this will be acknowledged where relevant, but in the context of electoral violence, actors not allied with incumbents tend to be the targets of violence, so for broad analytic purposes the state:nonstate::incumbent:opposition relationship is valid. There will of course be numerous occasions on which it will make sense to make more finely grained distinctions, and when this is the case the discussion will adopt appropriate language that reflects the nuances of particular situations.

most likely to undertake salient forms of electoral violence (e.g. Collier and Vicente 2012, 2014; Daxecker 2012). However, the data collected for this study suggest that across the globe, the majority of electoral violence is committed by state actors, and there are strong theoretical reasons to believe that the settings in which force is employed during electoral processes are shaped mainly by the state. The analyses presented here will frame electoral violence in terms of the incentives inherent in power structures of different types and will seek to ascertain the circumstances under which these institutions allow violence to occur, as well as the ways in which violence interacts with other forms of electoral manipulation. An argument is developed about electoral violence as a tool for regulating political exclusion, which is then tested on a range of quantitative and qualitative data from around the world using estimation techniques that enable the analysis of cross-sectional and longitudinal predictors of electoral violence simultaneously. The investigation also assesses the most efficacious approaches that can be taken by internal and external actors to mitigate this phenomenon.

Context and Argument

Peaceful, democratic elections are central to a fair society. Elections are institutions that establish a means of gaining power and legitimacy. But there are many ways in which competitive elections can be won: through open competition on the basis of alternative policy proposals, by means of vote buying and other types of electoral manipulation, or through the use of force. This volume provides a general investigation of the circumstances under which political actors will select combinations of these options.

Though the study of electoral violence remains underdeveloped, the problem is receiving increasing attention from students of comparative politics. Acts of peacetime violence have been the subject of human rights research for over 30 years now (Mitchell and McCormick 1988; Poe and Tate 1994), where the focus has been primarily on the violations of rights to physical integrity. More recently a number of scholars have considered the relationship between political violence, civil conflict, and the holding of elections.[2] There have also been a number of studies devoted specifically to

---

2. Askoy 2014; Bakke and Wibbels 2006; Birnir and Gohdes 2018; Brancati and Snyder 2012; Cederman, Gleditsch, and Hug 2012, 2013; Cheibub and Hayes 2017; Collier 2009; Condra et al. 2018; Flores and Nooruddin 2012, 2016, 2018; Goldsmith 2015; Harish and Little 2017; Harish and Toha 2018; Mansfield and Snyder 2005; Matanock 2017a, b; Salehyan and Linebarger 2015; J. Snyder 2000; Steele 2011.

violence that is directed at the electoral process itself, which is the topic of this study. Much of the existing empirical research has sought to identify the range of factors associated with electoral violence. These have been found by scholars to include socioeconomic variables, such as economic development and/or inequality,[3] and ethnic divisions or inequalities across ethnic groups.[4] Also found in many studies to be relevant are political factors such as competitive dynamics and closeness of the race,[5] electoral integrity,[6] electoral and other political institutions,[7] level of democracy,[8] informal institutions,[9] and international election observation.[10] A history of conflict has likewise been linked in several studies to levels of conflict in elections.[11] Other work has considered the timing of violence.[12] A further strand of research on electoral violence has focused on the actors involved, including strategies of mobilization and demobilization.[13] Despite the recent surge of interest in the interactions between electoral processes and conflict processes, much work remains to be done in this emergent subfield, given that there are also many questions left unanswered by these analyses, as well as findings that would profit from testing in a wider context.

3. Boone 2011; Boone and Kriger 2012; Fjelde and Höglund 2016; Klaus and Mitchell 2015; Salehyan and Linebarger 2015; Sisk 2012.

4. Brosché, Fjelde, and Höglund 2020; Claes 2016; Fjelde and Höglund 2016; Klaus and Mitchell 2015; Kuhn 2015; Mochtak 2018a; Mueller 2011, 2012; Wilkinson 2004; Wilkinson and Haid 2009.

5. Asunka et al. 2017; Claes 2016; Collier and Vicente 2014; Goldring and Wahman 2018; Hafner-Burton, Hyde, and Jablonski 2014; Höglund 2009; Salehyan and Linebarger 2015; C. Taylor, Pevehouse, and Straus 2017; Wilkinson 2004.

6. Boone and Kriger 2012; Dercon and Guttiérez-Romero 2012; Höglund 2009; Höglund, Jarstad, and Söderberg Kovacs 2009; Opitz, Fjelde, and Höglund 2013; Reilly 2011; Salehyan and Linebarger 2015.

7. Alesina, Piccolo, and Pinotti 2018; Burchard 2015; Claes 2016; Daxecker 2020; Fjelde 2020; Fjelde and Höglund 2016; Höglund 2009; Malik 2018; Reilly 2001; Wilkinson 2004.

8. Burchard 2015; Fjelde and Höglund 2016; Klaus and Mitchell 2015; Norris, Frank, and Martínez i Coma 2015; Salehyan and Linebarger 2015.

9. Alesina, Picollo, and Pinotti 2018; Berenschot 2018a; Boone 2011; Boone and Kriger 2012; Burchard 2015; Fjelde and Höglund 2016; Höglund 2009; Mares and Young 2016; Mueller 2011, 2012; Sisk 2012.

10. Asunka et al. 2017; Daxecker 2012; Smidt 2016.

11. Borzyskowski 2019; Harish and Toha 2018; Höglund, Jarstad, and Söderberg Kovacs 2009; Mueller 2012; Van Ham and Lindberg 2015; Wilkinson 2004.

12. Bhasin and Gandhi 2013; Davenport 1997; Hafner-Burton, Hyde, and Jablonski 2014; Straus and Taylor 2012.

13. Asunka et al. 2017; Bhasin and Gandhi 2013; Chaturvedi 2005; Christensen and Utas 2008; Collier and Vicente 2012, 2014; Hafner-Burton, Hyde, and Jablonski 2014, 2018; LeBas 2006; Straus and Taylor 2012; Young 2017.

Two of the main areas that would benefit from more extensive investigation are the power structures most conducive to electoral violence in a society in general, and the role of violence in the arsenal of strategies at the disposal of those involved in particular electoral contests that take place in that society. Though a number of previous analyses have touched on these topics, they have mostly either been based on individual case studies or regional investigations, or been large-N comparisons designed to ascertain general trends rather than to probe context-specific strategies. By drawing on a range of data sources and employing a variety of methods, this study develops and tests a novel integrated theory of electoral violence that links and elaborates on a number of propositions about the contextual determinants of this phenomenon. It also goes beyond existing work in shedding new light on the impact of interventions intended to reduce electoral conflict.

I start from the proposition that political violence is a tool for regulating political exclusion, and that when weak democratic institutions are combined with dysfunctional informal institutions, the scene is set for violent elections. The corollary of this argument is that violence can be avoided if democratic and/or informal institutions are so configured as to provide leaders with the incentives and the means to limit themselves to alternative electoral strategies. Let us unpack these claims. Violence is used by state actors (and their proxies) mainly as a tool to exclude other actors from political power in competitive elections, and violence is used by nonstate actors largely as a means of contesting such exclusion and seeking access to power. Elections are high-stakes affairs in states with weak democratic institutions and strong informal institutions of clientelism, patronage, and corruption. In such contexts, those in power control economic and legal as well as political resources, such that incumbents have ample reason to fear loss of power. In addition, they have reason to fear that if they lose a crucial election they will themselves be permanently excluded from ruling, as the victors may be reluctant to allow genuinely competitive contests in future. Political orders characterized by high levels of corruption and ineffectual democratic institutions are therefore ones that are strongly conducive to electoral violence. If electoral violence is largely a function of the way power is structured in different political orders, it follows that violence will no longer be such a viable strategy when corruption falls and democratic institutions are strengthened.

But if the structure of power determines whether violence is a viable electoral strategy, the use of force is only ever one of several tools that can be employed to regulate exclusion in the electoral sphere. The second core component of my argument is that violence is typically used in order to backstop other types of electoral manipulation. When there are insufficient disincentives to the use of force, state actors will most commonly use it as a means of supplementing and supporting electoral misconduct (the manipulation of electoral rules and procedures), as these are both cost-effective tools that state actors have at their disposal. Lacking access to misconduct, nonstate actors will often react by coupling the use of violence with vote buying and by seeking to use violence as a mobilizational device.

When force is used to skew electoral processes, this has a number of serious consequences for the political and social lives of the polities in question. Electoral violence remains a persistent obstacle to democratic consolidation; it can also have destabilizing effects on economic and political institutions (Alihodzic 2012; GCEDS 2012; Staniland 2014). The most obvious impact of electoral violence is the effect it has on elections themselves, undermining democratic decision making and potentially altering outcomes (Hafner-Burton, Hyde, and Jablonski 2018; Hickman 2009; Wilkinson and Haid 2009). Rather than being times of intense collective deliberation and discussion, elections can come to be viewed by the citizenry and the political elite alike as periods of attentive fear, which does not even appear in most cases to enhance levels of political knowledge (Söderström 2017). Evidence suggests that voters are strongly averse to the use of force in elections (Bratton 2008; Gutiérrez-Romero and LeBas 2020; Rosenzweig 2016), and voter concerns about electoral violence can, under certain circumstances, depress both turnout and support for democracy (Bratton 2008; Bekoe and Burchard 2017; Burchard 2015, 2018; Condra et al. 2018; Höglund and Piyarathne 2009; Gutiérrez-Romero and LeBas 2020). Commenting on the Filipino case, Patino and Velasco noted the effect of violence on citizen attitudes toward democracy: "In areas where violence is not an issue, voters choose among the best performers. Where violence proliferates, voters either cast their vote in view of ensuring their survival, or stay away from elections altogether. With violence and fraud, election loses credibility as a democratic exercise" (2004, 9). There is, in addition, evidence that electoral violence can alter the behavior of politicians. Alesina, Piccolo, and Pinotti (2018) found that in Italy the election-related use of force by organized crime syndicates impacted on politicians' willingness to discuss organized crime in the legislature. And it can under certain circumstances shape citizen attitudes, affecting in-group and out-group identifications (Gutiérrez-Romero 2014; Ishiyama, Gomez, and Stewart 2016; Wilkinson and Haid 2009).

Electoral violence can also lead to other types of instability. Several authors have shown that elections held in the wake of armed conflict can (re)activate political cleavages and stoke explosive unrest (Brancati and Snyder 2012; Chacón, Robinson, and Torvik 2011; Flores and Nooruddin 2012, 2016; J. Snyder 2000). This happened, for example, in Angola, where the 1992 election result prompted Jonas Savimbi and his National Union for the Total Independence of Angola (UNITA) movement to reignite a simmering civil conflict (Bratton and Van de Walle 1997; Fischer 2002; UNDP 2009). A similar process was observed in Congo (Brazzaville) in the mid-1990s, where electoral disputes sparked civil war (Fleischhacker 1999), and in Burundi where the country descended into civil war following the fraught 2015 elections (Söderberg Kovacs 2018). The use of force during elections is therefore a problem with wide ramifications for regime stability and political development.

Definition and Typology

Though citizens in contemporary democracies tend to associate elections with the peaceful resolution of political differences, violence has long lurked in the shadows of electoral processes. In nineteenth-century England, parties hired bands of ruffians to intimidate the supporters of their rivals (Tilly 1978). Mid-nineteenth-century Ireland saw priests attacked for seeking to exert electoral pressure on their parishioners (Hoppen 1996). Argentinean elections in the late nineteenth century were so violent that virtually all voters went armed to the polls and businesses closed for several days in advance of voting (Alonso 1996), while in early twentieth-century Costa Rica, President Ascención Esquivel at one point jailed a third of all electors in order to prevent them from exercising their franchise (Lehoucq 2004). In the 1960s, violent attacks were used to obstruct voter registration campaigns in the US Deep South following the full legal enfranchisement of African-Americans through the 1965 Voting Rights Act (L. McDonald 2003). And in contemporary Italy, force is used by organized criminal groups to sway electoral results (Alesina, Piccolo and Pinotti 2018).

WHAT IS ELECTORAL VIOLENCE?

Staniland (2014) noted that electoral violence suffers from poor conceptualization in the literature, with different authors meaning different things by the term. It therefore makes sense to start with an attempt to cut through the conceptual underbrush and map out what is intended by "electoral violence" and how the varieties of this phenomenon are conceptually related.

Force is used both strategically and nonstrategically in electoral contexts (Burchard 2015). This study will be concerned mainly with the strategic, or instrumental, use of violence in order to achieve desired ends. Not only is instrumental force more amenable to theorizing and analysis, it is also the case that eruptions of electoral violence that appear spontaneous are often in fact the result of strategic calculations by actors (Wilkinson 2004; Wilkinson and Haid 2009).

For the purpose of this investigation, electoral violence includes political violence that takes place during the electoral cycle and is linked causally to electoral processes, or, more formally, *coercive force, directed toward electoral actors and/or objects, that occurs in connection with electoral competition,* where "coercive force" includes *threats, unlawful detention, forcible curtailment of movement or displacement, and attacks that cause actual bodily harm.* The terms "electoral violence" and "electoral conflict" will be used interchangeably in this study.

It is worth commenting on a plausible objection to this definition: it incorporates all violence connected to the electoral process and involving electoral actors that occurs during the electoral period, regardless of whether the *stated* motive of the perpetrator was to interfere with the electoral process. Given that at election time the range of electoral actors is extensive, this might appear to be an overexpansive definition. The justification for casting the definitional net wide is that, regardless of intent, violence that occurs in the context of an election is likely to impinge on the election in some way, by shaping expectations of political processes, or by altering perceptions of relevant actors. Moreover, given that one can never be sure of the intention of the perpetrator of an act, it is more practical to specify the political relevance of that act with regard to its likely effect on the political process. Ursula Daxecker maintains that most forms of collective violence that occur during the electoral period have political motives (Daxecker 2014; cf. EC-UNDP Joint Task Force on Electoral Assistance 2011), but it is sufficient for our purposes to argue that they will in all probability *affect* the electoral process in some way. Finally, if we acknowledge that virtually all forms of collective violence in a society are likely to be affected by the electoral process, it is also necessary to recognize that the electoral process is bound to be affected by political conflict that is endemic in a society. The approach adopted here thus relies on both a temporal and a causal link between elections and violence, in keeping with other definitions of this phenomenon that have been offered in the literature.[14] It is, however, worth noting what this definition does *not* include: it does not encompass ordinary criminal activity that takes place during the electoral process, or opportunistic violence that may take place in the aftermath of elections as citizens take advantage of the postelectoral political hiatus to plunder and settle scores.[15]

As will be detailed at greater length in chapter 2, strategic violence typically includes the obstruction of some aspect of the electoral process, actions whose aim is instilling fear, or protest. This can involve efforts:

- to prevent people from contesting elections (through threats and intimidation, arbitrary detention, or incapacitating physical attacks, including murder)
- to disrupt electoral campaigns (through threats and intimidation, forcible interference in campaign activities, destruction of campaign materials, or incapacitating physical attacks on activists and supporters)
- to prevent people from voting (through threats and intimidation, displacement, disrupting of polling)
- to prevent aggrieved parties from pursuing legal challenges to declared electoral results or to impede public protests against fraudulent elections
- to impede the conduct of elections (through attacks on polling places, polling staff, or polling materials, or threats and intimidation)
- to protest against electoral irregularities.

In this sense, violence is generally designed to lock selected actors out of the benefits of open electoral competition or to protest against exclusion attempts of this type. Less commonly, violence is used in order to force people to vote and/or force them to support a particular candidate/party, though a survey of existing studies of electoral violence suggests that this is unusual as ballot secrecy raises the cost of monitoring compliance.[16]

14. See, for example, Birch and Muchlinski (2019), Daxecker (2014), Höglund (2009), Söderberg Kovacs (2018), and Straus and Taylor (2012).

15. I thank an anonymous reviewer for encouraging me to think through this aspect of my definition.

16. An example of the use of violence to alter vote choice comes from Sierra Leone, where Christensen and Utas documented self-reports from the perpetrators of violence of their aims. One informant explained his motives as follows: "You know, we have to make people understand how to vote. We have so many illiterates, they know nothing about politics and they don't know their rights. Their understanding is slow. That's why we tell them how to vote. . . . [I]t's like sensitization. If we don't do it by force they will never understand. I am fed up with violence, but for now I am

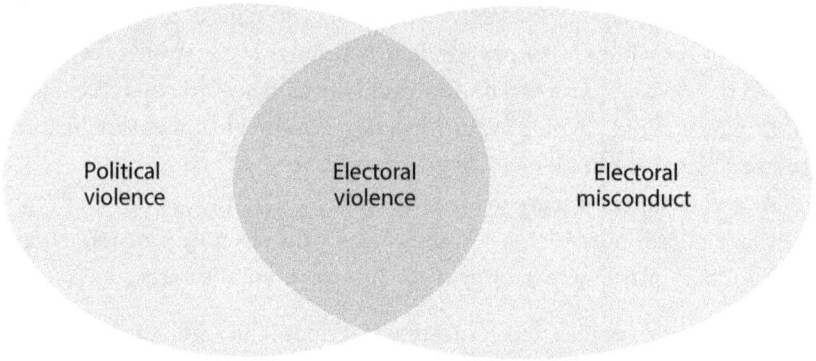

FIGURE 1.1. Electoral violence and electoral misconduct

VARIETIES OF ELECTORAL VIOLENCE

In order better to categorize electoral violence, it makes sense to situate it in terms of other political concepts. Conceptually, electoral violence is located at the intersection of electoral misconduct and political violence. Electoral misconduct, also known as electoral malpractice, is "the manipulation of electoral processes and outcomes so as to substitute personal or partisan benefit for the public interest" (Birch 2011, 14). It takes both violent and nonviolent forms, though it is most often nonviolent. Most but not all forms of political violence that take place during the electoral period constitute electoral violence, and some but not all electoral misconduct is violent (see figure 1.1).

For the purposes of analysis, it is convenient to subdivide electoral violence directed at people into threats and coercion on the one hand, and attacks causing actual bodily harm (lethal or nonlethal) on the other. Threats and coercion interfere directly with the electoral process by depriving people of their political rights and impeding their ability to take part freely in electoral (and other) activities. Physical attacks are forms of violence that are typically more severe, in that they cause physical suffering to the victims, and in this sense they fall more neatly into traditional typologies of political violence and conflict.[17] A third politically relevant form of electoral violence is attacks on property and other objects, including, for example, the

---

left with no choice. If they don't vote for the APC, they will have no rights in the end. They will continue to be second-class citizens" (quoted in Christensen and Utas 2008, 535).

17. That said, some forms of coercion can be of comparable or even greater severity to victims, such as forced displacement that deprives them of their homes.

TABLE 1-1. Examples of Electoral Violence by Type

	Threats and Coercion	Attacks	Violence against Objects or Property
State-perpetrated	Obstruction of voter access to polling stations by state proxies (hired thugs)	Violent police disruption of opposition campaign rallies	Destruction of opposition campaign materials by state actors
Nonstate-perpetrated	Threats of violence against rival candidates	Murder of a rival candidate	Torching of polling stations; electorally motivated rioting

destruction of polling places and the vandalism of campaign materials. Most of the data sources employed in this study include information only on the two forms of violence perpetrated against people—threats and coercion, and attacks—which will therefore be the primary focus of this analysis, though violence directed against objects will also be discussed in case studies and examples. This typology can be illustrated by the matrix in table 1.1, which includes examples of each type of violence.

A final conceptual distinction that is difficult to operationalize precisely but that is theoretically relevant for understanding electoral violence is the distinction between electoral contexts where violence is unexpected and those where it is expected. In most polities, elections are generally peaceful events that are only occasionally marred by widespread violence. It is undoubtedly the case that in any election there are isolated instances of coercive force being used in connection with the electoral process, but widespread electoral violence is uncommon in most contemporary states. There are, however, a number of states—examples include the Philippines, Jamaica, Bangladesh, Sierra Leone—where violence is woven into the fabric of electoral traditions, and widespread conflict involving numerous deaths takes place each time there is an election. Under these circumstances, violence is a mode of competition, a campaign tool. Another slightly different case is that of Mexico prior to the mid-1990s, where the preelectoral and electoral periods were generally calm, but rioting invariably erupted after the results of the election were announced, as opponents of the dominant Institutional Revolutionary Party (PRI) sought to gain minor concessions through the use of mass force in events commonly known as *concertacesiones* (Eisenstadt 2006). In all these cases, violence was expected, and it played an integral part of elections-as-usual. The expectations and strategies of actors in the electoral process will invariably be affected by the level of uncertainty surrounding the occurrence of violence, a point that will be addressed when electoral strategies are discussed. I will make an analytic distinction between contexts in which electoral violence is endemic, those where it is rare, and those where it is episodic, bearing in mind that in reality cases are spread across a gradient ranging from situations in which elections are almost certain to contain major violence to those in which violence is extremely unlikely to occur.

It will by now have become clear that patterns in the use of force vary considerably from country to country; it thus makes sense at this point to provide a number of concrete examples. In some contexts electoral violence takes on distinct regional or temporal patterns. For example, elections in Tanzania tend to be relatively peaceful, with the exception of the islands of Zanzibar, where eruptions of electoral violence are common. Historically, elections in Northern Ireland have also been at risk of conflict, though campaigning and voting has for the most part been conducted peacefully in other parts of the United Kingdom since the mid-nineteenth century. Côte d'Ivoire has since the early 1990s experienced some of the most violent elections anywhere in the world, yet it is largely free of the violence that accompanies the candidate nomination process in many parts of Africa (Goldring and Wahman 2018; Mac Giollabhui 2018; Reeder and Seeberg 2018; Seeberg, Wahman, and Skaaning 2018; Wanyama and Elklit 2018).

As with many forms of contentious politics, electoral violence tends to follow established repertoires (Tilly 1978), which are available to actors over successive elections. Not all elements of the repertoire will be employed in each electoral contest, but the range of likely uses of force is generally known to all major actors. There are, of course, unexpected eruptions of new forms of violence that occasionally intrude into elections in ways that few participants had anticipated, as, for example, when the Madrid train bombings killed 191 people days before the 2004 Spanish election. But the range of likely types of electoral violence tends to remain relatively stable over time in given electoral contexts.

In states such as Kenya, Zimbabwe, and Colombia, the forced displacement of voters by political leaders and security services is a common means of preventing citizens from exercising their franchise (Boone and Kriger 2012; LeBas 2006; Steele 2011), while in countries such as Zimbabwe, Egypt, Fiji, and Jamaica, state actors generally engage in subtler forms of harassment such as intimidation designed to discourage voting for specific candidates or to make citizens wary of attending the polls altogether (Blaydes 2011; Boone

and Kriger 2012; Figueroa and Sives 2002; Fischer 2002). In states such as
Belarus, Indonesia, Russia, Togo, Ukraine, Zambia, and Zimbabwe, candidates for election have often been victims of violent attacks (Bratton and
Van de Walle 1997; Harish and Toha 2017; C. Ross 2011; UNDP 2009; Wilson
2005b), whereas in Chad, Nigeria, South Africa, and Uganda, violence has
been observed in particular during the candidate nomination process (Seeberg, Wahman, and Skaaning 2018). In some cases such attacks have resulted
in the death or near death of prominent political figures, as when former
prime minister of Pakistan Benazir Bhutto was killed in 2007 while on the
campaign trail, when Ukrainian presidential candidate Viktor Yushchenko
was poisoned during the 2004 electoral campaign (Wilson 2005a), when
Togolese military forces loyal to President Eyadéma shot prodemocracy
campaigners and took the prime minister hostage in the run-up to the elections of 1993 (Bratton and Van de Walle 1997), or when two presidential
candidates were assassinated prior to the Haitian elections of 1987 and on
election day itself troops killed several dozen voters lining up to cast their
ballots (O'Neill 1993). Confrontations between the supporters of rival parties during electoral campaigns have been very common since the introduction of competitive elections, and they have featured prominently in contexts
as diverse as Yemen, Benin, Uganda, Fiji, the Seychelles, Pakistan, and the
Gambia (Fischer 2002). Such conflicts take place at virtually every election
in countries such as the Philippines and India (Fischer 2002; Patino and
Velasco 2004; Wilkinson 2004; UNDP 2009). In Bangladesh and Pakistan,
polling stations have frequently been torched on election day, and polling
officials kidnapped (Akhter 2001; Staniland 2014, 2015). In Indonesia, violence against state officials such as electoral administrators is also common
(Harish and Toha 2017). In Latin American countries such as Colombia and
Guatemala, drug lords use violence to ensure electoral outcomes that will
enable them to pursue their trade unfettered by the formal institutions of
the state (Creative Associates International 2009, 2013; S. Taylor 2009); the
Italian Mafia uses similar tactics (Alesina, Piccolo, and Pinotti 2018). The
severity of the phenomenon can vary from the mild voter intimidation that
is common across a large variety of electoral contexts to large-scale murder
and maiming that have been witnessed, for example, in Sierra Leone, where
at the time of the 1996 election electors' fingers, hands, noses, and lips were
cut off in order to prevent them from voting (Fischer 2002). Postelection
violence such as that witnessed in Thailand (2001), Kenya (2007/8), Ethiopia
(2005), Côte d'Ivoire (2010), Haiti (2010), Nigeria (2011), and Honduras

(2017) has also been frequent following disputed polls (Bratton and Van de Walle 1997; Claes and Stephan 2018; EC-UNDP Joint Task Force on Electoral Assistance 2011; Fischer 2002; Höglund 2009).

As these examples attest, there is a huge diversity in the forms taken by electoral violence, and a wide range of different actors can perpetrate it. As noted above, actors will be divided into state and nonstate in this study. State actors include public servants (electoral officials, civil servants, members of the security services), as well as incumbent politicians and affiliates of the party/parties in power. State actors also include proxies such as thugs hired to intimidate voters or disrupt campaign rallies. Nonstate actors include the affiliates of opposition parties, civil society groups, and eligible voters. International actors can also in theory be involved in electoral violence, as, for example, when international electoral observers are attacked, or when the citizens of foreign countries get caught up in electoral conflict, but the numbers of international actors involved in such episodes tend to be so small as to make this category difficult to analyze empirically.

Data and Global Patterns

Until recently, political scientists had very limited ability to study electoral violence cross-nationally, using the standard quantitative tools of the trade. Yet in recent years a number of new data sets have been released covering aspects of this phenomenon in different regions and/or countries of the world. These data sets are based on media reports (Daxecker, Amicarelli, and Jung 2019; Raleigh et al. 2010; Salehyan et al. 2012), election observation reports (Birch 2011; Borzyskowski and Wahman 2019), and expert and mass surveys (Inglehart et al. 2014; Norris, Frank, and Martínez i Coma 2014).

For the purpose of this study, global data are required, however. Fortunately, several cross-national data sets are now available that greatly expand the options open to comparative scholars of electoral violence. Though some of the indicators contained in these data sets are based on slightly different ontologies of electoral violence than that offered here, they provide useful measures that go a long way toward capturing the underlying phenomenon analyzed in this investigation. All these measures include violence that takes place during the electoral period and is connected to the electoral process, which are the core elements of the definition set out above.

One such source is the National Elections across Democracies and Autocracies (NELDA) data set (Hyde and Marinov 2012, 2015), which includes a dichotomous indicator of whether or not there was "significant violence involving civilian deaths immediately before, during, or after the election" (*Nelda33*), as well as an indicator of government harassment of the opposition, *Nelda15*, which codes responses to the question "Is there evidence that the government harassed the opposition?" In the version 4 release of this data set, 19.79 percent of elections held between 1995 and 2012 were coded as having significant violence, and opposition harassment was recorded in 17.01 percent of cases.

The other useful source of global comparative data on electoral violence is the Varieties of Democracy (V-DEM) data set (Coppedge et al. 2018a, b), which covers the 1900–2017 period and is based on expert assessments.[18] The V-DEM data are for this reason not as vulnerable as the NELDA data to the systematic biases known to affect electoral-violence data based on media reports (Borzyskowski and Wahman 2019). Relevant indicators in this data set are those for intimidation and violence of the opposition by state officials, *v2elintim* (answers to the question "In this national election, were opposition candidates/parties/campaign workers subjected to repression, intimidation, violence, or harassment *by the government, the ruling party, or their agents*?"), and an indicator for violence by nonstate actors, *v2elpeace* (answers to the question "In this national election, was the campaign period, election day, and postelection process free from other types (*not by the government, the ruling party, or their agents*) of violence related to the conduct of the election and the campaigns (but not conducted by the government and its agents)?"). On these measures, 44.56 percent of elections between 1995 and 2012 were recorded as having at least some violence by nonstate actors, with 2.70 percent of cases displaying "widespread" violence and a further 6.35 percent experiencing "significant" levels of violence. A total of 50.83 percent of elections during this period experienced at least some state intimidation of the opposition, with "systematic, frequent and violent harassment and intimidation of the opposition by the government or its agents" recorded in 3.83 percent of elections, and "periodic, not systematic, but possibly centrally coordinated—harassment and intimidation of the opposition by the government or its agents" found in 8.01 percent of all contests. It must be noted, however, that the highest level of state intimidation on the *v2elintim* scale reflects a situation where "repression and intimidation by the government or its agents was so strong that the entire period was quiet," making this an imperfect measure of state-initiated violence per se (Coppedge et al. 2018a). In the version of the *v2elintim* indicator employed

---

18. Version 8 of the V-DEM data set is used in this analysis.

in this study, the top category on the scale is recoded to 0 such that the scale more accurately reflects the actual level of violence that occurred in a given electoral context.

The NELDA and V-DEM data sets are useful sources of information, and they will both be used in the analyses presented in this volume. Yet these data sets aggregate electoral violence to relatively high levels. For this reason, the Countries at Risk of Electoral Violence data set (CREV) will also be used in analyses of more recent elections (Birch and Muchlinski 2019). The CREV is aggregated from event data, and as such it provides counts of events of specific types for every election to provide a more fine-grained coding of electoral violence than other data sources. The CREV covers legislative and executive elections in 101 states between 1995 and 2013 and is compiled on the basis of event data extracted from the Integrated Crisis Early Warning System (ICEWS) data set (Boschee et al. 2015). Events are aggregated into two categories according to the typology set out above: major threats and acts of coercion, and physical attacks, each of which is coded by actor, specifically state versus nonstate. For the purposes of this data set, state actors are defined as those who are part of the institutions of the state or government, as well as governing parties and holders of executive offices such as presidents or kings. Nonstate actors are defined as those affiliated with opposition parties as well as members of groups outside the state.[19] The CREV data are disaggregated by month of the electoral cycle, including the six months before each election, the month of the election, and three months following the election.[20] According to these data, there were during the 1995–2012 period a mean of 86 violent acts initiated by state actors and their proxies against nonstate actors, and 68 acts by nonstate actors against state actors. It appears from both the V-DEM and the CREV data that state-initiated violence is more prevalent at elections than violence initiated by nonstate actors throughout the majority of this period.

The versions of these data sets used in this study exclude country-years in which the country in question was engaged in either a civil war or an interstate war.[21] This is partly because violence committed as part of the war effort is bound to contaminate the data, and partly because the dynamics

19. The CREV also includes data for international actors (as both perpetrators and victims of violence), but the analyses carried out here will focus on state and nonstate actors alone, as violence by or against international actors in most cases constitutes a negligible proportion of overall violence.

20. For full details of CREV construction, see Birch and Muchlinski (2019).

21. The V-DEM variables *e_miinterc* (armed conflict, internal) and *e_miinteco* (armed conflict, international) are used to filter countries at war. The original source of these data is the European Union Clio Infra data set, http://www.clio-infra.eu/ (accessed July 23, 2017). In addition, Syria

of electoral competition during wartime differ in fundamental ways from those of peacetime competition (Flores and Noorudin 2018; Steele and Schubiger 2018). Each of the indicators of electoral violence considered here measures the phenomenon in a different way and each offers useful information. Despite the slightly different understandings of electoral violence subtending these different indicators, previous research has indicated that the measures are correlated (Birch and Muchlinski 2019).[22] The data sets will be thus used in combination in the pages that follow, though, as we shall see, certain data sets are better suited to some analyses than others.[23]

In this study, the unit of analysis is the election cycle, and statistical analyses will, where relevant, use data points from the first round of multiround elections.[24] The first round was selected for analysis as it marks the end of the preelection period and the start of a postelection period (in relation to the first round). Interround violence and violence occurring after the second round are captured by most of the empirical measures employed here, and the use of a single round reduces intraelectoral dependencies in the data.

I start my overview of global patterns in electoral violence with a sweeping panorama of patterns between 1945 and 2012, as evidenced in the NELDA and V-DEM data sets, both of which cover this entire period. As shown in figures 1.2 and 1.3, both data sets indicate that electoral violence is a significant global problem; however, they exhibit distinct patterns, reflecting different variable definitions and measurement approaches.

2012 is removed from the data set; though it is not coded as having been at war in this data set, the country was at the time of the 2012 elections experiencing considerable internal strife.

22. The biserial correlation between *Nelda33* and the CREV measure of aggregate attacks is .53; the correlation between *Nelda15* and the CREV measure of state threats and coercion is .23; both relationships are highly significant statistically. The polyserial correlation between the V-DEM *v2elintim* measure and the aggregate CREV measure of state-to-nonstate violence is .20. The polyserial correlation between the V-DEM *v2elpeace* indicator and the CREV aggregate measure of attacks is .35 and that between *v2elpeace* and nonstate-to-state attacks is .32. Again, all associations are highly significant statistically (Birch and Muchlinski 2019). See Birch and Muchlinski (2019) for detailed comparative analyses of the CREV data and regional data sets.

23. There are also several other event data sets that cover electoral violence, including the Armed Conflict Location and Event Dataset (ACLED; Raleigh et al. 2010), Social Conflict in Africa (SCAD; Salehyan et al. 2012), and Electoral Contention and Violence (ECAV; Daxecker, Amicarelli, and Jung 2019). These data sets are less well suited to the purposes of this analysis, however, owing to lack of global coverage. Moreover, given that the main variables of interest in this study are national-level characteristics of states and elections, it makes sense to employ national-level data.

24. When lags are included in models, these lags will thus refer to the (first round of) the previous election held in the country in question. Only 260 of the 2,083 elections (12.5 percent) included in the 1945–2012 data set are multiround elections.

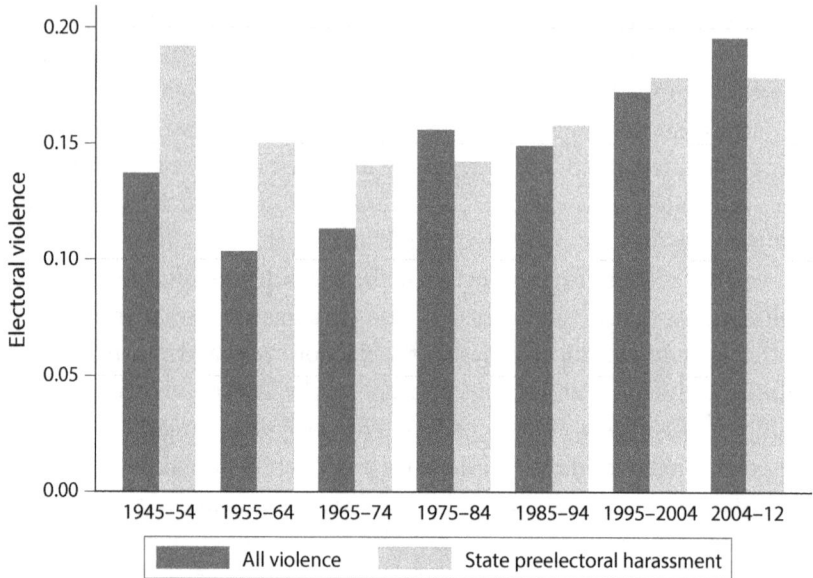

FIGURE 1.2. Trends in NELDA indicators of electoral violence (share of elections exhibiting the form of violence in question), 1945–2012

According to the NELDA data (figure 1.2), which pick up the most egregious forms of overall electoral violence and preelectoral harassment by state actors, elections became more peaceful between the end of the Second World War and the late 1960s, before increasing gradually in violence in the subsequent period—which includes the phenomenon commonly referred to as the "third wave" of democratization, starting in 1974 (Huntington 1991). The V-DEM nonstate-violence indicator remains broadly stable over the entire period, while the state-intimidation variable exhibits a decline over more recent decades (figure 1.3). These varying trends can undoubtedly be attributed to conceptual differences in the variables being measured as well as methodological differences in data collection. The reliance of the NELDA data on media reports may partly account for why an increase in both types of violence is observed in recent years; political liberalization, economic development, and technological change may have led to an increased number of violent incidents being *reported* in the latter period, especially in the final years when social media was increasingly being used to crowdsource allegations of electoral wrongdoing.[25]

25. A recent paper by Borzyskowski and Wahman (2019) points to similar effects that generate biases in media-based electoral-violence data.

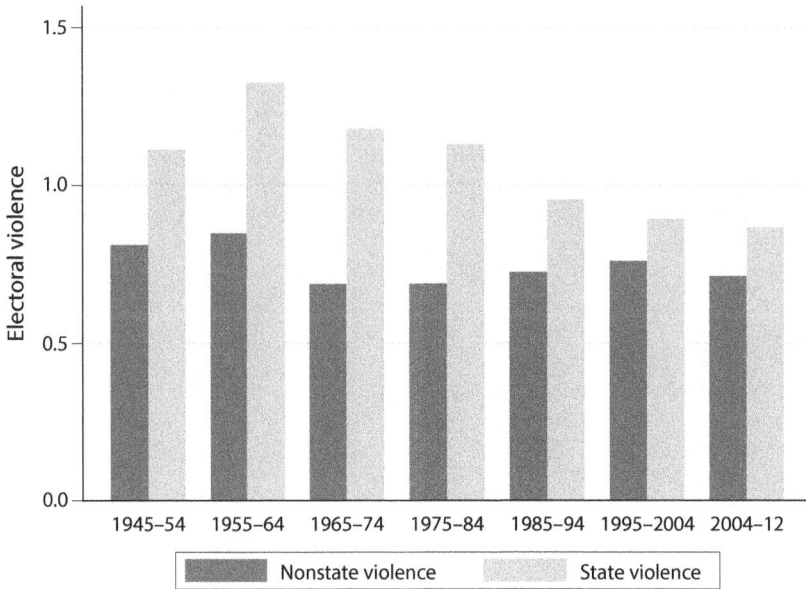

FIGURE 1.3. Trends in V-DEM indicators of electoral violence, 1945–2012

NB: The ordinal versions of these variables are used to enhance ease of interpretation; both variables are inverted such that a higher score corresponds to greater levels of violence.

Common to both data sets is the relative *stability* of global rates of electoral violence; the temporal variations reported here cover at most 15 percent of the range of the respective variables. Thus, despite the dramatic global changes associated with postwar decolonization, Cold War superpower rivalry, the collapse of the Soviet Union, the third wave of democratization, and the digital revolution, electoral violence has played a major role in a relatively steady portion of the world's elections during the entire modern era.

In addition to trends over time, it also makes sense to consider the global distribution of electoral violence. The preponderance of academic writing on this topic takes as its geographic focus the African continent, and from reading the literature one could be forgiven for thinking that electoral violence was mainly an African phenomenon. Yet examination of the cross-national data tells another story. Table 1.2 displays mean electoral-violence scores from the three global data sets—NELDA, V-DEM, and CREV—broken down by world region. The data are presented both for the maximum available time period for each indicator and for the most recent decade (2003–12), in order to provide a snapshot of contemporary patterns.

TABLE 1-2. Distribution of Electoral Violence by Political Region

	NELDA Overall Violence[b]		V-DEM Mean Violence[c]		CREV Mean Violence[d]	
World Region[a]	1945–2012	2003–12	1945–2012	2003–12	1995–2012	2003–12
Former communist Eastern Europe and Central Asia	.074	.093	0.816	0.610	1.644	1.549
Latin America	.209	.187	0.997	0.635	3.156	2.681
The Middle East and North Africa	.240	.403	0.994	0.897	3.969	2.904
Sub-Saharan Africa	.213	.203	1.406	1.308	3.485	3.339
Western Europe, North America, Australia, and New Zealand	.016	.027	0.050	0	0.633	0.697
East Asia	.033	.043	0.957	0.375	0.365	0.349
Southeast Asia	.291	.219	1.221	0.931	4.967	4.952
South Asia	.519	.600	1.500	1.536	7.653	6.766
The Pacific	.294	.750	0.412	1.000	1.399	1.437
The Caribbean	.212	.143	0.864	0.286	2.764	N/A

Figures in cells are regional means calculated on the basis of country means, to ensure each country is weighted equally.

[a] The definition of regions used here follows the 'political regions' indicator that forms part of the Quality of Government data set (Teorell et al. 2017).

[b] Using *Nelda33*.

[c] Mean of *v2elintim* and *v2elpeace*.

[d] State-to-nonstate + nonstate-to-state (as % of events recorded).

There is a remarkable similarity in the tales told by these three data sets, given the variations in country coverage and measurement strategy subtending them. According to all three measures, South Asia stands out as the region of the world where elections have been the most violent in recent decades, and Southeast Asia is also an area where the use of force is prevalent at election time. Sub-Saharan Africa is the second most violent region in the V-DEM data set, though it places only third in the CREV data set and fifth in the NELDA regional rankings. In all three data sets, the Caribbean is shown to have relatively high levels of violence over the more extended time periods, although electoral conflict appears to have abated in recent years. Though Latin America sits in the middle of all three rankings, violence in this region is notably higher than it is in other areas of the world where competitive, credible elections predominate, such as western Europe, North America, Australia, New Zealand, and East Asia. Not surprisingly, the Middle East and North Africa also have relatively high levels of electoral

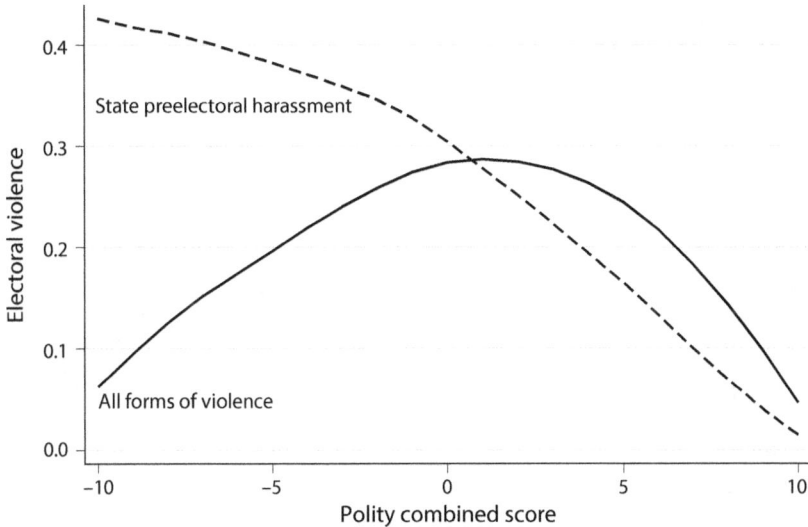

FIGURE 1.4. Patterns of electoral violence by level of democracy (NELDA), 1945–2012

conflict, whereas elections in the Pacific region have been carried out in relative peace in recent decades according to two of the three measures. All in all, these data suggest that electoral violence displays strong regional characteristics, and that heavy focus in the existing academic literature on Africa has led to a neglect of other areas where elections are also conflictual. It is worth noting too that though levels of violence are on all three scales low in East Asia, as well as in Europe, the Americas, and Australasia, there is no world region where elections have been entirely peaceful for an extended period. The use of force to interfere with electoral processes is a truly global phenomenon that warrants systematic comparative analysis such as that undertaken in this volume.

It is in addition constructive to consider patterns of violence at different levels of democracy. Previous research has identified a connection between political violence and democratic competition in countries that are poor (Collier and Rohner 2008; Flores and Nooruddin 2016; Hegre et al. 2001; Salehyan and Linebarger 2015) and those that have weak states (Brancati and Snyder 2012; Fein 1995; Mansfield and Snyder 2005), which are often in practice the same countries. In studies of electoral conduct, a link between hybrid regimes and violent elections has also been noted by some scholars. Fjelde and Höglund (2016) found a curvilinear relationship between democracy and electoral violence, while Norris, Frank, and Martinéz i Coma (2015) underlined the risk of violence in elections held in hybrid states; this pattern

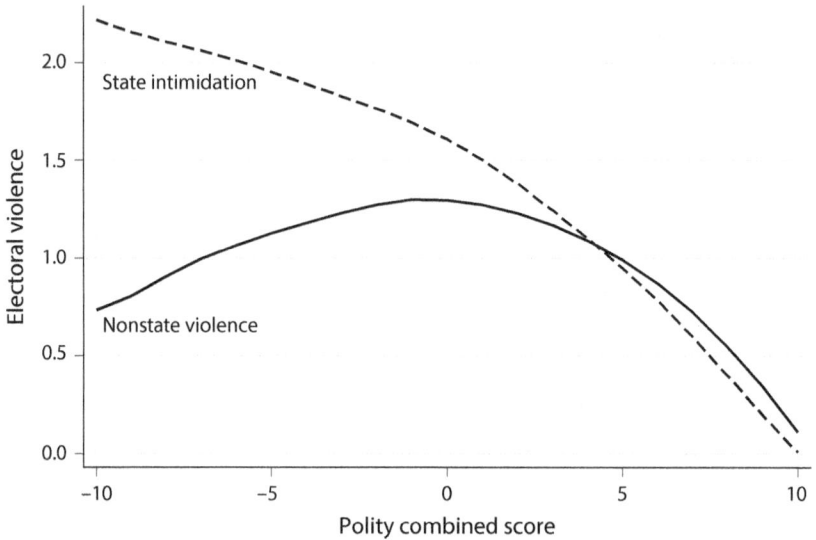

FIGURE 1.5. Patterns of electoral violence by level of democracy (V-DEM), 1945–2012

was found also in a detailed study of electoral violence in postcommunist Europe by Mochtak (2018b).[26]

Analysis of the three data sets employed here confirms this finding, but with some important nuances. Figure 1.4 plots the NELDA overall-violence measure (*Nelda33*) and the preelection state-violence measure (*Nelda15*) against the Polity IV combined "polity" score, which ranges from −10 in the most autocratic states to 10 in the most democratic (Marshall, Gurr, and Jaggers 2016). Figure 1.5 plots the V-DEM state- and nonstate-violence measures against the same scale. These figures exhibit a marked similarity; in both cases, state-initiated electoral violence declines monotonically with increases in democracy. The NELDA overall-violence measure and the V-DEM nonstate-violence indicator show an inverted-U-shaped pattern that peaks in the upper half of the Polity scale. The CREV data, depicted in figure 1.6, also indicate that elections tend to experience more violence in hybrid and transitional states than is the case either in established democracies or in authoritarian regimes; the patterns for all four types of violence are similar, though state threats peak at a lower level of democracy than

26. Burchard (2015), however, found a monotonic relationship between levels of authoritarianism and levels of electoral violence in the African context. Van Ham and Lindberg (2015) also failed to find a curvilinear relationship between government intimidation at election time and democratization in Africa.

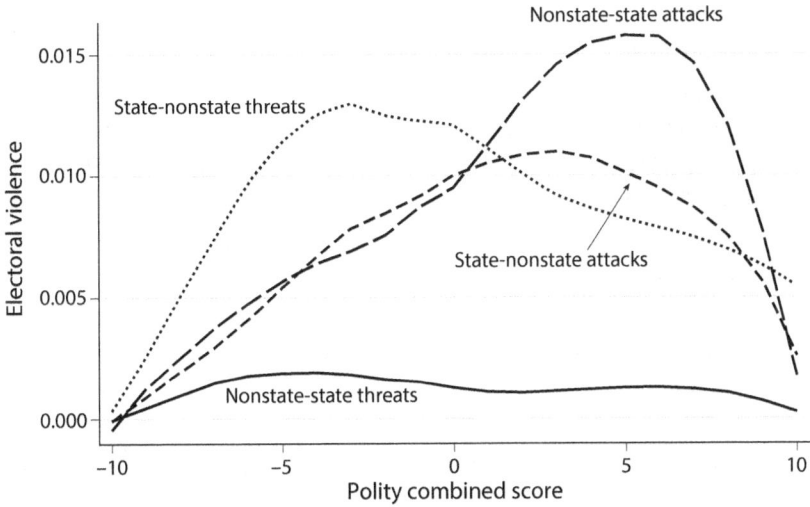

FIGURE 1.6. Patterns of electoral violence by level of democracy (CREV), 1995–2012

NB: Data are for electoral-violence events as a proportion of all reported events.

attacks by either state or nonstate actors, and threats by nonstate actors are less sensitive to level of democracy than the other three measures. We can summarize these findings by saying that electoral violence exhibits clear patterns that vary by regime type, suggesting a link between electoral strategy and modes of rule that will be explored in greater detail in the following two chapters. The analyses in these chapters will also break down the broad syndrome of democracy into its component parts in order better to assess their relationship to violent elections.

Chapter Preview

Following the initial overview of the topic of electoral violence and descriptive account of this phenomenon presented in this chapter, chapter 2 develops the study's main argument as to the incentives under which state and nonstate actors will employ violent means of shaping electoral outcomes, in addition to alternatives such as vote buying, fraud, or programmatic competition. This argument posits that electoral violence is shaped by the balance of democratic institutions and corruption, which conditions the costs of being excluded from power and the benefits of winning office. The chapter will also set out an account of why violence might be used to amplify and/ or complement other types of electoral manipulation, including vote buying and misconduct. The observable implications of this argument are detailed in the form of a series of testable hypotheses.

The hypotheses regarding state violence are elaborated in chapter 3 with respect to the choice situations faced by leaders at election time, and tested empirically on the basis of global data sets of electoral violence and covariates drawn from a variety of sources, supplemented by case studies based on qualitative data. The quantitative analyses carried out in this chapter confirm the connection between the structure of power (the relative strength of democratic and informal institutions) and electoral violence, and find also a strong empirical link between state-initiated violence and electoral misconduct in contexts where democratic constraints are lacking. Case studies of Zimbabwe, Syria, Belarus, and Paraguay show how state-initiated electoral violence forms part of political economies regulated by informal institutions of corruption and patronage.

Chapter 4 tests the argument's expectations vis-à-vis nonstate violence, again demonstrating a strong and consistent empirical association between violence committed by nonstate actors and corruption, together with a link between this form of violence and vote buying suggestive of carrot-and-stick tactics. This chapter also explores the use made by nonstate actors of violent electoral protest as a mobilizational device, and the techniques whereby politicians enlist vigilante groups and proxies to carry out high-risk forms of violence. Case studies of Pakistan, Ghana, Kyrgyzstan, and Côte d'Ivoire help to probe these casual mechanisms and to analyze the production of electoral violence.

Chapter 5 turns from the study of global patterns to a focus on the strategic dynamics inherent in different geographic contexts and different time periods. The chapter considers variations in electoral violence across the electoral cycle, over time, and across regions within countries. The analysis of strategic interactions between actors over the course of the electoral cycle suggests that retaliation can be a factor in the use of physical force, especially in the two months leading up to polling day. Case studies of the Philippines, Tanzania, Jamaica, and Ukraine demonstrate that uneven state capacity and the geography of partisanship help to account for geographic variations within countries in levels of electoral violence. The Tanzanian and Jamaican case studies also show how the way in which leaders and citizenries respond to each other's behavior over time can generate cycles of violence that reforms often fail to fully break.

Implicit in the academic study of electoral violence is the assumption that it is a problem to be addressed by programs specifically designed to reduce conflict. It is thus necessary in any comprehensive account of this phenomenon to devote careful consideration to the strategies that have been employed to mitigate electoral violence. This topic is taken up in chapter 6 by means of quantitative data analysis and case studies of electoral-violence-prevention techniques. In quantitative analysis, the chapter finds that electoral governance matters more than formal institutional design in efforts to contain electoral violence. Macedonia and Haiti are the focus of case studies that serve to deepen our understanding of these patterns, demonstrating the importance of electoral-authority capacity and political will in enabling effective violence control strategies.

The concluding chapter, chapter 7, summarizes the main findings of the volume and draws out their implications for political science as well as for policies on institutional design, electoral administration, electoral assistance, and diplomacy. The chapter considers the circumstances under which different strategies of electoral-violence prevention are likely to be successful and it provides a series of empirically grounded recommendations for the policy and practitioner communities.

2

Carrots and Sticks

TOWARD A THEORY OF ELECTORAL VIOLENCE

Force has been used to resolve political disputes for millennia. The question of why violence might be employed in an electoral context is of considerable interest. If actors have chosen the institution of elections as a means of mediating conflict, why would they then resort to coercive measures to pursue their electoral ends? I posit that the answer to this question can be found in the fact that states with violent elections tend to be characterized by weak democratic institutions and strong informal institutions, by which I mean the corruption, patronage, clientelism, and state capture afflicting a wide range of states (Helmke and Levitsky 2006; Kitschelt and Wilkinson 2007; Rothstein and Varraich 2017), and that informal institutions of this type often rely on electoral violence to sustain them.[1]

The first component of the argument to be developed here is that the balance of democratic institutions and corruption shapes the demand for electoral violence. In electoral authoritarian and hybrid regimes, rulers are reluctant to open themselves to the risk of democratic competition. There

1. The term "informal institutions" will be used throughout the study to designate the democratically harmful institutions of clientelism, patronage, state capture, and corruption, rather than constructive informal institutions that help support democracy. In Helmke and Levitsky's (2004) terminology, these are "competing" informal institutions rather than "complementary," "accommodating," or "substitutive" informal institutions.

are two main reasons for this: Politicians in all less-than-democratic states face serious commitment problems. They know that if they give up power democratically in the hopes of ushering in an extended period of democratic alternation, there is a significant risk that those who assume power will curb democracy and prevent any further alternation. This is the risk of "one person, one vote, one time." The second reason is that loss of power in such contexts opens leaders to economic and legal sanctions as well as to a spell in opposition. The stakes of elections are high, as political power tends to entail considerable economic opportunities via corruption, defined as the abuse of public office for private gain, together with legal immunity, whereas loss of power risks exposing politicians to loss of wealth and legal protection, possibly even exile or death. The *demand for electoral exclusion* will thus be higher in states with weak rule of law, weak democratic institutions, and high levels of corruption. Incumbents' demand for exclusion is mirrored by oppositions' high *demand for electoral inclusion*. In other words, I expect the relationship between corruption and electoral violence outlined here to be broadly symmetrical, applying both to those in power and to those in opposition.

Though a number of previous scholars have posited and/or observed a link between patronage and electoral violence (e.g. Berenschot 2018a, b; Boone 2011; Boone and Kriger 2010; Daxecker 2020; Fjelde and Höglund 2016; Höglund 2009; Mueller 2011, 2012; Sisk 2012; Söderberg Kovacs 2018; Staniland 2015; C. Taylor, Pevehouse, and Straus 2017; Wanyama and Elklit 2018), very few have made an explicit connection between electoral violence and corruption. Scholars of corruption have long been aware of the role of violence in the enforcement of illicit exchanges (e.g. Dal Bó, Dal Bó, and Di Tella 2006; Della Porta and Vannucci 1999; Johnston 2005, 2014; Sundström 2016), and I argue that the insights of this literature are relevant for understanding the role of electoral violence in excluding opponents and maintaining political orders based on informal institutions and corrupt exchange.

Violence is thus a tool regulating exclusion. However, it is only one of several possible tools that can be used to this end. Others include particularist rewards and the manipulation of formal electoral institutions and procedures (electoral misconduct). The second principal argument of this study is that electoral violence cannot be understood in isolation, as it is typically employed to backstop, amplify, or complement other forms electoral manipulation, including procedural misconduct (fraud, bias, administrative malfeasance) and vote buying, both of which can be understood as extensions of corruption (Bozeman, Molina, and Kaufmann 2017; Della Porta and Vannucci 1999; Fisman and Golden 2017; Johnston 2005, 2014). Specifically, violence is used to facilitate the form of electoral manipulation to which actors have most ready access; incumbent elites tend to use violence in order to facilitate misconduct, whereas oppositions are more likely to deploy violence as a support for vote buying.

In corrupt states with weak rule of law and low state capacity, all forms of manipulation are resources that can be used to achieve political ends. Actors also have legitimate resources, of course, including their track records of previous performance, candidate popularity, policy offers, and co-optation of the opposition, which are employed alongside illicit resources. But licit campaign tactics are low cost and readily available in most contexts, so they do not typically present those contesting elections with strategic choices. The same cannot be said for violence, which is costly and risky; it can therefore be expected to be used relatively sparingly and to be used in contexts where the exigencies of electoral competition require it. Other manipulative tools will generally be preferred to violence, provided they suffice; violence—or the threat of violence—is kept as an *additional* strategy to be deployed as and when required. Incumbents control the levers of the state, including the administration of elections. The various types of legal maneuvering, partisan administration, and fraud collectively known as electoral misconduct are techniques very commonly used in electoral authoritarian or hybrid states (Birch 2011; Cheeseman and Klaas 2018; Kelley 2012; Norris, 2015; Schedler 2013; Simpser 2013). As this analysis will demonstrate, activities of this sort are often intimately linked to state-initiated intimidation, coercion, and violent attacks, which serve to amplify the effects of misconduct and to quell scrutiny of the electoral process. Oppositions and other nonstate actors who do not have access to state institutions need to consider alternative manipulative strategies, the most accessible of which are the carrot of vote buying and the stick of violence, which can be expected to be used in conjunction. Though incumbents can and do also buy votes, this is a costly strategy that may well be avoidable if the combination of misconduct and selective repression is effective.

The contours of this component of the argument are set out schematically in table 2.1 and developed more fully in the sections to follow. In contexts of high corruption, the incumbent always has access to all three forms of manipulation, but can generally be expected to favor misconduct over vote buying for reasons of cost, and will use violence and the threat of violence as required in conjunction with misconduct. Nonstate actors may or may not have access to sufficient material resources for vote buying to be a viable electoral option, but

TABLE 2-1. Options for Manipulation by Actor

		Control of State Institutions	
		Yes	No
Access to Material Resources	Yes	Vote buying, misconduct, violence	Vote buying, violence
	No	None	Violence

where they do, the two tactics can be expected to be employed in tandem. In other circumstances, actors' only option may be the use of force.

In elaborating these claims, the chapter will begin by considering the relationship between power structures and electoral violence. The next section will set out the logic behind state-initiated violence, followed by consideration of the use of force by oppositions and other nonstate actors in the third section. The fourth section will be devoted to theorizing the production of violence. A final section will conclude.

Power Structures and Electoral Violence

In many competitive electoral states, formal democratic institutions are widely disregarded and the distribution of political and economic resources is instead governed via corrupt means by informal institutions of patronage, clientelism, and state capture. These terms may be seen to imply isolated occurrences of devious behavior within the context of rule-governed legal regimes, whereas in many states corruption dominates both the political and economic spheres, undermining state capacity and structuring the political order. In contexts of dominance by informal institutions and corruption, those who control the levers of political power also control vast economic resources, as access to opportunities to generate wealth is guarded by political elites who typically allocate such opportunities to their allies in order to shore up their support bases, to those who offer them kickbacks, or in some cases to opposition elites whom they seek to co-opt. Legal mechanisms are highly politicized in these settings, such that incumbent allies enjoy virtual immunity from prosecution, whereas legal sanctions are applied often without justification against the political opponents of those in power. Finally, the public sector itself is a considerable source of patronage and wealth in states dominated by informal institutions and corruption, especially in underdeveloped contexts where private-sector enterprise is limited and the state is heavily reliant on foreign aid, most of which passes through state coffers (Acemoglu and Robinson 2012; Berenschot 2018b; Helmke and Levitsky 2006; Kitschelt and Wilkinson 2007; Mungiu-Pippidi 2015; North, Wallis, and Weingast 2009; Rothstein 2011; Rothstein and Varraich 2017).

Under these circumstances, the stakes of winning political power are extremely high, as those who lose power typically lose not only the right to make and implement policy, but also personal opportunities to engage in wealth-making activities, economic and social support for their group, and protection under the law (Bratton 2008; Fjelde and Höglund 2016). Losing power in corrupt and less democratic regimes can be catastrophic both personally and collectively; unlike in well-governed democracies where those who lose elections retire or pursue other career paths, electoral losers can face imprisonment, exile, or even loss of life, and the groups that form their political support bases can expect to suffer considerable economic hardship or potentially persecution (Burchard 2015; Fjelde and Höglund 2016; Höglund 2009; Sisk 2012). Put simply, the stakes of elections are far higher in such societies. When the stakes are high, actors can be expected to use all means at their disposal to win electoral contests, including violence.

Moreover, violence is often used as an adjunct to corruption, in as much as violence is a tool typically employed to enforce corrupt exchanges and to silence potential whistle-blowers. Popular phrases such as *plata o plomo* (silver or lead) in Latin America and "guns, goons, and gold" in the Philippines are testimony to the intimacy with which the carrot and the stick are intertwined in political orders based on informal institutions and corruption. The literature on corruption makes an explicit connection between corrupt transactions and the use of coercive force that can help to shed light on the link between force and specifically electoral violence. Johnston opened a major comparative study of corruption with the claim that "corruption is tenacious—often sustained by powerful incentives and, at times, protected by violence" (2014, 1). In a detailed study of corruption in Italy, Della Porta and Vannucci described the dynamic in that context: "since trust is not always sufficient to enforce illegal agreement, coercion may be needed as an additional resource. Organized crime is therefore often an actor from whom corrupt politicians buy the resources of physical violence they need to punish 'lemons,' free-riders, or those who threaten to denounce the corrupt system" (1999, 22). Likewise, in a study of South Africa, Sundström showed how "officials who refuse bribes face intimidation by both citizens and colluding colleagues. This illustrates how violence may function as a mechanism to enforce corrupt contracts between bureaucrats and criminal citizens" (2016, 593). Numerous other studies have also found that corrupt exchanges often rely on violence as a guarantee (e.g. Bozeman, Molina, and Kaufmann 2017; Dal Bó, Dal Bó, and Di Tella 2006; North, Wallis, and Weingast 2009). The argument put forward here is that this logic should extend also to electoral violence, which provides elites with a powerful tool to distort electoral accountability. Of course there may also be cases where the high costs of using violence are a stimulus to corruption, but as the above survey suggests, the evidence overwhelmingly suggests that corruption is a cause of violence, and that corruption itself is caused by structural factors such as level of economic development, inequality, and dependence of the economy on natural-resource extraction (Aidt 2019; Chang and Golden 2010; Fisman and Golden 2017; Montinola and Jackman 2002; Triesman 2000).

At the same time, violence will be kept in check if democratic institutions restrain the abuse of power and penalize the use of illicit force. Though corruption is found even in many democracies (Fisman and Golden 2017), democratic mechanisms go some way toward curbing the use of violence to enforce corrupt exchanges and to prevent whistle-blowers from denouncing corrupt transactions. When accountability institutions are strong, the real threat of legal penalty and/or social sanction embodied in democratic institutions raises the cost of corruption as well as that of violent means of facilitating it.

This argument yields two observable implications:

H1: Corruption tends to promote electoral violence.
H2: Democratic institutions tend to curb electoral violence.

These general incentives apply symmetrically to both state and nonstate actors; those who win gain a lot and those who lose suffer considerably, bearing in mind that state and nonstate actors have access to different electoral resources, which will condition their approach to the use of violence as an electoral tool. There is also every reason to believe that both these relationships should hold across space and across time. Though corruption and democratic institutions both tend to change slowly, they do evolve, and this change should be associated with variations in how violent elections are. Likewise, we should expect to see at any given point in time more violent elections in states that are more corrupt and benefit from fewer democratic constraints.

Choices for Incumbents: Carrots, Sticks, and Cheating

In devising the ideal package of electoral strategies, leaders must balance the desire to win elections against the risk of losing legitimacy should they employ violent tactics. The risk of losing legitimacy has two components, external and internal. External legitimacy will be lost if the international community perceives that elections have deteriorated and judges a country to be moving away from democracy. In the present context, however, it is internal legitimacy that in most cases represents the most immediate threat to a ruler's ability to maintain power. If violence is too blatant, the leader risks provoking a legitimacy crisis and being faced with protests that could potentially result in loss of power. The protests that follow blatantly rigged and/or violent elections can unseat the leader, though in most cases it will be possible to use force to repress them. In any case, large-scale popular protests represent a non-negligible risk that the leader will be deposed in a disorderly and possibly violent fashion. As Cox (2009) and Fearon (2011) note, such an outcome is one that fully "rational" leaders ought to avoid at any cost, but it is a risk that loss-averse leaders may be prepared to run.

CHOOSING FROM THE MENU OF MANIPULATION

So far I have made general references to high-risk contexts, but I have not specified what these might entail. At first blush, it would seem to appear that the advent of electoral competition in any form would represent considerable risk to incumbent authoritarians. However, such leaders have proven adept at using a variety of manipulative strategies to ensure that they are able to win elections (Birch 2011; Cheeseman and Klaas 2018; Schedler 2002a, 2013; Simpser 2013).

Conceptually, the strategies of leaders are shaped by risk perceptions and resource endowments. This is why, all else equal, we would expect elites to use the manipulation of electoral procedures and vote buying over violence, as these strategies are associated with lower risks to legitimacy as well as lower risks to life and limb. The use of violence always entails significant danger for any actor, no matter how powerful. In addition to the legitimacy costs just noted, the principal risks of using violence include the danger of retaliation by opponents in the form of violence before, during, and after elections, and the risk of punishment at a future point in time (Bratton 2008; Gutiérrez-Romero and LeBas 2020; Hafner-Burton, Hyde, and Jablonski 2018; Rosenzweig 2016; Van Ham and Lindberg 2015).

It makes sense to consider the mix of repressive strategies that leaders can be expected to employ in this light. There has been some discussion in the literature on electoral violence as to whether fraud, violence, vote buying, and other forms of electoral manipulation are substitutes or complements. Collier and Vicente see the various strategies as substitutes. These scholars have demonstrated via formal modeling that incumbents will always have greater incentives to use fraud than violence, a hypothesis that is supported by evidence from Nigeria (Collier and Vicente 2012, 2014). Claes, by contrast, views the use of force as a more attractive strategy for incumbents, while still framing the two as alternatives: "In the face of an impending defeat or uncertain outcome, political incumbents or challengers may regard violence as a viable strategic alternative or complement to patronage and other types of persuasion" (2016, 11). Van Ham and Lindberg (2015) found in an analysis of African elections that vote buying is more likely to be used in more democratic contexts, while fraud and violence are more prevalent in less democratic circumstances. Also in the African context, Rauschenbach and Paula (2019) found in an analysis of seven states that parties employ intimidation to prevent opposition voters from voting, and they use clientelism to mobilize their own supporters.[2]

Yet there are also reasons to believe that electoral violence, vote buying, and fraud might vary in tandem. A review article on clientelism by Mares and Young (2016) emphasized the extent to which the purchase of political support relies on coercion to back it up. Moreover, informal institutions of patronage and clientelism reduce the risk of prosecution for regime allies, making violence more attractive for incumbents—and sometimes for opposition elites, if they believe they can bribe their way out of prosecution for criminal acts. Electoral corruption can also be used to buy off opponents. Indeed, Van Ham and Lindberg (2015) found that in their African sample government manipulation and vote buying covaried, even if there did appear to be a trade-off between vote buying and fraud. Existing research thus includes contradictory findings, and it leaves many basic theoretical questions unanswered.

The conjecture proposed here is that incumbent actors and others allied to the state are most likely to use violence *in combination* with the panoply of electoral misconduct techniques at their disposal, for reasons of relative cost as well as reasons to do with the logic internal to each strategy. Though manipulation of the rules governing elections remains a very common strategy through which leaders attempt to bias the playing field in their favor at election time, it is no longer the case that they can rely on such means to deliver a sure win; they must often resort to other measures as well. One of the most common second choices of leaders wishing to be assured of electoral victory is outright fraud, including ballot-box stuffing, mistabulation of

2. In a study that focuses on economic rather than physical intimidation, Frye, Reuter, and Szakonyi (2018) found that voter intimidation is more common where vote buying is more costly (cf. Frye, Reuter, and Szakonyi 2014; Mares 2015).

voting results, and other forms of blatant tampering with the polling process so as to alter the result. Yet many leaders also believe they will benefit from inviting international electoral observers to monitor their elections (Hyde 2011; Kelley 2012), and blatant election-day fraud is considerably more costly when international observers are present. Moreover, domestic observation has become more common in recent years, and the advent of mobile electronic technology has made it possible for domestic election observers to document incidents of fraud and instantly upload them anonymously to websites available throughout the world, thus disseminating evidence of wrongdoing without putting themselves at risk. Political and technological change has thus made it considerably more dangerous for leaders to rely on the traditional forms of electoral misconduct alone.

This leaves for the wily leader a range of strategies that fall in between the passage of the electoral law at the beginning of the electoral cycle and the announcement of the results at the end. In between the dual institutional mechanisms of rigging the legal framework governing elections and rigging the vote on polling day, there are a range of tactics still quite commonly employed to ensure the electoral victory of politicians unable to win power on the basis of their performance alone. These mainly consist of altering the behavior of those involved in the electoral process via illicit rewards or sanctions. Through the careful distribution of rewards to loyalists and the use of violent coercion against opponents, the leaders of a semidemocratic state can often increase their vote share sufficiently to ensure a comfortable margin of victory. Yet rewards are costly, so a judicious combination of misconduct and violence—or the threat of violence—is often a preferable alternative for the incumbent.

Violence is also commonly used in order to facilitate misconduct, as when officials are coerced into complying with projects involving the manipulation of electoral procedures or voters are threatened with violence if they denounce electoral wrongdoing. In this sense, manipulation can rely on the known *availability* of violence to ensure that it operates smoothly and effectively.

If voters and others in society fear violence from the state during the course of electoral competition, this fear can be expected to alter their behavior; they may be more reluctant to take part in election-related activities, and, crucially for incumbents, less likely to cry foul when they witness wrongdoing. Instilling fear in the population is thus a useful means of fending off scrutiny, and in the absence of effective scrutiny, fraud and other forms of misconduct are more easily undertaken. As Kalyvas said, "fear does not suffice to sustain rule in the long term . . . , however, it operates as a first-order condition that makes the production of loyalty possible" (2006, 115). Violence thus facilitates and paves the way for electoral misconduct and increases the chances that leaders will be able to manipulate the electoral process unchallenged.

Violence can also be used by incumbents as a means of conditioning the population into believing that support for the regime is the only logical option. In the classic Weberian state where democratic institutions are strong, the state holds a monopoly on the use of coercive force, and it exercises this monopoly impartially to the benefit of all equally (North, Wallis, and Weingast 2009). But as institutions weaken, so does the state's monopoly on the use of force, and the impartiality with which force is used by the state. This is because the weakening of impartial democratic institutions is typically accompanied by the strengthening of informal institutions of clientelism that view the state as a source of resources which can be plundered to the benefit of themselves and those in their network. As Mungiu-Pippidi argued (2015), spoliation remains the norm across much of the world.

In states with weak democratic institutions and strong informal institutions, termed by North, Wallis, and Weingast (2009) "natural states," and by Acemoglu and Robinson (2012) "extractive" rather than "inclusive" states, rent seeking and corruption are strategies of rule that shape the political order, but they are also strategies for controlling violence via the allocation of selective incentives to those who cooperate with the leadership. "The natural state reduces the problem of endemic violence through the formation of a dominant coalition whose members possess special privileges. . . . By limiting access to these privileges to members of the dominant coalition, elites create credible incentives to cooperate rather than fight among themselves" (North, Wallis, and Weingast 2009, 17–18). Violence is therefore an inherent part of such orders, as incumbent elites maintain their positions precisely by credibly committing to protect their clients, and for such protection to be valued, violence must be a real threat. Thus the use of coercive force is a common "negative inducement" in clientelist regimes (Mares and Young 2016; Mignozzetti and Sexton 2018). If benefits accrue to "insiders" and violence is used against "outsiders" but not against insiders, this creates a strong incentive for citizens at all levels of society to act as insiders by supporting the ruling elites at election time.

In addition, the availability of resources is an important factor shaping leaders' choice of electoral strategy. Particularist strategies such as vote buying require a broad base of potential supporters, established networks through which supporters can be mobilized, reliable mechanisms for monitoring compliance, and resources that voters are willing to accept in exchange for their vote (Della Porta and Vanucci 1999; Larreguy, Marshall, and Querubín 2016; Rouquié 1978; Schaffer 2007; Scott 1969; Stokes 2005; Stokes et al. 2013). Vote buying therefore works best in situations where the leadership can rely on preexisting informal institutions, which represent a considerable sunk cost. Violence, by contrast, is a more flexible and agile tool that can be deployed relatively rapidly. The effective use of threats, coercion, and physical attacks requires a relatively small group of loyal supporters who are able and willing to use force—and the threat of force—against the population. Examples of such forces are the Duvalier's Tontons Macoutes in Haiti, Mugabe's "veterans" in Zimbabwe, and the remnants of the KGB and other security forces that have been used as private armies in several former Soviet states.

Thus, in contexts where the risk of retaliation or legitimacy loss is limited, violence may be viewed by ruling elites as an attractive alternative to vote buying as it is cheaper and easier to deploy. But, as noted above, violence is never entirely without risks, and for this reason it is unlikely to be used on its own; it is typically used by state actors to back up programs of electoral misconduct. Electoral misconduct often relies on violence or the threat of violence to be effective, as the fear generated by the use of force facilitates the successful manipulation of electoral procedures; put another way, the possibility of violence softens populations up for fraud, and ensures that if fraud fails the leadership will nevertheless achieve its ends. Likewise, electoral misconduct ensures that violence pays off. Electoral misconduct is the way in which leaders reap the benefits of violence. So when violence is the preferred appetizer or dessert selected from the menu of manipulation, electoral misconduct is often the main course.

An example of this relationship is gleaned from the 2016 election in Uganda, where Sjöberg reported that:

> The government . . . attempted to control information flows . . . and made use of administration and law in order to prevent the opposition from reaching out to the electorate. The more widespread use of intimidation and overt violence compared with the 2011 elections would suggest, however, that these measures were deemed to be insufficient (Sjögren 2018, 60)

Another example comes from an election observation report on the 2008 parliamentary election in Macedonia, showing how violence and fraud were used in conjunction:

> The SEC [State Election Commission] announced that voter turnout for the 15 June early parliamentary elections was 58 per cent. Of 2,741 polling station results tabulated on the SEC database, 75 showed abnormally high turnout figures—many in areas where there were reported incidents of violence or ballot stuffing. Two polling stations in Poroj, from where IEOM [International Election Observation Mission] observers had to be extracted by police, showed for instance 99 to 100 per cent turnout with almost all votes cast for DPA [Democratic Party of Albanians]. (OSCE-ODIHR 2008, 20)

These preliminary examples show how violence can be used to ensure that misconduct is carried to completion; a wider range of evidence will be considered in chapter 3.

The foregoing argument indicates that we should expect to see state violence and electoral misconduct go hand in hand, and that blatant fraud should virtually always be backed up by (the threat of) force:

> *H3: Significant electoral misconduct often necessitates and is accompanied by state-initiated electoral violence.*

The relationship between these two variables can be understood as a weak causal one. Whereas H1 and H2 posit strong causal links between electoral violence, corruption, and democratic institutions, the link posited between electoral violence and misconduct is partly one of co-occurrence and partly a causal relationship, in as much as misconduct can be expected in some cases to necessitate the use of force to back it up.

Opposition Reactions: Exit, Voice, or Disloyalty

Opposition forces face a rather different set of strategic considerations from those faced by incumbents. This choice can be framed in terms of Hirschman's (1970) classic analytic trio of "exit, voice and loyalty," but with a twist; in the context of corrupt and less-than-democratic states, "disloyalty" is a fourth option that is both logical and prevalent. Hirschman's conceptualization of choice was based on customers' relations with firms, and his assumption was that of a rule-governed society where consumers either continued purchasing products (loyalty), voiced their discontent with the unsatisfactory offerings (voice), or sought merchandise from an alternative supplier (exit). Hirschman's consumers do not loot, attack, or cheat the suppliers of the goods on the market. But if we relax the implicit rule-of-law assumption, looting, attacking, and cheating appear on the horizon as additional options, which I collectively term "disloyalty."

In the electoral arena, as in politics more generally, the universe of states is replete with oppositions that have effectively been co-opted by incumbents (Frantz and Kendall-Taylor 2014; Gandhi 2008; Gandhi and Przeworski 2007; Wintrobe 1998). If there is no viable prospect of challenging the regime in the short term, loyalty may appear a sensible solution, especially if it comes with access to resources and policy-making influence. It stands to reason that loyal oppositions are typically peaceful at election time. Violence is the product of other choices.

THE EXIT OPTION

If a party or other grouping outside the ambit of the state and the incumbent power holder decides not to be loyal in the electoral context, the first decision it needs to make is whether or not to contest the election. This choice will in part be conditioned by the party's anticipated vote share, but the main factor driving opposition action is undoubtedly in most cases the strategy, or anticipated strategy, of the incumbent. If the incumbent looks set to run a particularly fraudulent and/or violent election, the opposition has a strong incentive to exercise the "exit" option and boycott the election entirely. There are two reasons for this. First, if the opposition has little chance of winning the election, it can via a boycott potentially build popular support and accrue legitimacy to itself by publicizing the abusive actions of the incumbent. Such legitimacy gains are a benefit that can potentially be stored away for use at some future election when the prospects of victory appear more propitious. The second rationale for calling a boycott in the face of high levels of misconduct and/or violence by state actors is simple self-preservation. If the opposition has little prospect of making significant gains in the election but stands to be targeted with violence, it makes sense to withdraw from active electoral competition. Indeed, Beaulieu (2014) views election boycotts as a form of protest. If the opposition boycotts, it still has the option of using violence, which can highlight the boycott's aims. Beaulieu notes that election boycotts accompanied by violence are a regular occurrence in Bangladesh (Beaulieu 2014; cf. Beaulieu and Hyde 2009); the combination of violence and boycotts has also been found in a variety of countries, including Mali, Togo, and Egypt (Beaulieu, 2014).

THE VOICE OPTION

If the opposition does not opt to exercise "exit" and instead decides to contest the election, which is most commonly the case, it must then consider how to maximize its chances of making political gains. In an electoral authoritarian context where the prospect of outright electoral victory may be remote for the opposition, its main aim is typically to increase its support base. Commenting on elections in Senegal in the 1970s, Hayward and Grovogui noted that:

> The meaning of electoral success for the opposition was less in winning (which did not seem to be in the cards, given [President] Senghor's popularity and accomplishments), but in the demonstration of mass support. If one were successful in the latter, access to power for both the elite and their supporters was almost certain assured. (Hayward and Grovogui 1987, 264)

The first choice the opposition must make in seeking to achieve this end is whether to run a clean campaign (the classic "voice" option) in the hopes that it will be rewarded by the electorate for refraining from engaging in manipulation, or whether to mobilize support through illicit means.

Should the opposition decide to use manipulation, its menu is somewhat more restricted than that of the incumbent. Nonstate actors are bereft of control over state institutions that might be used to alter the outcome of the election directly. Most forms of electoral manipulation are thus not within the power of the opposition, which cannot alter electoral laws or procedures, or interfere easily with formal registration or voting arrangements. Though the opposition does in theory have the power to manipulate the media through media ownership or the bribery of journalists, provided there is sufficient media freedom, and it can engage in the "black arts" of libelous campaign messages (Ledeneva 2006; Wilson 2005b), there may be limits to the extent to which such practices will be tolerated by the incumbent, which may well crack down on blatantly illicit forms of campaigning. But like those holding the reins of power, the opposition still has access to both carrots and sticks; the main forms of manipulation available to the opposition are vote buying (and related varieties of particularism) and violence. Broadly speaking, we can expect nonstate actors to target the carrot of vote buying at their supporters where they have sufficient resources, and the stick of violence or intimidation against a range of groups depending on the situation. If the opposition can afford it, vote buying is very much more advantageous to opposition forces than the use of force. Particularistic distribution can generate genuine support among large sectors of the electorate who come to view the opposition as favorably disposed toward them and their communities, and in most contexts it carries limited risk of electoral backlash or formal sanction. This may be a manipulative means of mobilizing "voice," but it is a tried-and-tested approach that has been employed ever since the advent of elections in ancient times (Staveley 1972), and it remains common in the world today (e.g. Birch 2011; Hidalgo and Nichter 2016; Mares and Young 2016; Min 2015; Schaffer 2007; Stokes 2005; Stokes et al. 2013).

OPPOSITION ELECTORAL VIOLENCE AS "DISLOYALTY"

Yet often the opposition does not command the resources to purchase sufficient numbers of votes, especially in comparison with state actors who are in many settings free to plunder the public purse in order to extend largesse to the population. In order to compete, nonstate actors must often rely on violence both to supplement and to complement the provision of particularistic rewards. In states with high levels of corruption, oppositions in many contexts command considerable wealth via links with legitimate and illegitimate business, as well as through control of subnational government in some regions (Collier and Vicente 2012). Co-optation and coercion go hand in hand in clientelist societies (Mares and Young 2016; Mignozzetti and Sexton 2018; Staniland 2015), and we can expect this pairing to be employed also by nonstate actors seeking to secure electoral advantage, especially those with access to arms who in the electoral context can become "electoral armed groups" (Staniland 2015). Benefits are extended to groups of potentially compliant citizens; intimidation is used to enforce efforts at co-optation. The locus classicus of this link is perhaps the Philippines, where "guns, goons, and gold" have dominated elections for decades. A politician is reported to have admitted in relation to the 1992 elections: "If we cannot buy the votes, we will simply make sure they [the voters] are too scared to vote against us" (quoted in Linantud 1998, 306). Following the "people-power" revolution, electoral integrity further improved, but the oligarchic system of power perpetuated the widespread use of violence (particularly intimidation) together with vote buying (Patino and Velasco 2004; Quimpo 2005). Patino and Velasco described this nexus in the run-up to the polls:

> The "ora de peligro" (literally "hour of danger") is the most intense and anxiety-filled period, when last-minute interventions take place. This

begins two days before the actual election day. Here parties and candidates are concerned with defending their voter base while trying to break the voter base and machinery of their opponents. Vote buying and coercion intensify during the ora de peligro. Voters may be threatened to vote for a candidate or not to vote at all. Bailiwicks are assaulted or homes of ward leaders strafed or burned, and candidates or their campaign managers may be ambushed while doing the last rounds of negotiations. (Patino and Velasco 2004, 4)

The same systematic linkage between vote buying and violence has also been identified in Nigeria (Bratton 2008) and Kenya (Gutiérrez-Romero 2014), among others.

We can distill from this discussion the following testable proposition about the causes of electoral violence by nonstate actors—we should expect to see nonstate violence go hand in hand with vote buying, as these are the two strategies of electoral manipulation available to the opposition, and the opposition in a corrupt state typically must use all the means at its disposal to achieve its electoral ends:

> H4: Significant vote buying often necessitates and is accompanied by nonstate-initiated electoral violence.

As with the link between state violence and misconduct, this relationship can be understood as being "weakly" causal: vote buying is expected to co-occur with nonstate electoral violence as a strategy of preference for nonstate actors, and vote buying also *generates* nonstate violence in that purchasers of votes require an effective sanction to use against recalcitrant sellers.

The Production of Electoral Violence

So far I have considered the overall strategic incentives that state and nonstate actors have to employ violence for electoral ends. But once a decision is made to use force, considerable planning and logistical organization must be undertaken in order to implement that decision. The orchestration of a campaign of intimidation or violent attacks is no mean feat. State and nonstate actors alike must think carefully about whom they will call upon to perpetrate violence, what kinds of inducements they will afford the perpetrators, and how they will achieve their ends. Logistical preparations of this type can be expected to be conditioned by the extent to which violence is anticipated in advance. Each of these topics merits consideration.

ACTORS

Perpetrators. We can identify two main types of actor: principals and agents of violence.[3] The principals are typically candidates or party leaders (bearing in mind that this can also include incumbents). In state-capture contexts, such as Italy or Colombia, principals can also be criminal groups (Alesina, Piccolo, and Pinotti 2018; S. Taylor 2009). Candidates for office and their close associates rarely carry out violent acts personally. They virtually always act via proxies or agents of some kind in an effort to obscure their role. Official law-enforcement officials are a common agent, in as much as they can be deployed to enforce the law selectively and curb violent acts in some contexts but not others, depending on the political needs of their partisan paymasters (Mares and Young 2016; OSCE-ODIHR 2008; Roessler 2005; Wilkinson 2004). For incumbent leaders, electoral violence perpetrated by youth gangs or ad hoc groups of hired thugs may be perceived as a low-cost and low-risk means of retaining power in comparison with reliance on paramilitary forces, which might potentially foment coups (Reno 2011). Evidence from case studies suggests that the agents of violence can be party affiliates (Asunka et al. 2017), but they are often nonpartisan criminal gangs or ad hoc groupings of economically insecure young men enlisted by political brokers to commit violent acts on behalf of the principals (Christensen and Utas 2008; Figueroa and Sives 2002; Höglund 2009; Mares and Young 2016; Rauschenbach and Paula 2019; Söderberg Kovacs 2018). For example, Fischer said of Jamaica that "in the 1970s and 80s, criminal gangs were employed by the two major political parties to rustle up votes. Although recently these gangs have been more involved in illicit narcotics than politics, they maintain political loyalties through 'garrison' districts, party strongholds where votes are delivered through threat and violence" (2002, 22). Gutiérrez-Romero related a report from a Kenyan farmer, originally quoted by Human Rights Watch, who told how in 2007 gangs "get paid by politicians. They move from door to door asking people to support one candidate. We do not argue with them. We just agree with what they say because arguing with them can cost you a life or that of your family members" (quoted in Gutiérrez-Romero 2014,1503). Though the use of proxies may help leaders to

3. Intermediaries are also often required in order to recruit and manage the agents of violence and to keep them at one remove from their principals so as to afford a layer of protection should the identity of the perpetrators and details of their acts to be made public or reported to authorities. However, we know less about the identities and precise roles of intermediaries, as these are less well documented.

avoid official punishment under the law, as happened for example in Kenya following the 2007–8 violence (Cheeseman and Klaas 2018), it is rare that citizenries are unaware of who is behind efforts at intimidation and the use of force. This means that the perpetrators of electoral violence are unlikely to escape informal censure and retaliation from opponents, a point that will be discussed in greater detail in chapters 4 and 5.

Victims. There is some evidence that victims of electoral violence are likely to be those who can most easily be threatened and are least likely to denounce violence by appealing to the legal system for justice or to the media for publicity. In a study of vote buying and intimidation in Guatemala, González-Ocantos and colleagues (2020) found that poor and rural voters were for this reason most likely to be victims of intimidation, a finding supported in relation to nomination violence in Zambia by Goldring and Wahman (2018). In a study of India, by contrast, Wilkinson (2004) showed urban areas to be more vulnerable to violence, a relationship identified also in Paraguay and Afghanistan by Mignozzetti and Sexton (2018), who found voters in urban areas, particularly temporary migrants, to be more vulnerable to coercive forms of clientelism, and in Burundi by Nindorera and Bjarnesen (2018), who provided evidence to suggest that urban voters are easier to mobilize in violent election-related protests owing to their more jaundiced view of governance. Bratton (2008) showed that although violent intimidation affects all socioeconomic groups in Nigeria, it is most concentrated among the least educated, a finding supported by Toros and Birch's (2019) analysis of familial electoral coercion in Turkey. Several scholars have also identified a relationship between poverty and the experience of electoral violence in African studies (Bratton 2008; Burchard 2015, 2018; Dercon and Gutiérrez-Romero 2012; Rauschenbach and Paula 2019). It thus appears that violence affects the disadvantaged disproportionately owing to the lower risks associated with using this tool against the poor.[4]

RECRUITMENT AND REMUNERATION OF AGENTS

In some contexts no inducement is required in order to motivate groups to use force against their fellow citizens. This might be the case among groups of youths who positively welcome an opportunity to undertake violent acts

---

4. There is some contrary evidence, however. Kuhn and von Borzyskowski (2020) found in an African study that the most knowledgeable in society (as proxied by newspaper readership) are most at risk of electoral violence given that they pose the greatest risk to perpetrators, and they may also be most difficult to convert through vote buying.

in the belief that these have been sanctioned by some higher authority that will protect them from possible negative consequences. In other cases, individuals might be willing to exact revenge on their enemies and might thus not require any kind of reward. Under such circumstances, violence itself is its own reward. In other cases, the opportunity to loot may be offered as a selective incentive to those who engage in violent acts; the victims of violence are thereby commandeered into paying for their own victimization, and the perpetrators' putative paymaster is saved the cost of employing those who work for him or her. Often, however, some additional benefit must be provided to those who commit violence in the service of electoral actors. This can be simply a monetary payment or it can be a promise of a reward with a job or other benefit following the election should the paymaster be victorious. In the latter case, violence forms part of a web of patronage activities; it is a political service that a client performs for his or her patron in exchange for protection, welfare benefits, or employment. This type of reward is likely to be sufficient only in cases of long-standing patronage ties, or if there is a high probability that the paymaster will in fact win the election. So if the opportunity to engage in violence may itself be a sufficient selective incentive for some individuals, in other cases the possibility of looting in connection with violent acts may provide rent-seeking opportunities analogous to those available to the brokers in vote-buying institutions (Christensen and Utas 2008; Larreguy, Marshall, and Querubín 2016; Stokes et al. 2013). In as much as the use of force is not always attractive, committing violent acts carries significant risk of retaliation, and it is repugnant to many people, the sponsors of violence may face recruitment problems. They may also face agency problems similar to those faced by the sponsors of vote buying. Indeed, agency problems have been identified by Stokes and colleagues (2013) as one of the main reasons for the decline of vote buying in many contexts. Thus the recruitment and remuneration of perpetrators will always be a challenge for principals, and logistics need to be seen as a major additional cost of violence.

MICROLEVEL CAUSAL CHANNELS

The causal mechanisms through which electoral violence exerts impact on the electoral process need to be considered in relation to the logistical challenges just elaborated. To conceptualize these microcausal channels, we can draw on the vocabulary of the electoral-systems literature and think of electoral violence as acting via distinct "mechanical" and "psychological" channels. The mechanical effect of electoral violence is direct physical damage or displacement of individuals and property, including candidates, activists, observers, polling personnel, voters, campaigning materials, and polling stations. A useful catch-all term for the mechanical channel through which violence operates is "obstruction," as virtually all such activities are designed to interfere with candidacies and/or campaigns. At the limit, obstructive violence can be aimed at the entire electoral process, but it is more commonly geared toward obstructing campaign or voting processes in regions controlled by rivals. Examples include attacks on candidates, attacks on campaign rallies, vandalism of campaign materials, obstruction of voter access to polling stations, and the capture of ballot boxes.

In all but a very small minority of elections, the effects of direct physical action of this sort are experienced by only a fraction of the population. They may well be important individuals who are central to the electoral process, such as presidential candidates, but such targeted actions are typically intended to affect the behavior of a small elite or small groups. Even when large numbers are affected—as with population displacements in Kenya or Zimbabwe—still only a minority of the overall population is typically touched by such actions.

By contrast, the psychological effect of electoral violence is to alter the behavior of larger and less precisely targeted groups by instilling fear in the population and in categories of the political elite, such as campaign activists, prospective candidates, and politicians. Fear can be used as a tool to mobilize, demobilize, or change behavior. Anecdotal evidence suggests that the most common form of fear-based violence is voter intimidation, and that using fear to demobilize voters believed to favor a rival party or to prevent the abstention of one's own loyalists is more common than attempting to use fear to shape vote choice, given the greater ease with which electoral participation can be monitored and verified (Bratton 2008; Burchard 2015; Cheeseman and Klaas 2018). This channel can be termed "intimidation."

For power holders, intimidation is a relatively "cheap" and effective tool, for two reasons. First, the deployment of force or threats of force is transient—confined largely to the period shortly before, during, or after elections—yet its impact is long-lived. Unlike vote buying and fraud, which must be repeated at each election in order to be effective, intimidation instills fear in people that can last for years with minimal need to top up with repeated action (Cheeseman and Klaas 2018). The long-term effects of fear-inducing forms of violence also mean that actors have the power to choose when to use them; they can afford to wait to deploy them when they have the necessary resources and think they can get away with it, knowing that their effects will linger for extended periods after the initial application. This has been observed, for example, in Zimbabwe, where incumbent success the 2013 polls has been attributed to the "dividend of fear" accrued through successive voter experiences of violent elections (Seeberg, Wahman, and Skaaning 2018). Intimidation also has the advantage that it can be dispensed to large numbers at once; the one-to-one transactions required with most forms of vote buying, or the alteration of individual votes required with many forms of fraud, are not necessary with intimidation. In this sense, the use of intimidatory violence may, when viable, seem like a good investment to many actors. Previous research suggests that we may expect variations in timing and targeting in relation to the electoral cycle and political factors. Hafner-Burton, Hyde, and Jablonski (2014) showed that incumbents are likely to use preelection harassment when faced with possible electoral loss. Bhasin and Gandhi (2013) found that state violence is focused mainly on opposition elites before elections, and on opposition voters after elections. Variations such as these will be examined in chapter 5, but the available evidence suggests that the generation of fear is one of the principal aims of state actors in perpetrating electoral violence.

For groups not in power, a campaign of mass intimidation could be very risky: it is difficult to administer undetected and such a campaign is likely to attract severe formal sanctions from the state. We can thus expect the widespread use of intimidation to be more frequent by state than by nonstate actors, as indeed is suggested by figure 1.6 in chapter 1. It is telling in this regard that the NELDA data set includes a variable designating harassment by state actors, but no equivalent for nonstate actors.

Another form of "psychological" violence more attractive to groups in opposition is the mounting of a demonstration, riot, or other violent mass event with the aim of putting pressure on the incumbent or state agencies to alter allegedly unfair election rules or to overturn the result of an election. Violent repression that may be used to quell such events also falls in the realm of psychological violence. When demonstrations of this type pit state against nonstate actors, they often serve as proxies for more routinized forms of negotiation and competition (Beaulieu 2014). The channel through which demonstrations or riots operate may be termed "protest."

The mechanism behind protest violence differs from the fear inducement of intimidation. Though protesters may seek to scare incumbents into acceding to their demands with the threat of political disorder or seizure of power, and state forces may attempt to repress violence by frightening protesters with displays of force, such episodes are best understood as jockeying for power and legitimacy in the eyes of third parties, such as the nonprotesting public, the military, or foreign powers. The victor is typically the side that is able to command the support of such third parties, as was the case in Serbia in 2000 (Birch 2002a), in Madagascar (Randrianja 2003), and in Mexico (Magaloni 2010). For the opposition, anger rather than fear is most useful in mobilizing regime opponents (Young 2017).

There are also other reasons to believe that nonstate actors are more likely to select forms of violence linked to mass mobilization rather than engaging in "surgical strikes" and other highly targeted attacks. This is because of the risks associated with the use of force at election time. The state has both the capacity and the incentive to crack down very hard on any illicit use of force, especially force that interferes with electoral competition. Moreover, if the opposition is known to engage in violent acts itself, any legitimacy advantage it maintains may well be squandered in the face of the scrutiny afforded by the media.

It may in some contexts be rational for opposition-allied forces to undertake targeted attacks against state candidates and campaign activities in areas where this can be expected to lead to material electoral benefits, but the most potent strategy for the opposition is to mobilize its supporters onto the streets. Mass mobilization both spreads the risk of repression and makes it possible for the opposition to portray the mobilization as the result of legitimate grievances against state injustices (Tilly 2004). Mass mobilization may or may not lead to violence, but during a highly charged electoral campaign when rival groups of party supporters confront each other, violence often results. Likewise, mass protests against fraud following the announcement of the results of an election often lead to at least some violent disorder; Beaulieu (2014) reported that 61 percent of the postelectoral protests included in her 1975–2006 sample turned violent, including those in states as diverse as Armenia, Cambodia, Kyrgyzstan, and Zambia. Previous research has found that violence itself can be a powerful mobilizational device (Bueno de Mesquita and Smith 2010; Kalyvas 2006), suggesting a possible feedback effect whereby mobilization leads to violence, which leads to further mobilization.

To sum up the discussion of causal mechanisms, we have delineated three different channels through which violence operates: obstruction, intimidation, and protest. There are of course other less common uses of violence, such as cattle raids or kidnap for ransom designed to raise election campaign funds, as reported in Kenya and the Philippines respectively (Meier, Bond, and Bond 2007; Patino and Velasco 2004), but a thorough reading of the relevant case-study literature suggests that obstruction, intimidation, and protest are the most prevalent channels for electoral violence.

This survey of the actors, management challenges, and causal channels inherent in the production of electoral violence demonstrates the variety and complexity of this phenomenon. It also enables us to formulate straightforward hypotheses. Given the "cheapness," flexibility, and efficacy of intimidation, this will be an attractive option for state actors considering using violence for electoral ends. An added advantage of intimidation is that in as much as it often falls short of causing outright physical harm, its perpetration does not carry the same degree of risk as forms of direct obstructive violence that result in actual bodily harm to individuals or physical damage to property. The CREV data set, which distinguishes by actor between threats and physical attacks, indicates that state actors engaged in at least some threatening behavior in 89.91 percent of elections in this data set, whereas there were reports of state-initiated attacks in 71.14 percent of elections in the data set. These numbers fall quite considerably when only elections with 10 or more incidents are included; in 53.47 percent of cases there were 10 or more state threats, and in 38.33 percent there were 10 or more state attacks. State actors are more likely to threaten violence than to undertake physical attacks.

The opposition, for its part, will normally face considerable risks if it uses violence of any sort liberally. It will thus have a strong incentive to bide its time and wait for a propitious moment, such as a close race where the incumbent has clearly lost popular support and is at risk of electoral defeat. Indeed, nonstate actors reportedly threatened violence in 58.04 percent of the elections included in the CREV data set (and in 25.08 percent of cases there were 10 or more such incidents), whereas they are reported as having carried out at least one physical attack in 87.45 percent of cases (with 10 or more incidents in 57.57 percent of elections). Thus, in contradistinction to state actors, attacks are the most common mode of electoral violence for nonstate actors. When the opposition does opt for violence, protest violence involving mass mobilization will often be an attractive option:

H5: Nonstate actors in opposition can be expected to favor forms of violence associated with mass mobilization, including protest violence, which will typically lead to countermeasures by state actors.

So far we have explored the motives of state and nonstate actors in relative isolation from each other. But real-world situations are characterized by strategic interactions, as actors adjust their strategies in response to those of their opponents, and this is an important aspect of microlevel causal channels that needs to be taken into consideration in the study of electoral violence. There is scattered evidence from case studies and regional analyses that this is the case. Tit-for-tat retaliatory violence has been observed, for example, in Kenya, Nigeria, Sri Lanka, Timor-Leste, and Zimbabwe (Bekoe and Burchard 2017; Dercon and Gutiérrez-Romero 2012; Fischer 2016; Höglund 2009; Klaus and Mitchell 2015; Kriger 2005; cf. Van Ham and Lindberg 2015). If the use of force at election time is in general a function of strategic interactions among actors, then this suggests a final hypothesis:

H6: Actors' use of electoral violence will increase when they are the object of violent acts by their electoral opponents.

A final consideration follows from the observation that electoral violence is extremely diverse in its manifestations. The general expectations set out here in the form of six hypotheses can be expected, if they are confirmed, to capture a good deal of the overall "shape" of electoral violence as a political phenomenon. Yet beneath the regularities we can discover in global data sets, there will by myriad exceptions, variations, and unexpected occurrences that also form an important part of any political activity, and perhaps an even more important part of strategies that are illicit, such as the use of force to skew electoral outcomes. Though it makes little sense to frame this characterization of electoral conflict as a formal hypothesis, it will be necessary to bear in mind in the chapters to come that there is tremendous variety in the types of intimidation, coercion, assault, murder, and vandalism that afflict elections, and also the political purposes to which such actions are put. The discussion in chapter 5 will reflect most explicitly on the diversity of electoral violence, but this is a theme that is threaded throughout the empirical evidence presented in the other chapters as well, and one that it is important never to lose sight of when considering specific instances of the phenomenon.

Conclusion

Elections are institutions that establish a means of gaining power and legitimacy. But there are many ways in which elections can be won. They can be won through open competition in which parties (or other political forces) present their track records and proposals for the future of the country, and voters select parties on this basis. But very often this open model of electoral competition proves unattractive for those who hold the reins of power in a state, and unpopular leaders frequently seek to use the resources at their disposal to make it easier for them to win elections.

Although widespread fatal electoral violence is still the exception rather than the norm in most countries, this phenomenon is coming to be seen by international actors as a significant global challenge and a threat to democratic institutions. In the past decade, the United Nations Development Program, the International Institute for Democracy and Electoral Assistance, the International Foundation for Electoral Systems, the United States Agency for International Development, and the United States Institute for Peace have all launched major electoral-violence initiatives (Claes 2016; Creative Associates International 2013; Fischer 2002; International IDEA 2009, 2011; Kammerud 2011; UNDP 2009). In the wake of the extreme violence witnessed in the 2007–8 Kenyan elections, a report by the Kofi Annan Foundation identified conflict at election time as one of the most significant threats to democracy today: "While this violence is not uniform in its causes or characteristics, it represents a major challenge to the integrity of elections around the world." The report goes on to add that "violence is not simply a problem for new democracies during the transition phase. There is no guarantee that election related violence will disappear over time as a country gains more experience with the electoral process. Instead, electoral violence is a function of weak or corrupt institutions" (GCEDS 2012, 24–25).

For the reasons set out above, it is logical to assume that in most contexts the state is the first mover in the decision to employ violent electoral tactics. State actors control the levers of electoral administration and they control the principal repressive institutions of the state; they often also have the power to decide the date of the election, so they have a significant advantage in terms of logistical planning over nonstate actors, who are typically obliged to react to state electoral initiatives. That said, the opposition can does have the power to make important choices. The most important choice is whether to take part in the election at all. If the opposition decides to boycott an election on the grounds that it is unlikely to be sufficiently fair, it must then decide whether to sit the election out peacefully or seek further to undermine the legitimacy of the electoral contest through efforts to sabotage that process via violence. Though the use of violence in any form may compromise opposition legitimacy, the extent to which this will result depends in large measure on the perceived legitimacy of the regime and the electoral process it is leading. If the incumbent's electoral strategy is highly violent, counterattacks by the opposition may be tolerated or indeed welcomed by large sectors of the population. In chapter 3 we turn to the empirical analysis of state-initiated electoral violence, before considering nonstate violence in chapter 4. These two chapters together will be used to test hypotheses H1–H5, while chapter 5 will test H6 and explore variations on the general relationships set out here. We will await chapter 6 for the development of hypotheses relevant to electoral-violence prevention, as this involves a discrete set of considerations.

3

Coercive Electoral Governance

THE USE OF FORCE BY STATE ACTORS

This chapter begins empirical testing of the hypotheses set out in chapter 2. Specifically, we are interested in finding out how state-initiated electoral violence is related to how power is structured in society by democratic institutions and corruption, and the way in which state violence is linked to other forms of electoral manipulation, including misconduct and vote buying. The analysis will also consider the types of violence employed by state actors to achieve electoral ends.

But first it makes sense to ask why we expect state actors to be responsible for violence at elections. One possible explanation for the forceful undermining of democratic electoral institutions is that those who decide to hold an election are not in the main those who deploy violence. This is the position, implicit or explicit, of a number of scholars who have studied the phenomenon. Violence may, as Collier and Vicente (2012, 2014) argued in the African context, be mainly a form of contentious politics, and as such a tool of the opposition, which is bereft of control over the formal institutional levers of power that might be used to engage in fraud (cf. Norris, Frank, and Martínez i Coma 2015). The use of electoral violence could thus be a response to an electoral process that is viewed as illegitimate because it is wracked by abuse. Moreover, opposition elites may not hold the same degree of normative commitment to elections as an institution if they have not been included in discussions over electoral procedures. They might view the use of violence to achieve their electoral goals as an acceptable strategy, given the circumstances in which they find themselves. If there are groups or organizations that are opposed to the use of elections per se, or opposed to the body to which elections are being held, violence may be seen as a suitable means of disrupting the electoral process. Alternatively, violence may be used by oppositions to protest against fraud and other forms of manipulation by state actors. Indeed, the link between state-enacted fraud and opposition-led violence has been demonstrated in a number of regional and case studies (Boone and Kriger 2012; Daxecker 2012; Höglund 2009; Höglund, Jarstad, and Söderberg Kovacs 2009; Opitz, Fjelde, and Höglund 2013).

However, the data presented in chapter 1 indicate that across the globe the majority of electoral violence is committed by state actors, a finding that is supported also by the work of other scholars.[1] Though the CREV data cited in that chapter suggest that nonstate actors are more likely than state actors to undertake attacks, the aggregate figures for state violence exceed those for nonstate violence in both the CREV and the V-DEM data sets, the only sources that disaggregate the two. When we think about the circumstances under which violent acts are carried out, this stands to reason, as there are strong theoretical grounds for believing that the context in which coercive methods are employed during electoral processes is shaped mainly by the state. States traditionally monopolize the legitimate use of force; they are thus in a position to allow or punish violence perpetrated by their own members and by others. The literature on political violence supports this contention. In a detailed study of collective violence, Tilly summarized a range of previous analyses and noted that "repressive [state] forces themselves are the most consistent initiators and performers of collective violence," and he went on to add that "the chief source of variation in collective violence is the operation of the polity" (Tilly 1978, 177, 182). Except in cases of extreme state weakness, public bodies will therefore almost always play a large role in shaping the incentives for any actor to use force during elections. There may be exceptions to this generalization when states are very weak, but in the vast majority of contexts, state actors can be assumed to play the greatest role in structuring the incentives in a society for electoral violence.

This chapter begins with a theoretical discussion of the choice situation in which state actors find themselves. The second section provides a descriptive

---

1. Studies by Fjelde and Höglund (2016) and Straus and Taylor (2012) have both found that state actors commit the majority of preelectoral violence.

overview of the data, while the third section presents the large-N explanatory models. Case studies of Zimbabwe, Syria, Belarus, and Paraguay follow in the fourth section, and a final section concludes.

Choices for State Actors

State and state-affiliated actors, including incumbent political leaders, have the greatest degree of latitude in selecting electoral strategies, and in particular deciding whether to use violence. They control the levers of power, the electoral administration, and often the timing of elections. They also enjoy a monopoly on the legitimate use of force. At the same time, their choice is conditioned by a range of factors, the most noteworthy of which are risk and resources. Leaders want to win elections, but this is not all they can be expected to want. More than winning elections, they should want to remain in power, and even more than remaining in power, they should want to remain alive (Cox 2009). They do not want to be subject to violence, which is always a very real risk for those who use abusive techniques against their citizens. The question then arises as to why leaders would hold elections so violent that the ensuing backlash threatens to remove them from power and in some cases even puts their physical well-being in danger.

Part of the answer is that when the leaders of less-than-democratic states perceive they are in danger of losing power, they are likely to engage in excessively risky forms of electoral manipulation, including violence, as demonstrated empirically by Hafner-Burton, Hyde, and Jablonski (2014). Larry Diamond has also noted that leaders will undertake the greatest amounts of violent repression when they are vulnerable: "When long-time authoritarian rulers face serious challenges (as in Malaysia and Zimbabwe recently), they may turn to their nastiest levels of repression, deploying levels of violence and intimidation that are unnecessary when political domination can be more subtly secured at the ballot box" (2002, 33). The question arises, however, as to why leaders would ever run the risks associated with electoral violence, especially when international observers are present to document it. Leaders ought, in theory, to select packages of electoral misconduct in which the greatest emphasis is put on "upstream" forms of manipulation, such as passing laws that advantage them in electoral terms, and cajoling or bribing voters into choosing the incumbent or incumbent-backed electoral option. The short answer is that in most cases this is precisely what they do. Leaders generally design strategies of electoral misconduct that enable them to win elections peacefully and to retain power (Birch 2011). However, this is not always the choice they make. They do sometimes opt for riskier forms of electoral manipulation, including violence.

Cox (2009) and Fearon (2011) have both argued that the leaders of authoritarian states risk holding elections so as to gain information about the strength of their rivals and thereby reduce the chances of violent removal from office through popular rebellion. Such information also helps the citizenry gauge leader strength, provided elections are fair enough. As Fearon said, "both parties may be better off if they commit to an independently monitored electoral system, because elections reveal more accurately and publicly what would happen in a rebellion" (2011, 1663). It follows that, over time, elections ought to become increasingly democratic as leaders will, if they behave strategically, refrain from the most blatant forms of electoral abuse and allow the scrutiny of elections in order to prevent threats that might put them at risk of violent removal from office. A similar argument was articulated by Staffan Lindberg, who detailed what he described as "democratization by elections":

> Iterative, multiparty elections change the cost of both repression and toleration and are thus key events that affect the cost-benefit analysis for the incumbent as well as for reformers. . . . If large numbers of the electorate turn out for elections and vote for the opposition, the cost of electoral manipulation and intimidation goes up. A more massive scheme of fraud and use of force needs to be put in place and shielded from outsiders, the risk of adverse reactions from the international community increases, the risk of post-electoral protest and violence goes up, and so on. At the same time, the benefits for the opposition elites of daring to mobilize citizens for protest increase. (Lindberg 2009, 325–26)

Lindberg acknowledged that in some cases elections can serve to reproduce and strengthen authoritarian regimes, but he argued that over time the cost of repeated repression at election time goes up, leading many authoritarian rulers to democratize eventually. This explains why leaders sometimes hold elections that are "too free" from the point of view of their narrow electoral interests, causing them to lose office and, under the right conditions, bringing to an end a period of authoritarianism.

The problem with both these authors' arguments is that although they can undoubtedly help to explain certain individual cases, it is unclear that they help us to explain aggregate patterns over time, as there is little evidence of a clear upward trend in recent years in the integrity of elections in semiauthoritarian states, once the democratization of central Europe in the

1990s is taken into consideration (Birch 2011). Something else must be going on to counteract cases where elections serve as a motor of democratization.

It is thus instructive to consider the roles of risks and resources in shaping the conditions under which actors might favor coercion over particularism as a preferred strategy of behavioral manipulation. Most political elites in authoritarian and semiauthoritarian settings can be expected to use some combination of the two methods, rewarding their supporters and coercing likely opponents (Blaydes 2011; González-Ocantos et al., 2020; Rauschenbach and Paula 2019; Van Ham and Lindberg 2015). Yet over and above this basic expectation, there are a number of factors that can be expected to be associated with a propensity to opt for violent over particularist measures. If "carrots" and "sticks" are in some senses alternatives, elites will have to select a balance that will serve their needs, depending on their resources and capabilities at any given point in time. I have argued that political elites well endowed with established clientelistic support bases will most likely rely primarily on corruption and other particularistic means to secure victory, but they will resort to violence and the more egregious forms of fraud if they face unusual or unexpected electoral risks. It follows that where leaders have limited established support networks and/or fewer resources to distribute, they are more likely to employ violence.

Overall Patterns

The empirical analysis of electoral violence begins with consideration of the overall distribution of different types of electoral manipulation commonly employed. To this end, I have taken the transformed ordinal versions of the V-DEM electoral-violence indicators and an indicator for vote buying from the V-DEM data set (*v2elvotbuy*, inverted so that higher values correspond to greater vote buying), together with a measure of electoral misconduct that has been purged of both violence and vote buying, and I have collapsed these indicators by country mean over the 1945–2012 period.[2] Each measure is dichotomized so as to create dummy indicators designating high levels of the manipulative tool in question. The top points on the four-point

2. This measure is constructed along the same lines as the V-DEM clean-elections index indicator, but with violence and vote-buying variables excluded. Specifically, the index is an additive scale (Cronbach's alpha = .916) composed of the following V-DEM indicators: electoral-authority autonomy (*v2elembaut*), electoral-authority capacity (*v2elembcap*), electoral-register accuracy (*v2elrgstry*), and "other irregularities" (*v2elirreg*), including "use of double IDs, intentional lack of voting materials, ballot-stuffing, misreporting of votes, and false collation of votes" (Coppedge et al. 2018a, 44).

state-violence scale (representing 15 percent of all cases) are included in the state-violence dummy; the nonstate-violence dummy includes the top three points on the five-point ordinal scale underlying this measure (reflecting 20 percent of the sample). The dummy variables for high levels of electoral misconduct and vote buying include the highest 20 percent of cases on each of these interval scales. Through this procedure it was possible to develop measures of high levels of manipulation on each of the four indicators for a total of 164 states. Table 3.1 sets out the countries that have various combinations of high scores on these four indicators.

Several important relationships immediately stand out from this table. First, the most common combinations are no excessive manipulation of any kind (43 cases, too numerous to list here) or high levels of all four forms of manipulation (21 cases). Together these polar opposites make up nearly half (40 percent) of all the cases included, suggesting that different forms of electoral manipulation tend to hang together. Second, it is relatively rare to see high levels of electoral misconduct in the absence of high levels of violence; there is not a single case of high misconduct alone where no form of violence is employed at high levels, and only eight cases with high levels of misconduct and vote buying, but no extensive violence.[3] Thus, as predicted in chapter 2, electoral violence is the handmaiden of other forms of electoral impropriety.

It is somewhat more common for vote buying to be alone prevalent—there are 16 rather heterogeneous cases where this is true. Violence is unlikely to be widespread in the absence of other forms of electoral abuse, but there are five cases where both state and nonstate violence are rife but not misconduct or vote buying, and 11 cases where nonstate violence alone predominates. In 7 cases—which with 2 exceptions are all communist or former communist countries—state violence is the only major problem. In the remaining cases, violence goes hand in hand with misconduct, vote buying, or both. Within this group, there are two clear pairings: as predicted in chapter 2, high levels of state violence are common in conjunction with high levels of misconduct, either together with vote buying (26 cases) or on its own (10 cases). Nonstate violence, by contrast, is commonly found together with vote buying, and there are only 4 cases where high levels of nonstate violence are accompanied by high levels of misconduct without state violence also being prevalent. Thus Collier and Vicente's (2012) conjecture that the rational state ought to favor fraud while rational oppositions should hit back with violence is reflected in only 11 states.

---

3. Curiously, these include Germany. It is not immediately obvious why Germany is so categorized. It is possible that this is because of a coding error in the V-DEM data set.

TABLE 3-1. Electoral Violence, Misconduct, and Vote Buying: Global Patterns 1945–2012

	State Violence	Nonstate Violence	State and Nonstate Violence	Neither State nor Nonstate Violence
Electoral Misconduct	Belarus Djibouti Swaziland Syria Uzbekistan	Benin Ethiopia Tajikistan Tanzania	Guyana Laos Liberia Serbia Somalia	
Vote Buying	Romania	Georgia Ghana Pakistan PNG Philippines Vietnam Senegal	Armenia Azerbaijan Jordan Malaysia Niger Uganda	Algeria Angola Australia Bhutan Bosnia and H. Burkina Faso Chile Costa Rica Czech Republic Guinea Bissau Japan Kuwait Solomon Islands Taiwan Turkey Venezuela
Electoral Misconduct and Vote Buying	Mali Mauritania Paraguay Tunisia Turkmenistan	Comoros Congo Gabon Honduras Iraq Madagascar Morocco Mozambique	Bolivia Cameroon CAR Chad Colombia Côte d'Ivoire Cuba DRC Dominican Republic Egypt El Salvador Equatorial Guinea Guatemala Guinea Haiti Iran Kenya Lebanon Libya Mexico	Afghanistan Bahrain Czechoslovakia Germany Kazakhstan Kyrgyz Republic Portugal Yemen

TABLE 3-1. (*continued*)

	State Violence	Nonstate Violence	State and Nonstate Violence	Neither State nor Nonstate Violence
Neither Electoral Misconduct nor Vote Buying	Brazil D. R. Vietnam East Germany Hungary Indonesia Poland Russia	Bangladesh Burundi Cambodia India Jamaica Lesotho Malawi South Africa South Yemen Sri Lanka Ukraine	Albania Bulgaria Mongolia Rwanda Zambia	43 countries

Cells in this table are populated according to high usage (in the top 20 percent of cases) of the forms of electoral manipulation in question. Bosnia and H., Bosnia and Herzegovina; CAR, Central African Republic; DRC, Democratic Republic of Congo; D. R. Vietnam, Democratic Republic of Vietnam; PNG, Papua New Guinea.

These data provide strong support for the argument that violence is a complement to other forms of electoral abuse, not a substitute. Yet it could be that this finding is due to the fact that the data presented here on violence, misconduct, and vote buying all come from the same source: V-DEM experts, whose overall view of a given election may affect the scores they provide on different measures of electoral probity. This fear can be allayed by examination of correlation coefficients between variables from different data sets, which reveals that a measure of electoral misconduct derived from the NELDA data set[4] is as significantly related to the V-DEM electoral-violence variables as are the V-DEM-derived electoral-misconduct and vote-buying measures. Similarly, the V-DEM electoral-misconduct and vote-buying measures are as significantly related to the NELDA electoral-violence measures as to the V-DEM electoral-violence measures.

While the data in table 3.1 provide a good feel for the texture of the relationships between electoral violence and other forms of electoral manipulation, they do not afford the precision required to test the hypotheses

4. This measure is an additive index created from the following NELDA indicators: "Before elections, are there significant concerns that elections will not be free and fair?" (*Nelda11*), "Were opposition leaders prevented from running?" (*Nelda13*), "In the run-up to the election, were there allegations of media bias in favor of the incumbent?" (*Nelda16*), and "Is there evidence that reports critical of the government's handling of the election reached large numbers of people?" (*Nelda28*).

elaborated in chapter 2. For this purpose, we turn to multivariate analysis, considering here the role of state-initiated violence in the electoral ecology, while reserving analysis of nonstate violence for chapter 4.

State Violence, Fraud, and Electoral Manipulation

We are now in a position to test the hypothesized relationship between forms of electoral manipulation on empirical evidence, using the electoral-violence data described in chapter 1 together with covariates from a range of sources. In order to do so, it is necessary first to develop indicators for our core independent variables: democratic institutions and corruption.

MEASURING DEMOCRATIC INSTITUTIONS

In chapter 1, the familiar "polity" score from the Polity IV data set was used to provide an overview of the magnitude of electoral violence at different levels of democracy. Yet, for the purposes of regression analysis where we are interested in examining causal relationships, it does not make sense to employ the polity score or any other aggregate measure of democratic performance, democratic rights, or democratic consolidation as an independent variable, as such measures invariably take account of electoral violence and other illicit uses of force to sway democratic decision-making procedures. It is highly unlikely that any country that had experienced high levels of electoral violence would ever receive a high score on any such measure, even if electoral violence were the only defect found in that country's democracy in a particular year, given the substantive importance of elections to democratic procedures. In order to avoid this form of endogeneity, it is necessary to use proxies for democratic performance that capture the constraints inherent in the institutional arrangements in a particular country without at the same time including any measure of electoral practices. For this, the commonly used Polity IV "executive-constraints" measure is chosen. The executive-constraints indicator measures institutionalized constraints exercised by "accountability groups," including legislatures, courts, and other formal sources of authority (Marshall, Gurr, and Jaggers 2016). This variable thus captures the extent to which the executive is bound by formal procedures that limit his or her authority; it is therefore a good indicator of the leader's freedom to manipulate at will elections and electorally relevant institutions such as the security forces and the courts. In theory it would be desirable to include a wider range of democracy measures, but this is precluded by the high correlations among them, as well as the high negative correlation between many of the democracy measures and corruption.

MEASURING CORRUPTION

Informal institutions of clientelism and patronage are typically dense networks of social ties that facilitate member access to state resources (Helmke and Levitsky 2006; Kitschelt and Wilkinson 2007). The most common manifestation of informal institutions, and the manifestation hypothesized in chapter 2 to be most closely related to electoral violence, is corruption.[5] The best known measures of corruption are the Transparency International Corruption Perceptions Index and the control-of-corruption indicator in the World Bank Governance Indicator data set, which rely on the same underlying data, derived largely from surveys of international business elites.[6] Yet these data sets cover the period since the mid-1990s only, they are largely measures of bureaucratic corruption involving bribery, and they have a number of well-known statistical properties that make them less than ideal for use as point estimates in longitudinal analysis (Dochev and Ujhelyi 2014; Sampford et al. 2006; Transparency International 2017).

A useful alternative is the V-DEM Political Corruption Index ($v2x\_corr$), which represents answers to the question "How pervasive is political corruption?" and:

> measures of six distinct types of corruption that cover both different areas and levels of the polity realm, distinguishing between executive, legislative and judicial corruption. Within the executive realm, the measures also distinguish between corruption mostly pertaining to bribery and corruption due to embezzlement. Finally, they differentiate between corruption in the highest echelons of the executive (at the level of the rulers/cabinet) on the one hand, and in the public sector at large on the other. The measures thus tap into several distinct types of corruption: both "petty" and "grand"; both bribery and theft; both corruption

5. From one perspective, clientelism is a broader concept than corruption, as the concept of clientelism designates not merely specific acts of illicit exchange, but entire structures of power. Rothstein and Varraich (2017), on the other hand, view clientelism and patronage as members of the family of related phenomena that they label "corruption." Conceptually, these concepts are very similar, as the core feature of each of them is a breach of the impartiality expected of democratic state institutions.

6. For details, see Kaufmann and Kraay (2016) and Transparency International (2017).

aimed [at] influencing law making and that affecting implementation. (Coppedge et al. 2018a, 230)

The index is calculated as the average of public-sector corruption (*v2x_pubcorr*), executive corruption (*v2x_execorr*), legislative corruption (*v2lgcrrpt*), and judicial corruption (*v2jucorrdc*). An added advantage of using the V-DEM corruption data is therefore that, in addition to the composite Corruption Index, the V-DEM data set includes these separate indicators reflecting the corruption of different branches of the state, enabling the analysis of the link between electoral violence and the infiltration of different branches by informal power structures.

The Public Sector Corruption Index represents answers to the question "To what extent do public sector employees grant favors in exchange for bribes, kickbacks, or other material inducements, and how often do they steal, embezzle, or misappropriate public funds or other state resources for personal or family use?" (Coppedge et al. 2018a, 235).[7] The Executive Corruption Index, *v2x_execorr*, is a measure of responses to the question "How routinely do members of the executive . . . or their agents grant favors in exchange for bribes, kickbacks, or other material inducements, and how often do they steal, embezzle, or misappropriate public funds or other state resources for personal or family use?" (232).[8] The V-DEM measure of legislative corruption, *v2lgcrrpt* ("Legislature corrupt activities"), represents answers to the question "Do members of the legislature abuse their position for financial gain?" (132).[9] The measure of judicial corruption, *v2jucorrdc* ("Judicial corruption decision"), reflects answers to the question "How often do individuals or businesses make undocumented extra payments or bribes in order to speed up or delay the process or to obtain a favorable judicial decision?" (151).[10]

---

7. The indicator is the mean of the point estimates of a Bayesian factor analysis model of the V-DEM indicators for public-sector bribery (*v2excrptps*) and embezzlement (*v2exthftps*) (Coppedge et al. 2018a, 235).

8. The index is calculated as the mean of the point estimates of the Bayesian factor analysis model of the two other indicators: those for executive bribery (*v2exbribe*) and executive embezzlement (*v2exembez*) (Coppedge et al. 2018a, 232).

9. The V-DEM codebook specifies that "This includes any of the following: (a) accepting bribes, (b) helping to obtain government contracts for firms that the legislator (or his/her family/friends/political supporters) own, (c) doing favors for firms in exchange for the opportunity of employment after leaving the legislature, (d) stealing money from the state or from campaign donations for personal use" (Coppedge et al. 2018a, 134). The indicator is coded on a five-point scale ranging from 0 (never) to 4 (commonly); the ordinal scale is converted to an interval scale by the Bayesian measurement model.

10. This five-point scale runs from 0 (never) to 4 (always) (Coppedge et al. 2018a, 151).

Table 3.2 presents a series of regression models based on these data. These models employ Bell and Jones's (2015) within-between random effects estimation strategy, which conditions the marginal effects of the covariates on the mean for each country by separately modeling cross-country ("between") variation as country means and interelectoral ("within") variation as deviation from the country mean for each variable. This strategy has the advantage over fixed effects that it enables the inclusion of slowly changing structural variables (which may be constant over time in some countries) and the analysis of both cross-sectional and cross-temporal effects, while at the same time avoiding the problem of possible correlation between residuals and explanatory variables that can affect standard random effects models.[11] All the models include year fixed effects to control for variations in incident reporting capabilities over time, as well as other secular changes and shocks that may have affected patterns of electoral violence. The dependent variables in Models 1 and 2 are binary NELDA indicators, and for this reason these are logit models. Model 1 is based on the overall-electoral-violence variable (*Nelda33*), on the grounds that, as shown in chapter 1, most electoral violence is state initiated. The dependent variable in Model 2 is the preelectoral-harassment variable (*Nelda15*), which taps state violence only but is restricted to that carried out in the run-up to the election. The dependent variable in the remaining models is an ordinal version of the V-DEM state-violence variable (*v2elintim*), transformed such that higher scores correspond to greater levels of violence. Models 3–7 are ordinal logit models. These models also all include controls often found in previous studies to be related to electoral violence: level of development (per capita GDP), the presence of international election monitors, and winner-take-all election types (presidential and legislative majoritarian).[12]

11. In the within-between model, the coefficients of the "within" variables are the same as those in a standard fixed effects model. For details of this approach see Bell and Jones (2015); see also Mundlack (1978).

12. See chapter 1 for a discussion of the relevant literature. The level of nonelectoral violence in a country is too closely correlated with the democratic constraints and corruption variables for it to be possible to include it in these models. Per capita GDP (logged) is taken from Bolt and Van Zanden (2014). Data for this variable are extracted from the V-DEM data set *e_migdppcln*. The variable for international election monitors is the "Election international monitors" (*v2elintmon*) indicator from the V-DEM data set (Coppedge et al 2018a, 73). Freedom from nonelectoral political violence is measured by the V-DEM Physical Violence Index (*v2x_clphy*), designed to answer the question "To what extent is physical integrity respected?" (Coppedge et al. 2018a, 229), and composed of measures of torture and political killings. Dummy variables for election type are included for presidential and legislative-majoritarian elections. These variables are derived from two sources: NELDA data on election "type" from version 4.0 of NELDA (Hyde and Marinov, 2012, 2015) is used to distinguish presidential from legislative elections. The data are collapsed

TABLE 3-2. State-Initiated Electoral Violence, 1945–2012

	Model 1 NELDA	Model 2 NELDA	Model 3 V-DEM	Model 4 V-DEM	Model 5 V-DEM	Model 6 V-DEM	Model 7 V-DEM
	All violence	Preelectoral					
CROSS-NATIONAL ("BETWEEN") EFFECTS							
Corruption index	4.477c	1.687	5.980c				
	(0.792)	(0.875)	(1.374)				
Public-sector corruption				5.906c			
				(1.331)			
Executive corruption					5.461c		
					(1.312)		
Legislative corruption						0.953c	
						(0.248)	
Judicial corruption							1.083c
							(0.296)
Executive constraints	0.176	−0.590c	−1.126c	−1.074c	−1.059c	−1.279c	−1.259c
	(0.109)	(0.132)	(0.189)	(0.189)	(0.198)	(0.175)	(0.184)
Per capita GDP (log)	−0.339a	−0.178	−0.212	−0.263	−0.492	−0.699a	−0.071
	(0.167)	(0.219)	(0.290)	(0.271)	(0.274)	(0.274)	(0.317)
International election monitors	−0.266	0.924	1.857b	1.701a	1.909b	1.993b	2.286c
	(0.628)	(0.678)	(0.721)	(0.727)	(0.724)	(0.729)	(0.702)
Presidential	−1.847a	0.318	−0.613	−0.285	−0.281	−0.565	−1.159
	(0.835)	(0.887)	(1.213)	(1.224)	(1.214)	(1.166)	(1.279)
Legislative-majoritarian	0.788	0.525	1.306	0.960	0.906	1.117	1.472
	(0.493)	(0.578)	(0.717)	(0.673)	(0.698)	(0.720)	(0.768)
LONGITUDINAL ("WITHIN") EFFECTS							
Corruption index	3.188b	3.460b	4.877c				
	(1.152)	(1.205)	(1.223)				

(continued)

	Model 1	Model 2	Model 3	Model 4	Model 5	Model 6	Model 7
Public-sector corruption	−0.038 (0.091)			5.121[c] (1.338)			
Executive corruption					5.159[c] (1.058)		
Legislative corruption						0.320 (0.197)	
Judicial corruption							0.912[b] (0.313)
Executive constraints	−0.542[c] (0.112)		−0.805[c] (0.122)	−0.785[c] (0.121)	−0.794[c] (0.123)	−0.999[c] (0.130)	−0.817[c] (0.122)
Per capita GDP (log)	0.191 (0.306)		−0.809[a] (0.360)	−0.696 (0.377)	−0.898[b] (0.350)	−0.983[b] (0.334)	−0.790[a] (0.327)
International election monitors	−0.144 (0.312)		0.149 (0.343)	0.091 (0.351)	0.129 (0.336)	0.268 (0.354)	0.305 (0.329)
Presidential	−0.380 (0.239)		−0.261 (0.164)	−0.274 (0.165)	−0.239 (0.162)	−0.285 (0.162)	−0.239 (0.161)
Legislative-majoritarian	0.185 (0.419)		0.423 (0.332)	0.344 (0.332)	0.481 (0.320)	0.446 (0.365)	0.408 (0.343)
Constant	1.627 (2.278)						
N	1668	1499	1735	1739	1739	1690	1735
Log pseudolikelihood	−577.201	−472.282	−1183.090	−1177.617	−1172.745	−1142.836	−1196.753
AIC	1308.402	1090.565	2532.180	2521.233	2511.490	2451.671	2559.506
BIC	1725.694	1478.381	2985.275	2974.502	2964.759	2902.567	3012.584

Cell entries are coefficients (robust standard errors). All models include year fixed effects (not shown). The dependent variable in Models 3–7 (*v2elintim_ord*) is transformed as follows: the values are inverted, and the highest value is then recoded to 0 to create a scale running from the lowest to the highest level of violence. Models 1 and 2 are random effects logit models. Models 3–7 are random effects ordered logit models; cut points not shown. AIC, Akaike information criterion; BIC, Bayesian information criterion.

[a] $p < .05$

[b] $p < .01$

[c] $p < .001$

Taken collectively, these models provide strong support for the dual hypotheses that corruption should be associated with an increase in state-perpetrated electoral violence and that democratic institutions should mitigate the use of force by state actors (H1 and H2 in chapter 2). Mean corruption within countries is strongly and positively related to electoral violence in all the models, with the exception of the NELDA preelectoral-harassment model (Model 2), where the relevant coefficient just barely fails to reach conventional levels of statistical significance. Variations in levels of corruption over time are also strongly and positively associated with electoral violence in all the models save that which employs the legislative-corruption indicator (Model 6). Thus corruption is a strong predictor of electoral violence in all seven models presented here, which between them employ different measures of state-initiated electoral violence and different measures of corruption.

A convenient way of assessing the magnitude of these effects is to consider predicted probabilities. As mean (cross-sectional) corruption rises from the bottom to the top of its observed scale and other variables are held at their means, the predicted probability of electoral violence according to Model 1, which relies on the binary NELDA overall-electoral-violence measure (*Nelda33*), rises from 2.16 to 43.64 percent; Model 2 predicts an analogous increase in the chances of preelectoral harassment (*Nelda15*) from 9.28 to 23.05 percent. The corresponding change predicted by Model 3, which relies on the more nuanced V-DEM state-violence indicator (*v2elintim*), is an increase from 2.14 to 29.58 percent in the chances of the highest level of violence. These models also demonstrate that variations in corruption from one election to the next condition electoral violence; the NELDA model for overall violence (*Nelda33*, Model 1) predicts that an increase from the bottom to the top of the range of the variable designating deviation from country means (longitudinal change) for corruption is associated with an increase in the probability of violence from 3.89 to 31.31 percent. The

---

by date via a .do file created by the NELDA team for this purpose, such that concurrent elections are a single case, which makes it possible to distinguish presidential from concurrent elections. Legislative elections are further broken down according to electoral system type, and a dummy variable is created for majoritarian electoral systems by employing the V-DEM lower-chamber electoral system variable, *v2elloelsy*. This indicator classifies electoral system into 13 types. The first 3 of these types (labelled 0, 1, and 2) are single-member district systems that reflect the winner-take-all logic. Legislative elections conducted under one of these systems are designated with the dummy variable "parliamentary majoritarian." The baseline category includes all elections types with multiple winners in each geographic area, including concurrent elections and elections conducted under proportional representation.

NELDA model for preelectoral harassment (*Nelda15*, Model 2) predicts that a similar shift is associated with an increase in the probability of preelectoral state violence from 4.74 to 31.72 percent. The corresponding change for the V-DEM state-violence indicator in Model 3 is an increase in probability of the highest level of violence from 4.88 to 28.75 percent. In sum, these results thus show that the level of corruption in a country is a strong and consistent predictor of how much state-initiated violence that country's elections are likely to experience, and that electoral violence is also sensitive to changes in corruption over time, as anticipated in chapter 2.[13]

The analysis of varieties of corruption presented in Models 4–7 tells much the same story as that evident in Model 3, which relies on the composite V-DEM corruption index. These models, which have as their dependent variable the more finely graded V-DEM electoral-violence indicator (*v2elintim*), show that an increase in mean public-sector corruption (*v2x_pubcorr*) from the bottom to the top of the scale pushes up the chances of the highest level of state violence from 2.40 to 30.42 percent (Model 4); a corresponding increase in mean executive corruption (*v2x_execorr*) results in a rise from 3.02 to 28.54 percent (Model 5); the change consequent upon an increase in mean legislative corruption (*v2lgcrrpt*) is from 2.34 to 28.32 percent (Model 6); and that which results from a rise in mean judicial corruption (*v2jucorrdc*) is a smaller shift from 1.80 to 2.12 percent (Model 7).[14] When it comes to interelectoral deviations from the means of these variables, the chances of the highest level of state violence increases from 5.57 to 31.23 percent for public-sector corruption (Model 4); from 4.93 to 28.04 percent for executive corruption (Model 5); from 11.72 to 20.11 percent for legislative corruption (Model 6); and from 5.88 to 26.76 percent for judicial corruption (Model 7). These figures are all broadly similar to those for the model that includes the overall-corruption index (*v2x_corr*), suggesting that the type of corruption is less important in predicting electoral violence than the presence of corruption, undoubtedly because different types of corruption tend to hang together.

The important role of executive constraints in shaping patterns of state electoral violence is also evident in these models. It may not be surprising that democracy should be a very powerful protector of the electoral peace, but it is useful to see that this effect holds even in the presence of corruption variables.

13. It is worth pointing out that the cross-sectional and longitudinal changes in predicted probabilities are not straightforwardly cumulative, as states at high levels of a variable have limited scope for increase.

14. The smaller coefficient magnitudes for legislative and judicial corruption are largely the result of the differences in variable construction described above.

The cross-sectional version of this variable is, as expected, significant and negatively signed in all the models in table 3.2, with the exception of Model 1, which relies on the NELDA overall-violence indicator (*Nelda33*), including nonstate as well as state violence. The longitudinal version of the executive-constraints variable is also significant in every model with the exception of that including the NELDA overall-violence indicator (*Nelda33*, Model 1). This suggests that changes over time in executive constraints help account for intertemporal variations in electoral violence, in accordance with the expectation that conjunctural political factors should largely explain why some elections in a country are violent whereas others are peaceful. In substantive terms, a rise in mean executive constraints from the bottom to the top of the observed range of this variable predicts a fall in the chances of an election experiencing preelectoral harassment (*Nelda15*) from 40.94 to 5.44 percent (Model 2). A similar change results in a drop in the probability of the highest level of violence as measured by the V-DEM state-violence indicator (*v2elintim*) from 40.50 to 2.35 percent (Model 3). An increase in over-time executive constraints results in a decline in the probability of violence as measured by the NELDA preelectoral-harassment indicator (*Nelda15*) from 50.76 to 3.71 percent (Model 2). According to Model 3, the same change results in a plunge in the probability of the highest level of state violence as measured by the V-DEM indicator (*v2elintim*) from 43.75 to 2.75 percent. Interestingly, modeling the executive-constraints variables as quadratics (not shown) indicates that the relationship between state violence and democratic constraints on the executive is broadly linear; chapter 4 returns to this topic, as the same cannot be said for nonstate violence.

Together, these findings suggest that corruption and democratic constraints both have strong impacts on state-initiated electoral violence. Corruption facilitates violence and democratic institutions constrain its use, as predicted by the theory outlined in chapter 2. It is also worth commenting on the control variables in these models. Per capita GDP is, as expected, negatively associated with electoral violence, but the coefficients for the relevant variables reach statistical significance in only about half the models. The presence of international election monitors is positively linked to electoral violence in some models, as anticipated in previous literature (Borzyskowski 2019; Daxecker 2014; Salehyan and Linebarger 2015); interestingly, it is the cross-sectional version of this variable that is significant, not its longitudinal counterpart, suggesting that when countries get into the habit of inviting observers, this may feed into the strategic thinking of political actors (for example, incumbents may plan in advance to crack down on the opposition after elections are over, as predicted by Bhasin and Gandhi [2013]). There is little indication, once other variables are controlled, that legislative elections held under winner-take-all majoritarian rules or presidential elections experience significantly higher (or lower) levels of state violence than the reference category in these models, which is elections where opportunities for winning are widely distributed (legislative elections held under proportional representation rules or concurrent elections).

The appendix to chapter 3 details robustness checks designed to test the impact of effects identified in previous research. The alternative models presented here find no support for a potential interaction effect between executive constraints and uncertainty as to the outcome of the election. This effect has been observed by Hafner-Burton, Hyde, and Jablonski (2014), but it is not in evidence in models including corruption terms. Another set of models tests for the interaction between ethnic power inequality and electoral system type found in an African sample by Fjelde and Höglund (2016); there is some evidence of an interaction between these variables, though one different from that found by Höglund and Fjelde. In neither case does the inclusion of these additional terms alter the basic relationship between corruption, democratic constraints, and electoral violence.

The next stage in the analysis is to add to the models in table 3.2 indicators for electoral misconduct and vote buying. A problem we face in this analysis is multicollinearity. The underlying power-structure variables of corruption, executive constraints, and freedom of expression are closely connected to electoral misconduct and vote buying, when we compare the over-time means of these variables. This is also true if we alter the proxies employed for the power-structure variables to indicators for rule of law, state capacity, or other measures of democratic institutions. This makes it problematic to include the country means for the power-structure measures in the same regression models as the country means for the electoral-manipulation variables. Given the strength of these relationships, the solution adopted here is to include only the longitudinal versions of these variables in the models. This makes sense substantively in as much as leaders have been hypothesized to select manipulative strategies based on features specific to individual elections. A further difficulty is that vote buying and electoral misconduct are also highly correlated; this is addressed by including them in separate models.

We start by analyzing the relationship between electoral misconduct and electoral violence in Model 1 in table 3.3, based on the NELDA indicator of state-initiated electoral violence (preelectoral harassment). The coefficient for electoral misconduct is positive and highly significant, confirming the conjecture set out in chapter 2 that misconduct and electoral violence should be complements, rather than substitutes. This model also provides evidence to support H3: that significant electoral misconduct often necessitates and is accompanied by state-initiated electoral violence. It will be recalled that this was framed as a "weak" causal relationship, in the sense that we expected to see an association between these two variables that has a causal aspect to it, in as much as the use of fraud and other forms of electoral abuse often relies on violence to back it up; this causal link will be explored in greater detail in the case studies later in this chapter.

Model 3 is an analogous model based on the V-DEM state-violence indicator, which is the most finely grained of the two measures and that which has the least missing data. Electoral misconduct is strongly and positively associated with state violence in this model also. A possible criticism of this model is that it relies on assessments of electoral violence and electoral misconduct by the same experts, whose overall evaluation of a given election might color their scoring of all aspects of electoral integrity, including both violence and misconduct. For this reason, Model 4 employs the V-DEM electoral-violence measure and the alternative electoral-misconduct measure constructed on the basis of NELDA variables. The NELDA data set does not include a full complement of misconduct measures, but as noted above the variables employed to create this alternative measure can be understood as a rough-and-ready substitute.[15] Again, this variable has a positive sign and is highly significant, confirming that the strong positive relationship between state-initiated electoral violence and electoral misconduct is not an artifact of data-set generation procedures.

Models 2 and 5 introduce vote buying rather than electoral misconduct. Readers will recall that chapter 2 predicted that electoral violence would hang together with both electoral misconduct and vote buying, but that electoral misconduct would be more closely associated with state-initiated violence and vote buying with nonstate-initiated violence. The weaker link between state violence and vote buying is clear from these models; though in both cases vote buying is a positive predictor of electoral violence—suggesting that, to an extent, state actors rely on this tool to back up violence—the coefficients are only weakly significant (below conventional

---

15. As described before, this measure is constructed along the same lines as the V-DEM clean-elections index indicator, but with violence and vote-buying variables excluded. Specifically, the index is an additive scale (Cronbach's alpha = .916) composed of the following V-DEM indicators: electoral-authority autonomy (*v2elembaut*), electoral-authority capacity (*v2elembcap*), electoral-register accuracy (*v2elrgstry*), and "other irregularities" (*v2elirreg*), including "use of double IDs, intentional lack of voting materials, ballot-stuffing, misreporting of votes, and false collation of votes" (Coppedge et al. 2018a, 44).

TABLE 3-3. State-Initiated Electoral Violence and Electoral Misconduct, 1945–2012

	NELDA State Preelectoral Harassment (*Nelda15*)		V-DEM Electoral Intimidation (*v2elintim*)		
	Model 1	Model 2	Model 3	Model 4	Model 5
CROSS-NATIONAL ("BETWEEN") EFFECTS					
Corruption Index	1.658	1.675	6.312[c]	6.009[c]	6.175[c]
	(0.875)	(0.872)	(1.468)	(1.392)	(1.400)
Executive constraints	−0.596[c]	−0.584[c]	−1.186[c]	−1.151[c]	−1.135[c]
	(0.133)	(0.132)	(0.197)	(0.189)	(0.190)
Per capita GDP (log)	−0.254	−0.196	−0.373	−0.213	−0.223
	(0.225)	(0.217)	(0.309)	(0.294)	(0.293)
International election	0.481	0.967	1.137	1.934[b]	1.927[b]
monitors	(0.694)	(0.689)	(0.784)	(0.726)	(0.746)
Presidential	0.131	0.200	−1.392	−0.672	−0.781
	(0.890)	(0.892)	(1.317)	(1.220)	(1.248)
Legislative-majoritarian	0.584	0.544	1.314	1.340	1.300
	(0.588)	(0.580)	(0.767)	(0.722)	(0.726)
LONGITUDINAL ("WITHIN") EFFECTS					
Electoral misconduct,	1.738[c]		2.445[c]		
V-DEM measure	(0.368)		(0.403)		
Electoral misconduct,				1.308[c]	
NELDA measure				(0.281)	
Vote buying		0.563[a]			0.516
		(0.227)			(0.291)
Corruption Index	0.145	1.742	0.336	5.006[c]	3.169[a]
	(1.280)	(1.370)	(1.395)	(1.244)	(1.570)
Executive constraints	−0.279[a]	−0.545[c]	−0.539[c]	−0.727[c]	−0.834[c]
	(0.125)	(0.112)	(0.141)	(0.123)	(0.124)
Per capita GDP (log)	0.324	0.252	−0.522	−0.721[a]	−0.739
	(0.318)	(0.306)	(0.379)	(0.364)	(0.382)
International election	0.110	−0.259	0.479	0.222	0.014
monitors	(0.324)	(0.305)	(0.381)	(0.339)	(0.352)
Presidential	−0.377	−0.396	−0.335	−0.257	−0.295
	(0.246)	(0.245)	(0.171)	(0.165)	(0.166)
Legislative-majoritarian	0.130	0.137	0.266	0.429	0.354
	(0.465)	(0.434)	(0.308)	(0.334)	(0.325)
Constant	1.145	1.294			
	(2.213)	(2.189)			
N	1499	1499	1735	1735	1735
Log pseudolikelihood	−455.263	−467.908	−1115.416	−1169.520	−1174.633
AIC	1058.526	1083.816	2398.832	2507.041	2517.266
BIC	1451.655	1476.945	2857.368	2965.577	2975.802

Cell entries are coefficients (robust standard errors). All models include year fixed effects (not shown). The dependent variable in Models 3–5 (*v2elintim_ord*) is transformed as follows: the values are inverted, and the highest value is then recoded to 0 to create a scale running from the lowest to the highest level of violence. Models 1 and 2 are random effects logit models; models 3–5 are random effects ordered logit models; cut points not shown. AIC, Akaike information criterion; BIC, Bayesian information criterion.

[a] $p < .05$

[b] $p < .01$

[c] $p < .001$

levels of statistical significance in the case of Model 5) and small in magnitude. The coefficients for the other variables in these models remain largely unchanged by the inclusion of the electoral-manipulation indicators.

The assessment of predicted probabilities provides further insight into the substantive impacts of the electoral-manipulation variables across models. Model 1 in table 3.3 indicates that an increase in deviation from country means in electoral misconduct from the bottom to the top of the scale for that variable increases the chances of an election suffering state violence (preelectoral harassment) dramatically from 1.00 percent to 74.49 percent. The analogous change in the highest level of state violence based on Model 3 is 0.76 to 58.69 percent, and that based on Model 4 is 11.19 to 23.01 percent. A similar increase in vote buying, by contrast, raises the risk of state violence from 7.21 to 31.18 percent in the NELDA-based Model 2. Thus, electoral misconduct is intimately associated with state violence, and this association is stronger than that for vote buying, though, as predicted, there is a positive association between state violence and both forms of electoral manipulation.

The cross-national findings presented here provide substantial support for the argument outlined above as to the structural conditions under which state actors will select violence as an election strategy; they also support the conjecture that violence is closely associated with the manipulation of electoral procedures. Thus violence is integral to other forms of electoral abuse, as the bivariate country-level associations in table 3.1 suggest. This is a fact that has largely escaped the extensive recent literature on electoral fraud, but it is one that is important for understanding how leaders of hybrid and semiauthoritarian states manipulate elections.

Large-N regression analysis is not capable of shedding light on the nuances of the relationship between electoral misconduct and state violence; for this purpose it is necessary to delve into individual cases where this relationship is found to be particularly strong. Case studies will also provide a means of probing the idea that threats and intimidation are the preferred electoral-violence method for state actors.

Case Studies

The evidence presented in the previous section indicates that violence is used by state actors in conjunction with other forms of electoral manipulation. I have argued that, generally speaking, violence is employed to back up electoral misconduct and vote buying, and that state actors are especially likely to rely on a combination of misconduct and violence when democratic institutions are weak and informal institutions are strong. Contextual variations in the cases chosen for analysis will allow us to assess these core claims.

The four cases selected to this end are Zimbabwe (1970–2008), Syria (1946–2011), Belarus (1991–2012), and Paraguay (1945–2012), which reflect different degrees of democratic competition. Of the four, Syria had the least scope for electoral contestation: no organized opposition was allowed, though in the post-1990s period independents could contest parliamentary elections, provided they passed a state vetting process. Belarus and Zimbabwe are examples of hegemonic authoritarian states where opposition parties were allowed to exist and to contest elections, but Alexander Lukashenko and his allies, on the one hand, and Mugabe's ZANU-PF (Zimbabwe African National Union—Patriotic Front), on the other, invariably won electoral contests. Paraguay underwent several distinct phases in the 1945–2012 period under analysis here: Alfredo Stroessner's military dictatorship during the 1954–89 period and the subsequent era of democratization and democratic consolidation. Even during the Stroessner period, electoral competition was allowed among three main parties, the dominant Colorados and two moderate opposition parties. In Syria, Belarus, and Paraguay, there is considerable evidence that blatant electoral misconduct and violence covary. Analysis of the interaction between these two types of electoral manipulation will shed light on the relationship between them.

ZIMBABWE

Zimbabwe under Robert Mugabe was one of the states that experienced the highest rates of electoral violence in the period considered here. At the time of the 2008 elections, 200 opposition supporters were murdered (Burchard 2015), and an estimated 30,000 farm workers were forcibly displaced in April 2008 alone in an effort by ruling party ZANU-PF to depress turnout by opposition supporters and to appropriate land that could be redistributed via patronage networks (Boone and Kriger 2010, 2012). One of the noteworthy characteristics of electoral violence in Zimbabwe is that voters have often been targeted directly, in addition to candidates and activists.

Mugabe was returned to power five times in multiparty elections after the southern African state declared independence from the United Kingdom in 1980; all these electoral contests involved the use of coercive force, though coercion increased notably after the turn of the century. During this period Mugabe and other leading members of his party were less willing to repudiate the use of force for electoral ends, and more often openly threatened to employ lethal violence against those who supported their opponents (Boone and Kriger 2012; Kriger 2005; LeBas 2006). In the 1980s, the newly independent government sought to purchase land from white farmers in order to redistribute productive assets to the indigenous African population. The economy faltered in the 1990s, however, and white settlers were at this point offered less money for their land and were increasingly subject to pressure to sell at below-market prices. At the same time, the ruling ZANU-PF party's hold on power began to weaken, as demonstrated by the party's inability to deliver victory in a 2000 referendum on changes to the constitution. At that point, land purchase gave way to land invasions and forcible appropriation by veterans and paramilitary gangs supported by ZANU-PF. Certain pieces of land were in some cases appropriated more than once and reallocated for political ends (Boone and Kriger 2012; Scarnecchia 2006). Through careful analysis, Boone and Kriger have demonstrated that displacement and intimidation were twin strategies designed to bring about electoral demobilization and mobilization respectively: "Violent displacement of farm workers was a deliberate electoral strategy from the start of the land invasions in 2000. . . . Meanwhile, workers [remaining] on the farms were subjected to violence and intimidation to ensure that they voted for ZANU PF" (Boone and Kriger 2012, 88). Scarnecchia also noted a dramatic rise in the use of violence for electoral ends during this period:

> The February 2000 defeat of ZANU-PF's constitutional referendum and the victory of many opposition parliamentary candidates in June 2000 signalled a crisis for the ruling party unlike any other electoral challenge. The paramilitary violence was particularly clear prior to the 2002 Presidential election. Opposition supporters and those perceived to be in the opposition were brutally beaten, sometimes killed, and often chased out of their jobs and schools. (Scarnecchia 2006, 222)

Techniques used during this period also involved forcible political reeducation, theft, destruction of property, and rape (LeBas 2006; Scarnecchia 2006). By one count there were over 200,000 incidents of political violence in the first half of 2000 (Kriger 2005).

The use of violence grew worse still over the first decade of the twenty-first century (LeBas 2006). On the basis of Afrobarometer data, Burchard calculated that fear of electoral violence was higher in Zimbabwe than in any other African country in both 2008–9 and 2011–13. At the time of the 2008 general election, nearly 90 percent of survey respondents expressed such fear (Burchard 2015). In that election, President Mugabe lost the first round of voting; a wave of violent attacks, torture, and arson occurred in the interround period, at which point Mugabe's opponent Morgan Tsvangirai withdrew from the contest owing to concerns that his supporters would be subject to violence (Goldsmith 2015).

Electoral politics in Zimbabwe under Mugabe thus combined both carrots and sticks, but the balance shifted over time from positive incentives to vote for the ruling party to negative incentives not to vote for the opposition (or not to vote at all—Zimbabwe has some of the lowest turnouts in Africa). The large land holdings of white settler farmers provided resources that the rulers of the fledgling state could purchase and redistribute in order to bolster their electoral support, and in the initial years of Zimbabwean independence, this vote-buying machine became established as a powerful patronage resource. The dilemma arose when the funds to buy land ran out and the bulk of relevant holdings had already been transferred out of white ownership. It was at this point that violent appropriation of land and the forcible displacement of black farmers began to be used as an electoral tool. Not only was displacement a powerful threat for those tempted to support the opposition, but once they were displaced, voters typically were no longer able to vote because of their physical distance from the polling places where they were registered. Displacement also provided ZANU-PF with fresh resources to redistribute, though the perceived value of those resources declined as it became evident that land tenure was insecure and the current holders of land risked reappropriation at a future date (Boone and Kriger 2012). The technique of land redistribution thus shifted over time from being predominantly a strategy of vote buying to being mainly a tool of intimidation and violence.

Zimbabwe provides an excellent example of the role of informal institutions in enabling violence. Lack of secure property rights and the propensity of the Mugabe regime to plunder private property for partisan benefit are classic signs of a state dominated by corrupt informal institutions. In this context, state institutions became tools to serve the private ambitions of politicians, rather than restraining their excesses. The regime was able to loot and coerce with impunity, as there were no effective mechanisms that could prevent such abuses of power. Therefore, though violence was not always used, it could be relied on when required. While the Mugabe regime was still confident of securing electoral victory through the distribution of particularistic benefits, the use of violence was less common, but when vote buying became more difficult, the regime shifted increasingly to violent tactics to secure victory.

SYRIA

Between attaining independence in 1946 and succumbing to civil war in 2012, the Syrian state experienced periods of relative freedom, but it was for the most part ruled by a dominant party regime that was highly clientelistic and repressive. Immediately following independence, there was a period of competitive elections and openness; in elections held during the 1940s, electoral violence was given a 1 on the 0–3 V-DEM ordinal electoral-intimidation scale. Yet this period of relative openness did not last long; the 1950s and early 1960s were marked by coups; military dictatorship; and the short-lived union with Egypt, the United Arab Republic (1958–61). In 1963 the Ba'ath party seized power, which it eventually consolidated in 1972 under the leadership of Hafez al-Assad. Throughout the period of his rule and that of his son from 2000, a perpetual state of emergency was in force and elections were tightly controlled, as were the media and civil society. During these years, state electoral violence rose to the highest point on the V-DEM electoral-intimidation scale, corruption shot up to near the top end of the *v2x_corr* corruption scale, and executive constraints plummeted to 1 before rising slightly to 3 in the latter years. During the 1972–2012 period, electoral misconduct hovered around 5 on a scale running from slightly less than 1 to slightly more than 6. Syria was by then a highly repressive state dominated by personalism and repressive control of the population (Brownlee 2005; George 2003; Weeden 1998).

From 1972 to 2012, the single most important clientelist network was the Ba'ath party (George 2003), which was constitutionally ensconced in a leadership role. The president was "elected" every seven years by plebiscite, with 99 percent approval typical. Though not technically a one-party state, Syria had between 1972 and 2012 a single "National Progressive Front" made up of the ruling Ba'ath party and a number of satellite parties. Together, the front presented joint slates at quadrennial parliamentary elections, meaning that there was no competition among them, and front members were invariable elected. From 1990, approximately a third of the seats in parliament were open to independents; wealthy Sunni business elites saw parliamentary representation as a means of securing access to patronage and the spoils of power in this Alawite-dominated regime (Blaydes 2011; George 2003). Some other independents were driven by more ideological motives, but though they contested elections under informal banners in the latter part of this period, formal opposition parties were not permitted.

For the privilege of being elected, wealthy business elites were prepared to spend liberally, and often engaged in vote buying (Perthes 1992). The ruling elite had little need for such tactics, however, as they controlled the electoral machinery. All candidates were screened before being allowed to run for election. Under these conditions, it is not surprising that voters were apathetic; informal turnout estimates suggest that as few as 4 to 20 percent of the eligible electorate participated in polls, though formal turnout figures were far higher.[16]

Given the lack of formal opposition parties and the vetting of candidates, one might not think that either fraud or violence would be necessary. But elections in Syria operated according to the "winning big" logic identified by Alberto Simpser (2013): the Assad regime devoted considerable resources to ensuring universal overt compliance with the formal doctrines of the Ba'ath regime and the leadership (Weeden 1998). Thus, fraud was used to ensure candidates and voters were all allegiant to the regime, and violence was employed to back up these efforts in the case of recalcitrance.

In an article on the 1990 parliamentary elections, Perthes claimed that "government employees had been taken to the polls collectively, and in general cast their votes in the open" (1992, 16). And for those who refused to comply, there could be serious repercussions. Similarly, George recounted the case of Sa'ad Jawdat Saeed from the village of Bir Ajman, who "voted 'no' in the July 2000 referendum to confirm Bashar al-Assad as President but he noticed that the polling station clerk had crossed out his reply and ticked the 'yes' box instead. When he protested, Saeed was detained by the local *mukhabarat* [secret service] and held for several weeks" (2003, 90). Thus the Assad regime was prepared to go to extreme lengths to ensure that, as far as possible, every villager expressed his or her electoral support for the president. In another case, a voter crossed out all the names of the National Progressive Front on the ballot paper in protest, and was imprisoned for two years when he refused to recant his action (George 2003). A further instance of abusive measures is that of a radical journalist who had managed to get on the ballot as an independent and have his victory announced at the close of polls, but was subsequently removed via a recount (Perthes 1992). Thus the manipulation of institutions was the main tool of control employed by the Syrian state to restrict competition, but to prevent citizens from manifesting protest against the limited choice on offer, various forms of electoral misconduct were used as well. When these failed, coercion was the fallback option that was called upon to ensure electoral compliance. During this period Syria was thus a case of fraud underpinned by repression in a highly authoritarian context.

---

16. George averred that turnout was "probably well below 20 percent" (2003, 90). Latif reported unofficial turnout figures of "between 4 and 10 percent" (2007, 1).

BELARUS

Belarus gained independence from the Soviet Union when the 70-year experiment with Leninism crumbled in late 1991. The prodemocracy, proindependence movement had been less well developed in Belarus than in many other Soviet republics, and independence took many in this small central European state by surprise. Alexander Lukashenko soon stepped into the breach; the 39-year-old former collective-farm director won the presidency in 1994 on a populist platform and has ruled the country ever since. Lukashenko has no formal connection with any political party, though the largest parties in the country all support him. Political competition is permitted but underdeveloped in Belarus, and though elections are in theory open, competition is restricted by means of a number of formal and informal procedures limiting contestation and hampering opposition activity. State patronage and corruption are holdovers from the Soviet period, as are restrictions on political rights.

Opposition candidates, activists, and voters have been systematically manipulated since Lukashenko came to power, and manipulation at election time has increasingly become violent. For the first decade and a half of his rule, Lukashenko was able to use largely nonviolent voter-suppression techniques. Starting in the mid-1990s, the president and his allies began to perfect tactics such as severe restrictions on campaign spending designed to ensure low-key campaigns, political pressure on the electoral commission to limit candidature, the co-optation of political parties, and the abuse of state resources (Mochtak 2018b; OSCE-ODIHR 2000a; Wilson 2005a). These techniques attracted the ire of international election observers, who consistently gave Belarus poor electoral-integrity ratings (Birch 2011), but the tactics employed largely fell short of widespread physical violence. The V-DEM state-violence indicator for Belarus was 0 in 1994, and then consistently 1 in the run-up to 2000. Though various types of electoral misconduct were observed, Belarus still scored slightly below the midpoint on the electoral-misconduct scale.

During the period of the "Bulldozer Revolution" in Serbia in 2000, the "Rose Revolution" in Georgia in 2003, and the "Orange Revolution" in Ukraine in 2004, however, the Belarusian opposition was galvanized and pushed for a change of regime. Prior to the 2001 presidential election, the traditionally fissiparous opposition overcame its internal divisions and united. It was nevertheless unsuccessful. It was at this point, facing a greater threat and unsure of the viability of the methods that had secured electoral hegemony in the 1990s, that the Belarusian leadership started adding more-violent techniques to its traditional panoply of electoral-manipulation devices. The election-monitoring mission report of the Organization for Security and Cooperation in Europe (OSCE) on the 2001 elections noted "a surge in allegations involving: acts of intimidation, arbitrary arrests and detentions, and confiscations/seizures of office equipment" (OSCE-ODIHR 2001, 14). The report went on to detail typical incidents of this type, which provide a flavor of the forms of harassment that were common in Belarusian elections of this period:

> Six members of the United Civic Party were detained for roughly 5 hours by militia while distributing opposition newspapers on 22 August in Minsk Oblast and the newspapers were reportedly confiscated. Specific examples of direct interference in the campaign of candidate Goncharik were also noted. For example, on the evening of 25 August, militia attempted to break into Goncharik's regional headquarters in Mogilev Oblast, but cut short their effort after confiscating campaign material and T-shirts bearing the slogan "Let's Say No to the Fool", deemed slanderous to the President. . . . Presidential Decree No. 11 further limited candidates' opportunity to organize public mass meetings with supporters. Domestic observers were especially targeted by security agencies. In one case, even an international long-term observer was targeted and harassed repeatedly. (14)

The report also confirmed as a causal factor for the repression the authorities' fear of a result similar to that in Serbia in 2000:

> The circulation of documents purported to originate from the State security services detailing the methods of "subversive organizations" funded by "the West" and planning a "Yugoslav scenario", and the suggested response to control and eliminate this scenario, typified an atmosphere in which campaigning was secondary to scare tactics. (14)

A similar pattern was documented in the OSCE's report on the 2004 parliamentary elections:

> As election day approached, police raids on campaign offices, the detention of a candidate, detention or harassment of campaign workers and domestic observers, as well as widely reported coercion applied to certain groups, particularly students, to take part in the election, produced a climate of intimidation. (OSCE-ODIHR 2004b, 2)

Following the election, opposition protests were held in Minsk for several days. On 19 October, the police broke up a demonstration, detaining approximately 40 people and beating prominent opposition figures (20).

Violence was ramped up even further at the time of the 2006 presidential elections, with the memory of the 2004 Ukrainian "Orange Revolution" fresh in the minds of incumbents and opposition alike. The climate during the campaign was tense, and there was routine harassment of opposition candidates, as had been the case in previous elections. Following the announcement of Lukashenko's victory, there were daily protests in Minsk for five days. The protests were broken up by police and between 500 and 1000 people were arrested, including 44 journalists and opposition presidential candidate Alexander Kozulin. The charges against those arrested ranged from terrorism to coup plots. On 17 March, President Lukashenko threatened in a televised speech to "tear [the opposition activists'] heads off . . . like those of ducklings" (OSCE-ODIHR 2006b, 14).

Not surprisingly, Belarus's state electoral-violence score on the V-DEM ordinal scale shot up from 1 to 3 in 2000, where it remained throughout the remainder of the period. The electoral-misconduct measure exhibited a smaller rise from 4.6 in 2000 to 5.0 in 2012. These data support the argument that when the Belarusian regime came under pressure, it continued to employ more or less the same types of electoral manipulation, but used greater force to back them up. During this period of heightened risk perceptions occasioned by successful "electoral revolutions" in other postcommunist states, the previously used techniques of fraud continued to be employed, but the violent components of those strategies were enhanced (Mochtak 2018b; OSCE-ODIHR 2001, 2004b, 2006b). Violent intimidation and harassment and repression thus served as supplements to electoral fraud, as suggested by the cross-national results above.

PARAGUAY

If Belarus is an example of state electoral violence on the rise, Paraguay offers a narrative of the decline in the exercise of state force in elections. At the conclusion of the Second World War, Paraguay was under the control of General Higinio Morínigo, who had banned political parties. Morínigo's power was soon challenged, however, by other groupings in the military. A tumultuous period followed that led to a civil war between rival factions of the armed forces in 1947—won by supporters of the National Republic Association, commonly known as the Colorado Party. Paraguay was between 1947 and 2008 controlled by Colorado, which succeeded in winning elections well into the period of democratization, beginning in 1989. Between 1954 and 1989, the South American state was a notoriously authoritarian military-dominant party regime ruled by General Alfredo Stroessner. "Stroessnerism" was based on an institutional triad of government, armed forces, and the Colorado Party, with the general at the apex of all three institutions. Riquelme commented that "a skillful combination of selective brutal repression and pervasive corruption accounted for [the regime's] longevity" (1993, 3), and Lambert noted that "corruption and clientelism in their diverse forms were tolerated and even encouraged as the economic base and principal mechanism of support" (2000, 381; cf. Bryce 1986; R. Snyder 1992). From the early 1960s, several opposition parties were allowed to contest elections and to win seats in parliament, which afforded them opportunities to access state resources, including generous parliamentary salaries (Nickson 1988), but other parties (including the communists) were outlawed, and politics was dominated by Colorado, which "functioned as a mass patronage machine" (Chehabi and Linz 1998, 71). Nickson delineated the contours of this relationship:

> Under Stroessner, the Colorado Party has been converted into a highly effective political machine. Its extensive network of branches (*seccionales*) throughout the country serves as a major system of patronage as well as a mechanism for the surveillance of political opposition. The civil service and security forces have become highly politicised under Stroessner. Access to employment in the public sector, to teaching posts in state schools and the national university, to jobs in state hospitals, in most public enterprises and also in the judiciary is limited, in practice, to members of the Colorado Party. In addition, since July 1955 officials serving in the armed forces have been obliged to join the Colorado Party and admission to the officer corps has become effectively restricted to children of Colorado families. (Nickson 1988, 240)

Of the four examples considered here, Paraguay thus represents the most institutionalized case of violence intimately coupled with corruption.

Elections were a crucial element of the Colorado Party's political hegemony. Schedler maintained that elections formed the "foundation" of hegemonic rule under Stroessner (Schedler 2013), and Nickson noted that opposition was contained by means of "a mixture of harsh repression and cooption" that engendered a "culture of fear" (Nickson 1988, 241; cf. Saguier 1979). Under the electoral law of 1967, opposition parties were guaranteed one-third of parliamentary seats, whatever their vote share (Nickson 1988). But beyond this sop to multipartyism, there was little in Paraguayan electoral practice that inspires confidence. Nickson detailed the range of types of electoral misconduct used in presidential elections held during the Stroessner period:

> During the election campaign, opposition candidates are denied access to radio and television and are refused the right of assembly for both private and public political rallies. Ballot-rigging is widespread. In rural areas, opposition members are refused inscription in the electoral register while the multiple inscription of Colorado Party members is widely practised. Secret ballot provisions are not usually respected in rural areas. Opposition representatives are regularly denied access to the counting of votes and, in some areas, the Colorado Party has ended up with more votes than the number of registered electors. (Nickson 1988, 241)

The data support this anecdotal evidence. The electoral-misconduct scores for the postwar period are all close to the top end of the observed range for this variable up to and including the 1988 election, while Paraguay is consistently rated 3 on the 0–3 V-DEM state-violence scale. During the Stroessner years, elections in Paraguay were both extremely coercive and extremely fraudulent.

In 1989, a coup led by General Andrés Rodríguez initiated a period of political liberalization which culminated in relatively democratic elections. The 1993 transitional election was generally peaceful, though there were attacks on opposition-supporting media outlets and polling organizations, and the border was closed for part of polling day (Riquelme 1993). There ensued a somewhat rocky consolidation period during which the Colorado Party continued to claim regular electoral victories, until finally succumbing to defeat in the presidential election of 2008, the last election in the data set employed in this analysis. During this period corruption levels remained relatively high, but executive constraints rose from the very bottom to the very top of the scale, and media freedom also rose to .80 on the 0–1 scale by 2008. During this time, electoral violence fell from 3 to 1, and eventually to 0 in the 2008 elections, and misconduct declined to around the middle of the range for that variable. Thus, while not entirely devoid of manipulation, Paraguayan elections were from 1993 on considerably more democratic than they had been during the Stroessner period (Nickson 2009).

The 1993 elections were therefore an uncertain turning point, when old practices lingered even as competition increased. Nagel reported that in the run-up to this election "prominent Colorado officials and military leaders made overt threats to 'take the elections by fraud' (or force) if necessary" (1999, 171), and members of the armed forces issued veiled threats in public to seize power if the Colorado Party was not victorious (Riquelme 1993). Riquelme recounted how at the time of the 1993 elections:

> At a Colorado Party meeting in Tobatí, Department of Cordillera, the Party chairman, Blás N. Riquelme, promoted the use of fraud, stating, among other things, (a) that this was not the time for theorizing because the Colorado Party was "at war" against the opposition, (b), that the election would be won "by assault", (c) that the party would establish a "special commission to commit fraud", (d) that it had the necessary resources in arms and money and, above all, the support of the Armed Forces, to implement this strategy. (52–53)

The same account noted that intimidation was most prevalent in rural areas and against members the indigenous population, who were threatened with violence if they did not support the Colorados. Nagel supported this view, noting that in 1993 and also the elections of 1996, "local Colorado cadres expended remarkable energy in harassing, intimidating and buying the campesinos [peasants] back into the fold" (1999, 169). Misconduct in the 1993 election included tampering with voter lists, reallocation of opposition supporters to remote polling stations, and the abuse of state resources; the military and the Colorado Party allegedly collaborated with electoral authorities in undertaking these acts (Riquelme 1993). But gradually over the subsequent years, a more assertive media and an increasingly active civil society combined with a re-energized opposition to put pressure on the authorities to deliver elections with integrity (Nickson 2009).

The Paraguayan example illustrates how under conditions of authoritarianism and corruption, violence and electoral misconduct went hand in hand, accompanied to some extent by vote buying, but gradually as power came to be structured along more democratic lines, accountability institutions held electoral actors in check, preventing most violence and limiting the use of misconduct.

These case studies have shown both the diversity and the common features of state-perpetrated electoral violence. In all four cases, electoral violence is embedded in political economies regulated by informal institutions. There are interesting variations in when and how state and state-sponsored actors use force to achieve their ends, but a common feature of all four cases is the very widespread use of strategies of intimidation by elites in public discourse, coupled with the rarer but nevertheless potent use of actual force. Given that the state has manifest ability to deploy violence at will, threats and other forms of intimidation are often sufficient. The case studies confirm that, as indicated in chapter 2, state actors prefer threats to attacks, yet when the threat of force is insufficient, they do not hesitate to use physical force to ensure electoral victory. The commonalities between the cases also support the findings of the large-N analyses carried out in the previous section: state-initiated violence is facilitated by corruption and checked by democratic constraints, and incumbent leaders in competitive authoritarian states tend to use violence to support electoral misconduct, although it can also be employed in conjunction with vote buying, as the Zimbabwean example demonstrates.

Conclusion

In an era in which democracy is in the normative ascendancy and international election monitors regularly troop to observe the polls of all but the most established democracies, the leaders of semidemocratic states have limited opportunities for fiddling elections. True, the spectrum of manipulative techniques is large and there remains a very wide range of mechanisms through which elections can be stolen, yet geopolitical realities have in recent decades vastly reduced the number of tools that can be safely employed to ensure electoral victory. In previous eras, elections could be reliably won by establishing rules of the game that themselves guaranteed victory for the incumbent political group. In today's world this is more difficult. States face significant diplomatic and other sanctions for restricting electoral competition (Hyde 2011; Kelley 2012). The result is that authoritarian leaders are increasingly resorting to manipulation—including fraudulent, particularistic, and coercive types—to achieve their ends.

The coercive form of electoral manipulation includes the range of electoral-violence strategies reviewed in chapter 1. This chapter has shown how leaders in states with weak democratic institutions and strong informal institutions often rely on violence to reach their goals, and that violence is typically used as a support for electoral misconduct, both to supplement and to facilitate fraud. Chapter 4 will examine how nonincumbent actors both react to state-initiated violence and initiate violence themselves. In so doing it will be possible to explore the wide range of different types of actor engaged in violent activities and the diversity of ends to which coercive measures are put.

Appendix to Chapter 3: Robustness Checks

The models presented in table 3.4 include tests for additional specifications identified in previous studies to be relevant to the use of electoral violence. These main findings reported in this chapter are robust to these variations in model specification.

An important global study by Hafner-Burton, Hyde, and Jablonski (2014) found, as confirmed here, that democratic constraints mitigate electoral violence. However, these authors also found the uncertainty of the electoral outcome to be linked to electoral violence. It is not entirely clear that uncertainly of the outcome is exogenous to violence, as severe violence in the run-up to the election could have the effect of repressing the opposition to such an extent that it is clear to all that the incumbent power holder has a high probability of winning. It is nevertheless worth testing this finding on the data employed in this study. The first two models in table 3.4 include a variable designating uncertainty, constructed, following Hafner-Burton, Hyde, and Jablonski, by inverting responses to *Nelda12*, which records answers to the question "Was the incumbent or ruling party confident of victory before elections?" (Hyde and Marinov 2015, 8–9). As with the specification adopted by these authors, the uncertainty variable is interacted with executive constraints (the same Polity measure as used by Hafner-Burton, Hyde, and Jablonski). The longitudinal versions of both variables are employed in this interaction, as the effect under consideration is specific to individual elections. The results of this analysis are presented in Models 1 and 2 of table 3.4; as can be seen, the interaction terms fail to reach conventional levels of statistical significance in either model, and the overall results described above remain unaltered. The main effect of uncertainty appears to be to reduce electoral violence, but, as noted, this could be endogenous to violent campaign activities.

Another well-known finding that is worth testing is that of the African study by Fjelde and Höglund (2016), which found there to be an interactive effect between ethnic power inequality and electoral systems in shaping electoral violence, such that high levels of inequality in majoritarian systems have a particularly large impact on the incidence of violent elections. Models 3 and 4 test for the effect of this relationship on the global sample employed here by adding to Models 1 and 2 in table 3.2 variables designating ethnic power inequality and an interaction term between ethnic power inequality and majoritarian electoral system.[17] The country means for both variables

17. The measure used for the ethnic-power-inequality variable is the V-DEM "Power Distributed by Social Group" indicator, *v2pepwrsoc*, defined as follows: "A social group is differentiated

TABLE 3-4. State-Initiated Electoral Violence, 1945–2012, Robustness Checks

	Model 1 NELDA	Model 2 V-DEM	Model 3 NELDA	Model 4 V-DEM
CROSS-NATIONAL ("BETWEEN") EFFECTS				
Corruption Index	1.555	6.307[c]	1.102	5.255[c]
	(0.876)	(1.356)	(0.858)	(1.430)
Executive constraints	−0.475[b]	−0.755[c]	−0.592[c]	−0.953[c]
	(0.152)	(0.206)	(0.142)	(0.197)
Per capita GDP (log)	−0.220	−0.278	−0.132	−0.301
	(0.222)	(0.267)	(0.208)	(0.296)
International election monitors	0.648	1.242	0.826	1.650[a]
	(0.724)	(0.648)	(0.635)	(0.755)
Presidential	0.026	−1.467	0.493	−0.240
	(0.923)	(1.227)	(0.897)	(1.296)
Legislative-majoritarian	0.396	0.667	6.010[b]	−1.192
	(0.613)	(0.671)	(1.991)	(2.677)
Ethnic power distribution			0.098	0.939[b]
			(0.283)	(0.328)
Ethnic power distribution × legislative majoritarian			−1.565[b]	0.683
			(0.574)	(0.748)
LONGITUDINAL ("WITHIN") EFFECTS				
Corruption Index	3.431[b]	4.763[c]	3.435[b]	4.048[b]
	(1.274)	(1.278)	(1.217)	(1.317)
Executive constraints	−0.477[c]	−0.768	−0.537[c]	−0.763[c]
	(0.117)	(0.115)	(0.119)	(0.127)
Per capita GDP (log)	0.116	−0.866	0.154	−1.067[b]
	(0.300)	(0.357)	(0.307)	(0.383)
International election monitors	−0.014	0.246	−0.153	0.272
	(0.327)	(0.369)	(0.320)	(0.364)
Presidential	−0.443	−0.125	−0.382	−0.235
	(0.260)	(0.169)	(0.245)	(0.161)
Legislative-majoritarian	0.344	0.647[a]	0.187	0.451
	(0.469)	(0.328)	(0.425)	(0.332)
Uncertain outcome	−0.922[b]	−0.894[c]		
	(0.308)	(0.217)		
Uncertain outcome × executive constraints	0.077	0.169		
	(0.178)	(0.149)		
Constant	2.505		−0.367	
	(2.253)		(2.474)	
N	1405	1625	1499	1735
Log pseudolikelihood	−426.226	−1068.468	−466.819	−1162.762
AIC	1004.452	2308.937	1085.637	2497.524
BIC	1403.285	2772.757	1489.391	2966.978

Cell entries are coefficients (robust standard errors). All models include year fixed effects (not shown). The dependent variable in Models 3 and 4 (*v2elintim_ord*) is transformed as follows: the values are inverted, and the highest value is then recoded to 0 to create a scale running from the lowest to the highest level of violence. Models 1 and 3 are random effects logit models; models 2 and 4 are random effects ordered logit models; cut points not shown. AIC, Akaike information criterion; BIC, Bayesian information criterion.

[a] $p < .05$
[b] $p < .01$
[c] $p < .001$

were used in this interaction, as both electoral systems and ethnic power distributions are slowly changing variables (indeed, many countries in the sample studied here experienced no electoral-system changes during the period under analysis). There is a somewhat unexpected negative interaction between state-initiated preelectoral harassment (*Nelda15*) and ethnic inequality under majoritarian systems, but no significant interaction effect in the model based on the V-DEM state-violence indicator. Crucially for the purposes of this chapter, the impacts of corruption and executive constraints remain largely unchanged in both models.

---

within a country by caste, ethnicity, language, race, region, religion, or some combination thereof. (It does *not* include identities grounded in sexual orientation or socioeconomic status.) Social group identity is contextually defined and is likely to vary across countries and through time. Social group identities are also likely to cross-cut, so that a given person could be defined in multiple ways, i.e., as part of multiple groups. Nonetheless, at any given point in time there are social groups within a society that are understood—by those residing within that society—to be different, in ways that may be politically relevant" (Coppedge et al. 2018a, 186). This indicator varies between 0 (power monopoly of the wealthy) and 4 (equal power distribution). The variable has been inverted for the purposes of the analyses conducted here, so that a higher score represents greater inequality.

4

Violence by Nonstate Actors

In chapter 3 we assessed the principal causes and dynamics of state-initiated and state-sponsored electoral violence. We saw that violence is used by state actors (and their proxies) mainly in contexts with high levels of corruption and weak democratic constraints, and that violence is often employed as a backstop to other forms of electoral misconduct by state actors. In high-stakes contexts where those in power control economic and legal as well as political resources, incumbent elites use violence to lock out of power groups they see as threats to their tenure, and that they are unable to manipulate through other means.

This chapter turns to nonstate electoral violence—electoral violence initiated by nonstate actors, including political opposition parties, "electoral armed groups" (Staniland 2015), communal groups, and other actors outside the control of formal state institutions. We are interested in understanding the circumstances under which nonstate actors resort to violent means to achieve their ends, how state-initiated violence and nonstate violence interact, and also how nonstate electoral violence is produced. The chapter starts by a conceptualization and typology of the phenomenon of nonstate electoral violence, before turning to the factors that shape its frequency and intensity across the globe. Case studies from Pakistan, Ghana, Kyrgyzstan, and Côte d'Ivoire serve to illustrate the arguments advanced, to tease out the causal mechanisms posited in the cross-national analyses, and to analyze the production dynamics of this type of violence.

The Concept of Nonstate Electoral Violence

In assessing electoral violence initiated by nonstate actors, it is necessary first of all to ascertain exactly what it is we are studying. It might be tempting to view electoral violence as epiphenomenal, in the sense that societies that are generally more prone to violence and/or conflict are also more likely to have violent elections. Were this the case, then electoral violence by groups in society would be an extension of other types of violence and not a discrete phenomenon. However, the evidence suggests that this is far from being true. Though elections that occur in the context of violent societies and civil war do tend to be more conflictual than others, electoral violence and civil violence are by no means coextensive, and nonelectoral violence explains only about 5 percent of electoral violence (Harish and Toha 2018). This finding suggests that violence perpetrated by nonstate actors in connection with the electoral process is indeed a separate phenomenon, not simply an extension of criminality or political violence. And if it is a separate phenomenon, then it is a phenomenon that requires a separate explanatory approach. However, it is also important to recognize that election-related violence by nonstate actors is a more varied phenomenon than state-initiated violence, in terms of both the actors involved and the ends pursued.

Chapters 1 and 2 delineated the common motives for electoral violence: obstruction of the electoral process, the generation of fear, and protest. I argued there that whereas state actors are more likely to put greater emphasis on the generation of fear, nonstate actors were more likely to emphasize protest, and to use electoral violence in conjunction with vote buying as part of a mobilizational strategy. Nonstate actors may also use violence to obstruct aspects of the electoral campaign, especially (but not exclusively) if they opt to boycott the contest.[1] Actors typically involved in such forms of violence include partisan groups, communal groups with strong identities and interests distinct from partisan entities, and illicit groups (e.g.

---

1. Burchard (2015) has identified a separate category of "incidental" or nonstrategic violence, not undertaken with a particular instrumental objective in mind, but violence that erupts spontaneously as part of the electoral campaign or other electoral process. This might happen, for instance, when heated debates between rival partisan groups get out of hand, when jostling at crowded polling stations results in violent clashes, or when peaceful rallies or protests turn violent as a result of state intimidation or other factors that incite the crowd. Such nonstrategic violence is less easy to theorize and analyze empirically, however, and while some nonstate violence is undoubtedly of the "incidental" type, the analysis undertaken here will be of strategic violence by nonstate actors.

organized crime syndicates or drug cartels) for whom violence is a commonly employed tool used to achieve a variety of ends.

Analytically, mobilizational violence can be understood as taking two principal forms: protests against state electoral manipulation and violence between competing informal groupings seeking to secure the loyalty of their clients. Protest violence during the campaign often focuses on electoral procedures—for example, that which erupted in Guyana in 1992 following a dispute over electoral registers and reported by Fischer:

> The Election Commission Headquarters was attacked by a stone-throwing band of People's Nation Congress activists discontent with voter registration lists. This group took on mob proportions and later that day stormed the office of the People's Progressive Party candidate Cheddi Jagan, the eventual winner in the presidential campaign. Widespread looting in downtown Georgetown ensued for several days. (Fischer 2002, 24)

Another example is Burundi, where dozens died and an estimated 175,000 were displaced in protests in the run-up to the 2015 election in which Pierre Nkurunziza sought a third term as president amid opposition claims he was not eligible (BBC 2015a; Reuters 2015).

More commonly, however, opposition protests against electoral misconduct occur after the election results have been announced (Beaulieu 2014; Brancati 2016; Kuntz and Thompson 2009; Norris 2014; Svolik and Chernyk 2012; Tucker 2007). Following the disputed 2007 presidential election in Kenya in which the "wrong" candidate, Mwai Kibaki, was widely believed to have been declared victorious, the supporters of his rival, Raila Odinga, protested with chants of "No Raila, no peace!" (Dercon and Gutiérrez-Romero 2012, 735). Schedler (2013) noted that postelectoral protest can have a number of functions: it can serve to inform and mobilize the population, as well as to put pressure on incumbent elites. Electoral protest can also send a signal to international actors that an election has not been accepted by large sectors of the domestic population and is therefore potentially problematic (Donno 2013; Hyde 2011; Hyde and Marinov 2012; Kelley 2012). In this sense, protest can contribute to the development of democracy. Yet postelectoral protests are often violent (Brancati 2016), and even when they are relatively peaceful, they frequently attract violent repression by agents of the state, as happened for example in the 2017 elections in Honduras, when police shot and killed over a dozen peaceful protesters who were demonstrating against electoral irregularities (Claes and Stephan 2018).

Violent protests against electoral misconduct are thus a major form of nonstate electoral violence, and they are also an important mobilizational tool for the opposition, which can and does employ them to generate mass movements in support of its cause, as has been witnessed in countries such as Serbia, Ukraine, Georgia, Madagascar, and Mexico (Beissinger 2007; Bunce and Wolchik 2010; Eisenstadt 1999, 2006; Kalandadze and Orenstein 2009; Kuntz and Thompson 2009; Magaloni 2006; Ó Beachain and Polese 2010; Tucker 2007). Indeed, this form of protest is credited with being the seed of modern modes of contentious politics; a protest against the failure of the British Parliament to seat John Wilkes after he had won an election in 1769 is cited by Tilly (1978) as the origin of the modern demonstration as a distinctive form of collective action.

The use of force in order to backstop clientelist electoral mobilization is the second main form of mobilizational violence. Violence by local bosses in Thailand is a good example of this. Kongkirati (2014) has shown how reforms introduced in 1997 made elections more competitive, leading local patrons to supplement their traditional vote-buying techniques with violence designed to draw support away from other local bosses and also from Thaksin Shinawatra's Thai Rak Thai party.

The "garrison process" in Jamaica that developed between the 1960s and 1990s provides another instance of this phenomenon. This term describes a system whereby competing networks of clientelist criminal groups form urban "garrisons" where the social and political activities of residents are limited and controlled. These mechanisms of social control are then employed to mobilize voters on election day for the party that is in alliance with the garrison in question (Figueroa and Sives 2002; Sives 2010). This coercive mobilization was so successful as to create high turnouts and virtually homogeneous voting districts: "In the 1993 election, for the parish of Kingston (part of the capital of the same name), 48 per cent of the boxes returned no votes for the losing candidate(s). In one constituency the figure rose to 98 per cent of those boxes where voting took place" (Figueroa and Sives 2002, 83).

Reno described the logic behind a similar phenomenon in the African context: "Corrupt and deeply disliked politicians have weathered public anger for decades. One reason for this survival is that their recruitment of armed youths gives them roles as local patrons" (2011, 212). The same author went on to explain how the use of coercive clientelism lowers the cost of purchasing votes:

If voters are allowed a genuine choice of who represents them in a patronage-based system, voters are liable to sell their vote to the candidate who can offer them the most material rewards for their loyalty. Electoral violence helps to quell these demands though intimidation and denying recruits to activists and, in extreme cases, forces voters to rely on their local power brokers to use gangs to protect them from other candidates' militias. (218)

Violence is thus a "cheap" tool that can be used to hedge against the possible high costs of vote buying, with the result being a combined "carrot-and-stick" strategy.

Obstructive violence is riskier for nonstate actors, owing to the possibility of formal state sanctions. Obstruction is a common tactic employed by illicit groups like drug cartels. In weak states such as Guatemala, which are subject to penetration by criminal groups, the use of violence as an electoral tool can be a strategy of state capture: "In Guatemala, the perpetrators [of electoral violence] are largely drug trafficking organizations (DTOs), in particular the Mexican drug cartel the Zetas, who employ homicide, physical assaults, and intimidation to capture local governments in order to maintain transit routes or safe havens for their illicit activities" (Creative Associates International 2013, 7).

Obstructive violence is also used by opposition groups, especially when engaging in boycotts. Akhter has documented how in Bangladesh at the time of the 1988 elections, "violence resulting from the physical confrontation between pro-election and anti-election camps led to the postponement of polling in 72 vote centres in Dhaka alone" (2001, 135–37). During the 1996 election campaign, "bomb blasts, violent street demonstrations, clashes between pro- and anti-poll activists and strikes became almost an everyday event. Anti-election activists assaulted several candidates, set fire to district BNP offices, and burnt a district election office" (164). On the day of a 1994 by-election, "one group of armed youth brandishing firearms was able to mark the ballot papers and stuff the boxes whereas the other group in a similar fashion broke the ballot boxes and burnt the ballot papers. . . . [B]oth the ruling and the opposition parties were engaged in violent actions" (162). And during the 1991 election, "48 persons died in electoral violence; most of the deaths were the result of bombing and gun fights, and attacks on the electoral processions of the rival groups" (188).

This section has provided an overview of the concept of nonstate electoral violence and examples of its most common manifestations. The next section goes on to test the hypotheses set out in chapter 2 as to the determinants of electoral violence by nonstate actors.

The Causes of Nonstate Electoral Violence

The overall logic of violence as a tool to exclude actors from power or to seize power should in theory apply symmetrically; the same aspects of the way in which power is structured in society increase the stakes of losing power for the state as well as the stakes of gaining power for the opposition. We therefore start the empirical analysis of nonstate violence with models based on those for state violence, employing as a dependent variable the (inverted) V-DEM *v2elpeace* indicator of nonstate violence (see table 4.1).

Model 1, which includes mainly structural variables, shows that corruption is both cross-sectionally and longitudinally a strong and highly significant predictor of nonstate violence, as was the case for state violence. The regulation of access to resources by corrupt informal institutions provides a powerful motivation for nonstate actors to use violence to achieve their ends. This may be in part because in corrupt states, groups out of power are linked to corruption networks of their own, which use violence to enforce exchanges, but it is also undoubtedly due to the fact that the possibility of accessing state resources via electoral means is a strong enough motive to make electoral violence a viable strategy in certain contexts. The symmetric relationship between corruption and electoral violence is thus confirmed, providing further support for H1, the conjecture that corruption should drive electoral violence. In order to use this model to calculate the impact of corruption on the probability that an election will be racked by high levels of electoral violence, it makes sense to amalgamate the top two categories in the four-point nonstate-violence scale, as the top category contains relatively few cases. Doing so indicates that a state with the lowest level of mean corruption has a 0.27 percent probability of experiencing high levels of nonstate violence, all else equal, whereas a state at the top of the corruption scale has an 18.44 percent chance of this outcome. Examining similar figures for variations over time, an increase in corruption from the bottom to the top of the scale is associated with a predicted rise in nonstate violence from 0.63 to 19.37 percent.

Interestingly, the executive-constraints variable is not significant in Model 1; however, Model 2 shows that this is because the relationship between executive constraints and nonstate violence is not linear. Figures 1.4, 1.5, and 1.6 in chapter 1 hinted at a curvilinear relationship between democracy and electoral violence, but such an effect was not evident in relation to state violence in chapter 3. When this variable is entered in quadratic form in the nonstate violence model, however, a curvilinear effect is revealed in relation

TABLE 4-1. Nonstate-Initiated Electoral Violence, 1945–2012

	Model 1	Model 2	Model 3	Model 4	Model 5	Model 6
CROSS-NATIONAL ("BETWEEN") EFFECTS						
Corruption	7.546c (1.495)	6.994c (1.488)	7.052c (1.523)	6.978c (1.492)	7.280c (1.529)	7.462c (1.557)
Executive constraints	-0.084 (0.215)	3.055b (1.080)	3.238b (1.117)	3.044b (1.086)	3.128b (1.101)	3.177b (1.144)
Executive constraints²		-0.370b (0.121)	-0.389b (0.125)	-0.370b (0.121)	-0.378b (0.123)	-0.389b (0.128)
Per capita GDP (log)	-1.461c (0.373)	-1.393c (0.346)	-1.518c (0.361)	-1.396c (0.348)	-1.423c (0.353)	-1.484c (0.361)
International election monitors	0.230 (0.960)	-0.258 (0.926)	-0.721 (0.935)	-0.227 (0.926)	-0.212 (0.942)	-0.184 (0.981)
Presidential	-2.954 (1.443)	-2.803a (1.419)	-3.361a (1.455)	-2.821a (1.425)	-3.218a (1.426)	-3.292a (1.467)
Legislative-majoritarian	1.340 (0.937)	1.845a (0.924)	1.863a (0.946)	1.863a (0.927)	1.858a (0.947)	1.884 (0.980)
Close race						1.165 (1.717)
LONGITUDINAL ("WITHIN") EFFECTS						
Electoral misconduct, V-DEM			1.476c (0.361)			
Electoral misconduct, NELDA				0.680a (0.341)		
Vote buying					0.885c (0.212)	0.753c (0.204)
Boycott						0.585c (0.174)
Close race						0.453 (0.249)
Boycott * close race						0.722a (0.352)
Corruption	6.789c (1.350)	6.591c (1.328)	3.720b (1.452)	6.654c (1.305)	3.640b (1.351)	3.084a (1.288)
Executive constraints	-0.162 (0.122)	0.488 (0.437)	0.734 (0.437)	0.522 (0.435)	0.517 (0.452)	0.473 (0.423)
Executive constraints²		-0.080 (0.054)	-0.083 (0.052)	-0.080 (0.053)	-0.085 (0.055)	-0.070 (0.052)

(continued)

	Model 1	Model 2	Model 3	Model 4	Model 5	Model 6
Per capita GDP (log)	-0.991[a] (0.481)	-0.905 (0.463)	-0.766 (0.501)	-0.861 (0.465)	-0.857 (0.489)	-0.836 (0.468)
International election monitors	0.332 (0.379)	0.300 (0.395)	0.533 (0.424)	0.349 (0.393)	0.072 (0.389)	0.142 (0.380)
Presidential	0.229 (0.199)	0.237 (0.195)	0.263 (0.192)	0.244 (0.192)	0.191 (0.196)	0.135 (0.188)
Legislative-majoritarian	-0.027 (0.451)	0.030 (0.434)	-0.046 (0.427)	0.047 (0.434)	-0.189 (0.436)	-0.219 (0.419)
N	1735	1735	1735	1735	1735	1735
Log pseudolikelihood	-1115.769	-1104.531	-1079.208	-1101.277	-1081.352	-1061.684
AIC	2399.538	2381.063	2332.416	2376.554	2336.703	2305.368
BIC	2858.075	2850.516	2807.328	2851.466	2811.616	2802.115

The models in this table are random effects ordered logit models; cut points not shown. Cell entries are coefficients (robust standard errors). All models include year fixed effects (not shown). The dependent variable in Models 3–6 (*v2elpeace_ord*) is transformed as follows: the values are inverted to create a scale running from the lowest to the highest level of violence. AIC, Akaike information criterion; BIC, Bayesian information criterion.

[a] *p* < .05
[b] *p* < .01
[c] *p* < .001

to nonstate violence. This relationship is displayed in visual form in figure 4.1. Though theory predicts that democratic constraints should operate more strongly on state than nonstate violence, it is clear that both types of violence are affected by formal constraints on the use and abuse of power. Yet in very undemocratic contexts, an increase in executive constraints can actually fuel nonstate violence, undoubtedly because such changes tend to go hand in hand with liberalization that affords more opportunities for oppositions to mobilize. Throughout most of the range of this variable, the association with nonstate violence is negative, as is the case for state violence. This can potentially be interpreted, following Borzyskowski (2019), in terms of the credibility effect that well-run institutions have in building confidence in democratic systems and quelling opposition unrest (cf. Birch and Muchlinski 2018). This effect will be explored more fully in chapter 6.[2]

Models 3–5 in table 4.1 include electoral misconduct and vote buying (longitudinal versions only, as in chapter 3). Models 3 and 4 suggest a significant relationship between electoral misconduct and nonstate electoral violence. These effects are far less pronounced than the dramatic shifts in state violence shown in chapter 3. An increase in the chances of violence from 0.98 to 10.39 percent (9.41 percentage points) is found for the V-DEM-based fraud measure, and an increase from 5.18 to 8.71 percent (3.53 percentage points) for the NELDA-based measure. This confirms the supposition that although misconduct goes hand in hand with all forms of electoral violence, the two strategies are most likely to be employed in tandem by state actors. Violence by nonstate actors is, by contrast, more likely to occur in protest against misconduct, but even serious election rigging will not always lead to violent protest, for the reasons discussed below.

Model 5 confirms the expectation articulated in chapter 2 that there should be a strong link between vote buying and violence by nonstate actors. Unfortunately, the V-DEM vote-buying variable does not distinguish between the purchase of votes by state and by nonstate actors, nor is there any available comparative indicator that does this. We must, however, assume that in elections with high levels of vote buying, both sides will engage in this practice, as the relevant literature suggests is the case (Rouquié 1978; Schaffer 2007; Scott 1969; Stokes 2005; Stokes et al. 2013). This model indicates that at the lowest level of vote buying, the chance of an

---

2. A model (not shown) to test for a possible interaction between majoritarian electoral systems and ethnic power distribution, analogous to that for state violence hinted at in chapter 3, showed no significant interaction effect.

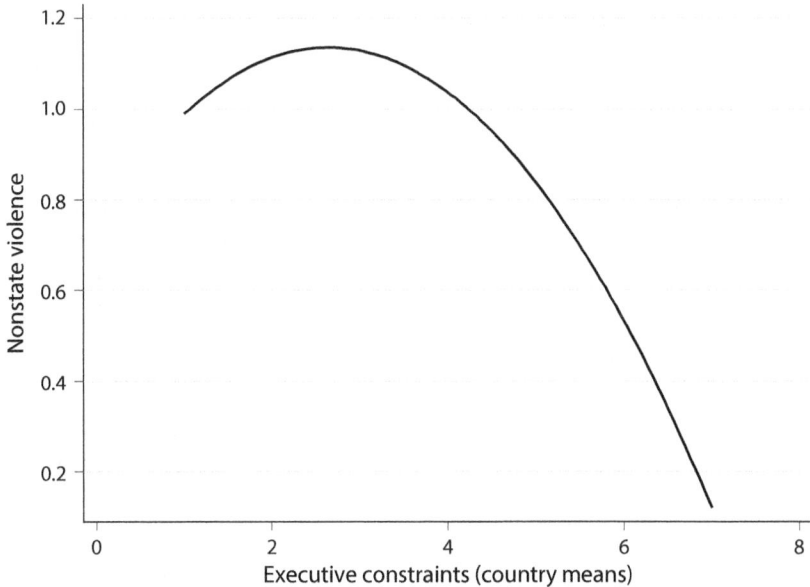

FIGURE 4.1. Executive constraints and nonstate violence

election experiencing high levels of nonstate violence is only 1.95 percent, whereas when vote buying is at the top of its observed range, the chance of high violence levels is 15.67 percent—an increase of 13.72 percentage points. There is thus a close connection between these variables, which will be explored in greater detail in the case studies below.

Thus, as found in chapter 3 in relation to violence committed by state actors, nonstate violence goes hand in hand with other forms of electoral manipulation, though in the case of nonstate violence there is, as anticipated, a closer link with vote buying than with electoral misconduct. The provision of particularistic rewards to voters can be a means of overcoming the effects of fraud by those linked to the state; it is also a strategy that can be used to mobilize popular support in a context where opposition groups may have limited opportunities to get their message across through the channels of parliamentary representation. At the same time, nonstate actors typically have limited resources, and there are large sectors of the electorate that will not be susceptible to their entreaties as they have ties to the state apparatus. The use of force is therefore often attractive to nonstate actors as a means of enforcing vote-buying "contracts," mobilizing support, suppressing participation by incumbent supporters, and obstructing incumbent campaign activities. This may be an especially viable strategy when nonstate actors are well endowed with funds from licit or illicit economic activity.

Votes are expensive, and the use of violence carries significant risks. This is true for state and nonstate actors alike, but these problems are especially acute for those not allied to the state, as they are more vulnerable to repression and they do not have ready access to state coffers in order to fill their campaign war chests. It is therefore reasonable to expect that nonstate groups will throw all their energy and resources—both carrots and sticks—into elections only when they have a realistic chance of winning. In other contexts they are likely to opt for the exit strategy, or boycott, as discussed in chapter 2. Boycotts may or may not be accompanied by violence; as the cases of Bangladesh, Mali, Togo, and Egypt attest, boycotts are in some cases carried out together with a program of violent activities (Beaulieu 2014). This suggests the inclusion of two additional variables in the model of nonstate violence: opposition boycotts and close races. Model 6 in table 4.1 includes these two variables, plus an interaction term between them.[3]

This model shows there to be interactive effect between boycotts and close races, as supported by a test of joint significance ($p < .000$). Figure 4.2, which is based on the interval version of the *v2elpeace* variable for ease of visualization, displays this relationship in graphic form. This shows that where boycotts accompany close races, the chances of nonstate violence go up, whereas the opposite is true when there is no boycott.

Another interesting aspect of the models in table 4.1 is that there is a strong and significant relationship between nonstate violence and mean per capita GDP, with richer states exhibiting less violence. The negative relationship between electoral violence and level of economic development is well established in the literature (Borzyskowski 2019; Norris, Frank, and Martínez i Coma 2015; Salehyan and Linebarger 2015), but it has not previously been noted that this link pertains mainly to nonstate violence. This could be due to the fact that in poorer states the private sector tends to be

---

3. The measure used for the boycott variable is the V-DEM "Election Boycott" indicator, *v2elboycot*. This indicator codes responses to the question: "In this national election, did any registered opposition candidates or parties boycott?" where "A boycott is a deliberate and public refusal to participate in an election by a candidate or party who is eligible to participate" (Coppedge et al. 2018a, 59). The indicator varies from 0 to 4, where 0 corresponds to "total" boycotts and 4 corresponds to "nonexistent" boycotts. The variable has been inverted for the purposes of the analyses conducted here, such that higher scores represent boycotts of greater magnitude and coverage. Margin of victory is calculated as the difference between the largest vote-winning party and the second-largest vote-winning party in legislative elections (V-DEM indicators *v2ellovtlg – v2ellovstm*) or the largest vote-winning candidate and the second-largest vote-winning candidate in legislative elections (V-DEM indicators *v2elvotlrg – v2elvotsml*). This variable is then inverted so that a higher value corresponds to a closer race, and, for the purposes of this analysis, a dummy variable is employed that designates a margin of victory of 5 percent or less.

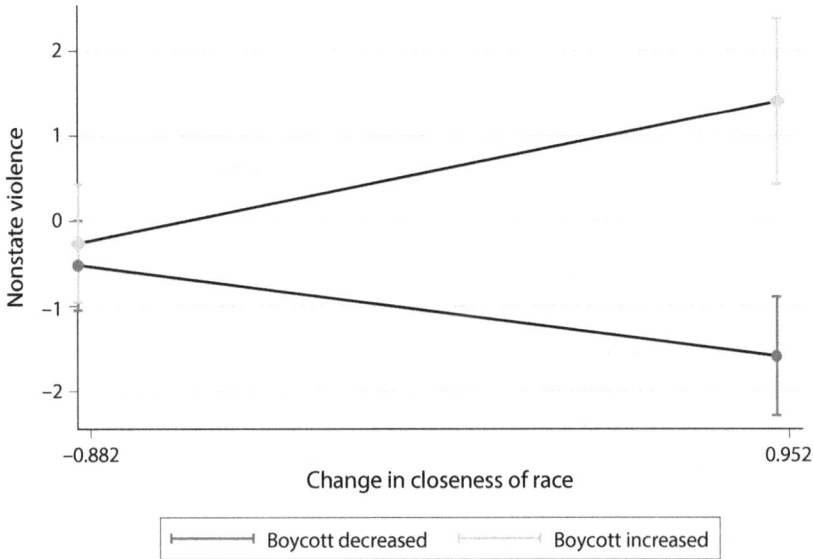

FIGURE 4.2. Boycotts, close races and nonstate electoral violence

NB: Figure shows predictive margins with 95% confidence intervals.

less well developed, so there are fewer options for wealth generation by nonstate actors, who therefore have more incentive to seek to secure control over state resources. There is also some evidence that presidential elections attract less nonstate violence than other types, whereas legislative elections held under majoritarian rules attract more, as predicted by some authors (e.g. Burchard 2015; Fjelde and Höglund 2016; Wilkinson 2004). No such consistent patterns were observed in relation to state violence, and it is not entirely clear how these findings are to be interpreted, though this is an area that would merit future study.

Protest and the Production of Violence by Nonstate Actors

One possible understanding of the role of boycotts is that is in some contexts they are not used simply as an "exit" strategy, but also as a form of protest. This is the approach adopted by Beaulieu (2014), and it suggests more detailed consideration of the relationship between protest and nonstate electoral violence. In addition to boycotts, protest activities include demonstrations, the articulation of grievances in the media, and direct appeals to politicians in the form of petitions and similar devices. Though these activities are not intrinsically violent, they do in many contexts include or result in violence of some kind.

The demands of postelectoral protestors can vary, as they may call for institutional reform, and/or a reconsideration of the result of the election just held (Schedler 2013). All their aims generally have a common core: to improve the conduct of elections in the country in question. The literature on the "color revolutions" in central and eastern Europe documents how in case after case, worsening electoral irregularities led groups of citizens to take to the streets in protest (Beissinger 2007; Bunce and Wolchik 2010; Kalandadze and Orenstein 2009; Ó Beachain and Polese 2010; Tucker 2007). These protests were less than successful in countries such as Azerbaijan and Belarus, but in Serbia, Georgia, and Ukraine, antifraud movements led to wholesale changes of power that improved the quality of electoral conduct (at least for a time). Magaloni's (2006, 2010) detailed analysis of several cases, especially that of Mexico, also provides valuable insight into the conditions under which leaders are prepared to commit to holding free and fair elections in the face of mass protest.[4]

At the same time, protest usually fails to dislodge authoritarian leaders. Where formal institutions are weak and power is personalized, elections are more likely to be high-stakes affairs in which losers run a considerable risk to personal security and of loss of wealth and status and permanent exclusion from the political system. Under these conditions, incumbent leaders frequently seek to retain their positions by repressing opposition elites and continuing to undertake electoral misconduct. In cases where large-scale electoral malfeasance has been the norm for a considerable time and incumbent elites are not particularly weak, they are typically able to repress calls for reform (as in 2012 Russia or 2009 Iran), and they are often able to remain in power, despite widespread unrest (Bhasin and Gandhi 2013; Schedler 2013; Simpser 2013). Following successful repression, leaders once again have the option of engaging in proactive reforms, as happened in Moldova in 2009 after the Communists quelled an attempted "electoral revolution" (Pop-Eleches and Robertson 2010), though they are generally unlikely to do so, assuming the underlying strength of their institutions has not changed. Without large-scale mobilization, authoritarian leaders may well seek to consolidate their forces and regain their strength.

---

4. In a series of case studies, Norris (2014) has provided useful conceptual insights into the potential for popular protest to lead to cleaner elections.

A number of scholars have pointed to the informational role of elections (Egorov, Guriev, and Sonin 2009; Gandhi and Lust-Okar 2009; Little, Tucker, and LaGatta 2015; Magaloni 2006; Maleski and Schuler 2011; Pravda 1978; Schedler 2013; Simpser 2013; Wintrobe 1998). In the absence of credible elections, authoritarian leaders face a problem of gauging their true popularity. It is important for the leadership of a regime to know what portion of the public supports it in order to be able to protect itself against popular revolts, identify potential areas of internal regime weakness, and determine the level of resources that it needs to devote to repression and/ or patronage. Information about the true support of the incumbent is also valuable to the opposition; if the opposition knows when the regime's support is on the wane, it will be in a better position to identify opportunities to mobilize for change.

Given the inherent risk of an unexpectedly poor electoral result, the incumbent leadership has an incentive to undertake electoral misconduct in order to ensure that the electoral results announced following the poll will enable it to retain power. Provided the incumbent is confident that it can manipulate elections sufficiently to allow it to win an election it calls, it makes sense for it to call elections on a regular basis so as to maintain up-to-date information about its true support. This calculation is in part due to the fact that the incumbent benefits from an information asymmetry in the electoral arena. The revealed level of incumbent support R, as reflected in published vote totals, is composed of both true support, S, and fraud, F: $R = S + F$. Only the incumbent leadership knows the ratio of S to F, as it has a monopoly over most forms of fraud, and the opposition typically finds it difficult to monitor and measure the amount of misconduct committed with any degree of confidence or precision. Knowing R and F enables the leadership to deduce S, a capability that is denied the opposition. This private information gives the incumbent leadership an advantage as it is able to misrepresent the level of malpractice it is engaging in and potentially convince the electorate that it has genuinely high levels of support. The opposition is disadvantaged in that it has no way of knowing exactly how much genuine support the leadership has and thus how difficult it might be to mobilize people to challenge the incumbent.

The opposition may seek to organize street demonstrations or other forms of protest to test the degree to which the population is convinced by incumbent claims. This is potentially a very costly signal in several senses—the opposition risks revealing weakness by trying and failing to mobilize sufficient support, it risks repression if it does mobilize large numbers of people onto the streets, and it risks revealing information about opposition networks and tactics. But if the opposition is convinced that the incumbent's genuine popularity is lower than what the incumbent claims, these costs may well be seen as worth bearing, especially given the potential benefit of revealing regime weakness. Indeed, Beaulieu sees electoral protest in terms of a bargaining failure of the sort elaborated by Fearon (1995), where information asymmetries and misrepresentation of strength on the part of both incumbent and opposition lead to failures to coordinate on acceptable political moves that manifest themselves as street demonstrations and boycotts as forms of electoral protest.

If street demonstrations and boycotts are alternative means of mobilizing people in protest against allegedly fraudulent elections, we ought to expect these tactics to be substitutes; if misconduct is suspected in advance of the election, a boycott (possibly accompanied by violence) many well be the preferred form of protest, and in that context postelection demonstrations are less likely to attract large crowds of angry voters who may adopt violent tactics. If, on the other hand, a boycott is not called and the opposition takes part in the election that is perceived to be fraudulent, angry and potentially violent protests will be more likely.

In order to examine in greater detail the relationship between boycotts, postelection protests, and nonstate electoral violence, it is useful to employ an indicator from the NELDA data set, *Nelda29*, which designates the occurrence of fraud-related protests. It is coded as a dummy variable with a value of 1 given a positive answer to the question "Were there riots and protests after the election?" The codebook notes to this item specify that "the riots and protests should at least somewhat be related to the handling or outcome of the election." This indicator is then modified by means of *Nelda30*, "If yes (nelda29): did they involve allegations of vote fraud?" so as to exclude protests that did not involve allegations of fraud (Hyde and Marinov 2015, 14–15).

Table 4.2 presents two models, based on a variation of Model 6 in table 4.1 above, that include postelectoral protests (Model 1) and postelectoral protests interacted with boycotts (Model 2). Model 1 in table 4.2 shows that, as expected, there is more likely to be nonstate electoral violence when there is postelectoral protest; this is true both cross-sectionally and over time. The interaction effect tested in Model 2 indicates that the presence of a boycott has a moderating impact on the propensity of protests to be accompanied by violence, as supported by a test of joint significance ($p < .000$). These effects are visualized in figure 4.3.

TABLE 4-2. Nonstate-Initiated Electoral Violence and Protest, 1945–2012

	Model 1	Model 2
CROSS-NATIONAL ("BETWEEN") EFFECTS		
Corruption	6.279[c] (1.646)	6.349[c] (1.653)
Executive constraints	3.062[b] (1.089)	3.118[b] (1.094)
Executive constraints^2	−0.377[b] (0.122)	−0.383[b] (0.122)
Per capita GDP (log)	−1.477[c] (0.363)	−1.475[c] (0.365)
International election monitors	−0.641 (1.030)	−0.633 (1.037)
Presidential	−3.285 (1.512)	−3.268[a] (1.520)
Legislative-majoritarian	1.320 (0.953)	1.347[a] (0.959)
Close race	1.041 (1.766)	1.052 (1.768)
Postelectoral protest	5.595[b] (1.772)	5.616[b] (1.771)
LONGITUDINAL ("WITHIN") EFFECTS		
Postelectoral protest	0.744[c] (0.220)	0.843[c] (0.221)
Postelectoral protest × boycott		−0.532[a] (0.250)
Vote buying	0.689[c] (0.208)	0.690[c] (0.207)
Boycott	0.546[b] (0.179)	0.580[c] (0.175)
Close race	0.302 (0.223)	0.270 (0.230)
Corruption	3.341[a] (1.365)	3.291[a] (1.384)
Executive constraints	0.442 (0.417)	0.454 (0.417)
Executive constraints^2	−0.068 (0.050)	−0.068 (0.051)
Per capita GDP (log)	−0.882 (0.469)	−0.845 (0.472)
International election monitors	0.061 (0.385)	0.097 (0.385)
Presidential	0.130 (0.187)	0.143 (0.191)
Legislative-majoritarian	−0.181 (0.443)	−0.191 (0.429)
N	1717	1717
Log pseudolikelihood	−1029.195	−1025.986
AIC	2242.390	2237.972
BIC	2743.637	2744.668

The models in this table are random effects ordered logit models; cut points not shown. Cell entries are coefficients (robust standard errors). All models include year fixed effects (not shown). The dependent variable in Models 3–7 (*v2elpeace_ord*) is transformed as follows: the values are inverted to create a scale running from the lowest to the highest level of violence. AIC, Akaike information criterion; BIC, Bayesian information criterion.

[a] $p < .05$
[b] $p < .01$
[c] $p < .001$

This analysis confirms the view that election boycotts and postelectoral protests form part of the opposition's strategic arsenal, and that both strategies can increase the chances that opposition members will resort to the use of force. Of the two, postelectoral protests are by far the most likely to lead to violence, but this is marginally less likely when the two strategies are combined, probably because nonparticipation in the electoral contest

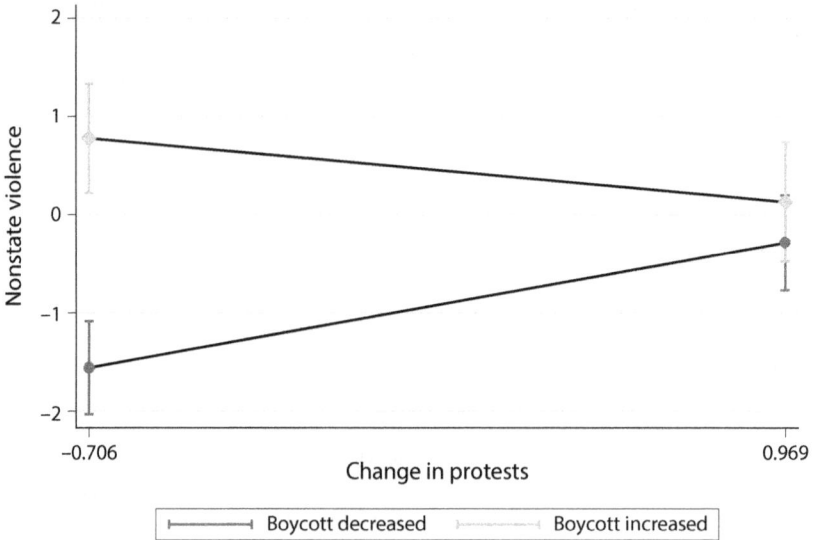

FIGURE 4.3. Postelectoral protests, boycotts, and nonstate electoral violence

NB: Figure shows predictive margins with 95% confidence intervals.

dampens popular grievance following the announcement of the results and thus makes it more difficult for opposition leaders to mobilize people to take part in protest activities.

Case Studies

As noted above and in chapter 2, nonstate actors in opposition can be expected to favor forms of violence associated with mass mobilization, including protest violence, which will typically lead to countermeasures by state actors. In the previous section, we found there to be a link between nonstate violence and vote buying that accords with the idea that nonstate actors mobilize support by means of both carrots and sticks. This section provides four case studies designed to analyze the relationship between protest, mobilization, and vote buying in greater detail.

The cases chosen to this end are Pakistan, Ghana, Kyrgyzstan, and Côte d'Ivoire. These cases have very different political histories: Pakistan and Ghana are both former British colonies, Côte d'Ivoire is a former colony of France, and Kyrgyzstan was part of the Soviet empire. Yet they share some similar characteristics as well: they are all "hybrid" states partway between democracy and authoritarianism; all have competitive multiparty systems, but their democracies are all in key ways flawed.

PAKISTAN

Popular mobilization employing both carrots and sticks has been a mainstay of party politicians in Pakistan for decades, and this technique is especially attractive to parties that are out of power and thus do not have recourse to state resources to assist their electoral campaigns. Pakistan has had a particularly fraught electoral history. Following independence from Britain in 1947, the state went 23 years before it held a general election in 1970. This event was so contentious it triggered a civil war between East and West Pakistan, which resulted in the secession of the former as renamed Bangladesh. The next election, in 1977, led to a military coup, and it was not until 1988 that multiparty elections began to be held on a regular basis, albeit punctuated by a coup in 1999. Pakistani elections have been uniformly violent, with force being used as a tactic by virtually all major parties (Reif 2009; Staniland 2015; Wilkinson 2000). The European Union (EU) election observation mission reported 13 deaths at the time of the 2002 election (EU 2002), but six years later an estimated 150 people were killed during the run-up to the 2008 election, including presidential candidate Benazir Bhutto (EU 2008). The 2013 election marked the country's first orderly transition of power from one civilian government to another, though approximately 150 people again died in election-related violence (EU 2013).[5] The victory of opposition leader Imran Khan in the 2018 election was marred by a series of polling-station bombings and other violence that killed an estimated 180 people (Barker 2018; EU 2018). This pattern translates into consistently high V-DEM scores for nonstate violence; all the elections held between independence and 2012 were rated 2 on the V-DEM ordinal scale for this measure, placing them in the top 20 percent most violent elections in this data set.

Some of Pakistan's election violence is connected to ongoing separatist struggles in the country and to Taliban activity in the northern areas bordering Afghanistan, but much of it also appears to be perpetrated by party-allied actors against their political opponents (Nellis and Siddiqui 2018; Siddiqui 2017; Staniland 2015; Wilkinson 2000). Violence is thus a tool that is used in Pakistan for a variety of political ends, not just to shape electoral results. But this does not mean that its role in elections is any less significant. On the contrary, violence and the threat of violence have major impacts on electoral contests in the country. Commenting at the time of the 2008 election, the

5. The Pak Institute for Peace Studies (2013) reported a higher number of 298 fatalities in attacks on candidates, party supporters, and voters.

EU observation mission report noted that "the threat of violence and an atmosphere of fear prevailed over the campaign period, seriously affecting the election environment" (EU 2008, 14).

There is abundant evidence that much Pakistani electoral conflict is linked to clientelist party machines. Pakistan has throughout its history as an independent state been plagued by high levels of corruption, weak parties, and personalized politics (Wilkinson 2000). Parties have been patronage machines that have often misused state power when they have held it, and manipulated electoral procedures to win elections; many of them also employ armed thugs, and elected representatives wield considerable influence over local police forces (Nellis and Siddiqui 2018; Wilkinson 2000). In an in-depth study of political violence in Pakistan, Siddiqui (2017) argued that force is likely to be used by parties in contexts where their internal structures are weak and their links with voters are clientelistic. This analysis aligns well with the overall argument proffered in this chapter that there should be a systematic connection between clientelist and coercive strategies by nonstate actors, including first and foremost opposition parties.

Karachi, Pakistan's largest city and commercial capital, has in recent elections been the site of much of the country's partisan electoral conflict. The city was for a number of years under the political control of the Muttahida Qaumi Movement (MQM) party that is alleged to have used violence liberally to control the streets of this megacity, assisted in the 1990s by a series of fitful electoral alliances with successive ruling parties at national level (BBC 2015b; Staniland 2015). As one study of political violence in Karachi noted, "the MQM and other parties consolidated their respective support bases among the city's various ethnic groups and successfully challenged the institutional hegemony of state security forces over many parts of the city" (Gazdar and Mallah 2013, 3100). Another study claimed that "political parties have created armed wings, criminal gangs are allied with political actors, and the military and police have both colluded with and tried to suppress key electoral armed groups" (Staniland 2015, 700). The forcible capture of polling stations by criminal gangs is a common technique in Pakistan, and at the time of the 2008 election there was evidence of a strong link between polling-station capture, turnout, and support for the MQM in Karachi (Gazdar and Mallah 2013). Informal institutional control—state capture—over the security sector has in this instance been extended to electoral administration, demonstrating clearly that the use of force is a tool of informal politics that relies on its control of local institutions to mobilize support, via a carrot-and-stick technique that Staniland refers to as "armed clientelism" (2015, 701).

A detailed analysis of violent attacks at the time of the 2013 elections by the Pak Institute for Peace Studies sheds further light on partisan patterns of perpetration in Karachi. Of the 245 violent attacks recorded by the monitoring activities of this group in the four-and-a-half month period spanning the election campaign and the immediate postelection period, 148 were terrorist attacks carried out by the Taliban and separatist groups, whereas 97 were partisan electoral violence involving clashes between party supporters, the majority of which (70) were in Karachi (Pak Institute for Peace Studies 2013). Contemporary news reports indicate that the conflicts were mostly between two opposition parties vying for local control: the MQM and cricketer-turned-politician Imran Khan's newer Pakistan Tehreek-e-Insaf (PTI) party, which was making inroads into the MQM's vote, fighting on an anticorruption platform (BBC 2013a). The EU election observation mission report on the 2008 election noted that Imran Khan had been forcibly prevented from entering Karachi to campaign (EU 2008). By 2013 that had changed, and his party was successful at winning seats in the city, but at the cost of prominent figures, including Zahra Shahid Hussain, vice president of the PTI, who was murdered on the eve of a rerun of the election in a disputed seat. The party blamed its rival the MQM, which has also been implicated in other attacks on PTI members (BBC 2013b; Khan 2015).

In the 2018 general election the PTI finally won victory at national level, but this followed an extremely violent preelectoral period when one attack killed 149 people, another led to 30 deaths, and several other attacks killed 1 or more people, many of whom were candidates (EU 2018). The EU observation mission report described the campaign as being characterized by both violent intimidation and clientelist vote-winning tactics. Discussing the latter phenomenon, the report noted that "influential landowners and representatives of extended families, the so-called 'electables,' were able to generate large political appeal and financial means to secure votes," further specifying that "an electable is a holder of a significant number of votes." (28). Again we observe the carrot going hand in hand with the stick.

These examples show how in Pakistan violence is used in conjunction with clientelism to mobilize votes, largely in the run-up to elections. Though by no means is all clientelist mobilization violent, the phenomenon of "armed clientelism" does appear to be characteristic of Pakistani electoral politics.

GHANA

If violence is used to mobilize votes in Pakistan, its use in Ghana appears designed rather to mobilize activists. The transitional 1992 election in this West African country also furnishes a good example of how electoral boycotts, protests, and violence are combined. Ghana is a country that is relatively stable and democratic by African standards; nevertheless, low-level electoral intimidation and disorder are regularly anticipated by the population and the shadow of violence lurks at polling time. Burchard (2015) reported that in the 2008–9 Afrobarometer survey, nearly 50 percent of Ghanaians claimed to fear violent elections; by the 2001–13 round of this survey, the figure had gone down to just over 40 percent, but this is still a substantial portion of the population. Throughout the post–Cold War period Ghana has experienced regular low-level campaign violence, which has meant that though the country's V-DEM nonstate-violence scores have fallen from 2 in the early and mid-1990s to 1 thereafter, the use of force persists in Ghanaian elections. State violence, by contrast, was rated 1 in 1992 and 1996 and 0 thereafter on the V-DEM ordinal scale.

Following independence from Britain in 1957, Ghana experienced a turbulent period of authoritarian and military rule that lasted until 1992. No elections held during this period were democratic, and the 1978 polls were violent (Gyimah-Boadi 1998). The 1981–92 period was one in which political parties were banned under the leadership of Flight Lieutenant Jerry Rawlings and elections were not held. This situation changed very rapidly when Ghana was swept up in the wave of democratization that rolled across Africa in the early 1990s.

In 1992 a new constitution was passed and parties were legalized. Soon thereafter, a presidential election was called. Standing as a civilian, Rawlings was duly elected president in what were considered internationally as relatively free and fair elections (Gyimah-Boadi 1999). Many within Ghana disagreed with this assessment, however, noting the regime's appointment of the electoral commission, and lack of time given to opposition parties to form and campaign in the five and a half months (May to November) between party legalization and the election. The result was a spate of deadly postelection rioting orchestrated by the opposition Alliance of Democratic Forces and New Patriotic Party (Gyimah-Boadi 1998, 1999). The opposition also decided to boycott the parliamentary elections held in December of 1992; though it later regretted this decision (Lindberg 2006), it did give the opposition the opportunity to experiment with protest. With the opposition temporarily locked out of power, the ostensibly democratic institutions established under the new constitution—the electoral commission and the commission on human rights—lacked legitimacy, which impeded the democratization process.

Prior to the 1996 polls, a number of reforms were undertaken to address the opposition's concerns about matters such as the quality of the electoral register, voter education, and electoral administrator training (Gyimah-Boadi 1998, 1999). Another key innovation was the establishment of the highly effective Inter-Party Advisory Group (IPAC), which was to serve as a negotiating and confidence-building forum where parties could air grievances to the electoral commission and solutions to problems could be debated; from 2005 this was supplemented by the National Peace Council, which served a similar mediation function. A further institutional development that helped to enhance electoral credibility was the establishment of domestic election-observer groups in the run-up to the 1996 polls. The combined impact of these changes was somewhat increased confidence in the electoral process and notably more peaceful elections in 1996 (Gyimah-Boadi 1999; Oduro 2012). Yet other institutional factors made electoral conflict more likely, including a slow legal process for resolving electoral disputes (Debrah 2011), and weakness and politicization of the security sector, which can in many cases be attributed to patronage. Oduro noted that in northern Ghana in 2008, "perpetrators [of electoral violence] feared neither prosecution nor arrest because they were protected by their political benefactors, who were leading personalities in party hierarchies" (2012, 223).

This quote suggests a third counterproductive institutional development during the post-transition period: the establishment of patronage-based parties that compete for power and for the opportunity to distribute the spoils of state control to their supporters. Ghana's two main parties are the National Democratic Congress and the New Patriotic Party, both of which emerged in the aftermath of the country's legalization of multiparty competition in 1992. Much of Ghanaian electoral violence has been perpetrated by party-affiliated youth groups colloquially known as "machomen" or "foot soldiers" (Bob-Milliar 2014; Schmitz 2018). The pattern of allocation of public-sector jobs following changes in power strongly suggests that active involvement in electoral campaigns is rewarded by preferential treatment in the postelectoral period (Bob-Milliar 2014; Democracy Watch 2010), and interviews with party activists confirm that they join a party largely in anticipation of particularist benefits rather than on ideological grounds, even if activism does not always guarantee the reward anticipated (Bob-Milliar 2012). One of Bob-Milliar's interviewees described the selective incentives offered to party activists as follows:

> Politics is everything in Ghana. If you want employment, you can be as qualified as anybody but only party membership card would enable you to be short listed; if you are sick party will care for you; if you want contract and other business dealings it is party; school for your children party will help; if you want to go Mecca party's protocol list is very important; in bereavement party's donation is assured; even if you want to marry a woman, party friends will provide funds. (quoted in Bob-Milliar 2012, 681)

There is considerable evidence that much electoral violence is carried out by party activists (even if only a minority of activists engage in this sort of behavior). Most violent episodes have involved clashes between supporters of rival parties at campaign rallies or on polling day, especially in highly competitive areas (Asunka et al. 2017; Oduro 2012). Conflict has been especially problematic in regions where there are particularly virulent chieftaincy feuds (Oduro 2012; Schmitz 2018). A compounding factor is the apparent willingness of political parties to allow local disputes to become politicized; Oduro went so far as to claim that the "culture of politicians' using chieftaincy disputes to further their political interests is the bane of peaceful elections [in Ghana]" (2012, 223).

Yet even in other areas, party youth activists are often deployed at election time to undertake intimidation on behalf of their partisan patrons. In Bob-Milliar's words:

> Foot soldier political activism is very contentious as it is driven by passion and aggression. Their brand of political activism has features of lawlessness, and the line between conventional participation and contentious politics becomes blurred. . . . The political activities that engaged the attention of foot soldiers may include taking part in pro- and antigovernment protests, attending meetings, canvassing for votes, and exercising public authority in diverse ways (e.g., providing security for their communities). (2014, 131–32)

Ghana's competitive clientelism is one in which intimidation of opponents, vandalism, and disorderly protest activity designed to serve electoral ends have become institutionalized. In the run-up to the 2012 elections the National Democratic Congress announced the creation of a "heroes fund" to support the families of party activists injured or killed "in the service of the party" (Gyimah-Boadi and Pempel 2012, 106). Ghana thus provides a good example of how opportunities to undertake violence in exchange for material rewards can be a powerful mobilizational device.

KYRGYZSTAN 2005

The Kyrgyz parliamentary election of 2005, which brought about the so-called "Tulip Revolution," is a good example of how violence can be used in conjunction with protest as a mobilizational device. Of the three successful "color revolutions" that occurred in the former Soviet Union during this period, the Tulip Revolution was the only one that led to bloodshed; six people died and there was an estimated $100 million of property damage due to looting (Tucker 2007). The state repression of postelectoral protests in Armenia, Azerbaijan, and Belarus was also violent, but in Kyrgyzstan violence orchestrated by the opposition was effective in bringing about regime change.

Regional tensions appear to have played a significant role in stoking unrest in the run-up to the elections. President Askar Akaev, who was from the more Russified, secular North of the country, had appointed many like himself to posts in his administration; as Akaev sought to centralize control of power in the early 2000s, local leaders hailing from the more traditional, religious South felt aggrieved and excluded (Lewis 2010; Ó Beachain 2010). Protest began in advance of the polls when several candidates from the South were denied ballot access, and daily street protests took place in the southern regions between the first and second rounds of voting (Herron 2009). Election observation reports following election day confirmed the opposition's suspicion that there had been malpractice of various kinds, including inaccurate voter rolls, lack of transparency in aspects of electoral administration, state interference in the media, and infringements on freedom of assembly and expression (OSCE-ODIHR 2005a). Following the announcement of the results, protest activity escalated in the South, especially in Jalalabad and Osh, and spread also to the capital Bishkek. In several places unsuccessful candidates seized control of local administrative buildings to protest against their defeat (Lewis 2010). The government reacted by repressing the demonstrators; repression increased the size of the protests, and it also prompted the demonstrators to use violent means themselves, including petrol bombs and arson (Herron 2009; Lewis 2010). Ultimately neither the president nor his security personnel were willing to ramp up coercion to the levels that might have been required to stamp out the protests (Hale 2005; Ó Beachain

2010). As the number of people on the streets swelled, so their demands grew, and they started asking for President Akaev to go, despite the fact that the elections had been for members of parliament, not the presidency. They also attacked the office of the presidential administration and looted government buildings in the capital (Herron 2009; Ó Beachain 2010). Akaev eventually resigned and the presidency was handed to southerner demonstration leader (and alleged financier) Kurmanbek Bakiev, whom Akaev had sacked as prime minister in 2002 following a crackdown on protests that had left five people dead (Ó Beachain 2010).

This series of events can be understood in terms of the dynamics of clientelistic mobilization intertwined with coercion in an election that reflected a succession struggle more than a democratic breakthrough (Hale 2005, 2006). By 2005 Akaev had been in power for 14 years, since Kyrgyzstan had gained independence in 1991. The fledgling post-Soviet state was heavily dominated by informal institutions, and a North-South divide was instrumental in shaping patronage networks (Lewis 2010; Ó Beachain 2010). The Russified North of the country was more closely integrated into regional (post-Soviet) political, social, and economic structures, whereas power in the less developed South was structured more closely around local kinship networks. Between 1991 and 2000, Kyrgyzstan had been relatively democratic by Central Asian standards, but as the new century dawned, Akaev started to tighten his rein on power. North-South tensions had led to sporadic electoral protests at the time of the presidential poll of 2000, and government repression of several opposition leaders in 2002 marked an upsurge of unrest. Electoral-system reforms in advance of the 2005 vote increased competition among local clientelistic elites; the number of seats in parliament was reduced, and the proportional-representation component of the system was eliminated, leaving only single-member district majoritarian races. David Lewis characterized the consequences of these changes thus:

> Local authority figures—clan leaders, local businessmen and many figures with links to organized crime, became the front runners in the new election campaign. . . . [T]here were many more such powerful local figures than could be accommodated in the new legislature. As a result, there were fiercely contested contests in almost all constituencies, between rival local leaders who all had recourse to considerable resources, not least the ability to mobilize popular protest in the case of real or perceived malpractice. (Lewis 2010, 50–51)

Lewis further specified the nature of the resources on which candidates drew, noting that campaign activities "included payment of money or provision of various services to key community leaders to ensure their community voted for the candidate. Very few candidates had much chance of getting elected without significant funding, running into hundreds of thousands of dollars" (52). Vote buying was also noted by election observers (OSCE-ODIHR 2005a).

The disarray in which the country found itself, with the security services reluctant to use force, meant that protest was cheap. As Lewis noted, "there was no cost attached to participation in demonstrations, and much greater cost in some communities (social ostracism, loss of access to local leaders) associated with opposing anti-governmental protests. It was noticeably easier to mobilize large groups of people in the periphery, outside Bishkek, than in the capital" (Lewis 2010, 59). The tight patron-client networks of southern Kyrgyzstan thus facilitated both the purchase of votes via community leaders and the mobilization of protest, as predicted by the theoretical framework set out in chapter 2, and as suggested by the quantitative analyses in table 4.1. This interpretation is confirmed by commentator analyses of the postrevolutionary situation in the Central Asian mountain state, where the change of leader appears to have enhanced the hold of informal institutions on power: "while Kyrgyzstan's political arena is now somewhat more competitive than it was under Akaev, this competition appears to have taken on a more lawless and covert character, with multiple assassinations of politicians-cum-businessmen and frequent mutual accusations among top officials of conspiracy and influence-peddling" (Hale 2006, 316). Violence, including violent postelectoral protest, was thus an integral part of clientelism in Kyrgyzstan in the mid-2000s, with positive and negative incentives closely aligned components of the electoral arsenals of would-be leaders.

CÔTE D'IVOIRE

Côte d'Ivoire provides another example of the interrelationship between electoral violence and protest, in this case protest that is associated with boycotts. The West African state was long known as an unusually stable African authoritarian regime under founding president Félix Houphouët-Boigny, who ruled the country for 33 years (Hartmann 1999). The situation changed dramatically when the country democratized in the early 1990s, and Côte d'Ivoire has since experienced nearly three decades of turbulence and strife. The small West African state gained independence from France in 1960 and embarked immediately on an extended period of personalist one-party politics under the hegemonic Parti Démocratique de la Côte d'Ivoire led by Houphouët-Boigny. Economic crisis, public protests, and international pressure converged to oblige Houphouët-Boigny to open his country to multiparty electoral competition in 1990. In 1993, Houphouët-Boigny died in office and was succeeded by his protégé, Konan Bédié, marking the beginning of a period of instability.

In Côte d'Ivoire, state repression at election time was rife throughout the authoritarian period, which lasted from shortly after independence until the democratic opening of the early 1990s. Thereafter the use of force as an electoral tool by state actors declined, from 3 on the V-DEM scale between 1965 and 1985 to 2 in 1990, 1995, and 2000 and 1 in elections held in 2010 and 2011.

The trajectory of nonstate electoral violence is the mirror image of this pattern: violence by nonstate actors was virtually nonexistent before 1990; the V-DEM score for this variable is a steady 0 for elections held during the two and a half decades between 1960 and 1985. This figure rose to 1 at the time of the 1990 elections, 2 in 1995, 3 in 2000, and 4 in 2010, before declining to 2 in 2015.

The advent of electoral competition thus brought with it political disruption. Following a brief opening in the early 1990s, Ivorian politics descended into an uneasy and strife-ridden competitive authoritarianism, which revived historic ethnic tensions between the predominantly Muslim North of the country and the largely Christian South. Electoral practices also suffered during this period. The 1995 presidential election was not contested by the main opposition parties, who called an "active boycott" that involved protests (Boone and Kriger 2012, 97). The election campaign was somewhat marred by violence, including land grabs and forced displacement in the West of the country (Boone and Kriger 2012; Straus and Taylor 2009), but following the victory of the incumbent on 95 percent of the declared vote, there was little unrest, as the boycott had ensured that this outcome was virtually a foregone conclusion.

The 2000 elections were more contentious politically and more actively contested by the opposition. The result was widespread violence. Following the disqualification of northern candidate Alassane Ouatarra on the grounds that his parents were not both Ivorian citizens, as required by law, several opposition parties decided to boycott the poll (Beaulieu 2014), though opposition candidate Laurent Gbagbo took part in the election. A dubious result gave victory to General Robert Guéï, who had assumed power following a coup in 1999. This was challenged by Gbagbo, who mobilized his supporters in a massive postelectoral protest following allegations of fraud, and there followed three days of street fighting in the capital Abidjan (Boone and Kriger 2012). Guéï eventually fled, whereupon Ouatarra's supporters challenged Gbagbo's claim to the presidency. Though Gbagbo ultimately gained control of the situation and assumed the presidency, a full-scale civil war erupted in 2002 over the perennial issue of land rights, and elections were not held again until 2010, following the Ouagadougou accords of 2007, which settled the dispute temporarily. Gbagbo's decision to contest the election had made the outcome more important for the opposition, which then fought hard to secure the victory it believed it had deserved.

The 10-year period between the 2000 and the 2010 elections did little to heal the wounds of war. The 2010 presidential election was certified by the United Nations as a means of affording credibility to the process (Bekoe 2018). International intervention helped ensure that the election was again contested by the opposition, but following the election, postelectoral protest by the defeated opposition led to one of the bloodiest events in the annals of electoral history, as protest took the form of attacks by rival gangs and militias, which led to reprisals as the violence escalated (Klaus and Mitchell 2015; Straus 2011), resulting ultimately in over 3000 deaths and a million displaced people, and sparking a near civil war in 2011. The violence was triggered by the refusal of Gbagbo to relinquish power, despite having clearly lost the election, and despite the fact that the result of the election had been certified by the United Nations Operation in Côte d'Ivoire (Bekoe 2018; ICG 2011). UN presence had failed to prevent a number of forms of electoral abuse by the incumbent, and the opposition's participation in the contest had again raised the stakes, contributing to the violence of the strife that ensued.

The 2015 elections were again boycotted by the main opposition parties (Smidt 2020), and postelectoral unrest was limited as there was widespread expectation of incumbent victory and clear postelectoral control of the country by incumbent political forces (Piccolino 2016).

Thus the Ivorian elections with the greatest amount of postelectoral protest-related violence, those of 2000 and 2010, were also those in which elements of the opposition participated actively, whereas the boycotted 1995 and 2015 elections experienced far more muted postelectoral protests and limited violence. Commensurate with the quantitative evidence presented above, opposition boycotts appear to have dampened appetite for extreme forms of protest following the polls, whereas opposition contestation appears to have increased the chances that aggrieved losers would resort to violence to challenge the result of what were perceived to have been fraudulent elections.

The examples of Pakistan, Ghana, Kyrgyzstan, and Côte d'Ivoire demonstrate the ways in which violence can be used by nonstate actors, mainly opposition parties, for electoral ends. Violence was employed in all four cases as a mobilizational device, with the emphasis in Pakistan and Kyrgyzstan on vote mobilization, in Ghana on the mobilization of the "foot soldiers" needed to win an electoral contest, and in Côte d'Ivoire on mobilization via boycott. In Ghana, Kyrgyzstan, and Côte d'Ivoire, the mobilization of anti-incumbent protests played a large role, whereas in Pakistan most violence took place as a part of clashes between competing groups of party activists. In all four contexts, violence was intimately tied up with clientelism in carrot-and-stick configurations. Bereft of state resources, oppositions cobbled together election strategies using the tools at their disposal—historic antagonisms, anger at incumbents, material benefits to supporters, and to activists the promise of rewards once in office—to win elections.

Conclusion

This chapter has probed the causes and dynamics of violence perpetrated by nonstate actors in connection with electoral processes. We have seen that violence is a tool commonly used by political oppositions as a mobilizational device. We have also seen that it is often combined with vote buying and other forms of clientelism. This carrot-and-stick approach makes maximum use of the resources available to political actors out of power—informal networks and power structures outside the state, as well as coercive capacity and money. In the run-up to elections this is typically manifest in terms of efforts to manipulate voters' expressed preferences. It can also take the form of street protests, before and/or after elections, which can lead to violence. Nonstate actors are in many respects constrained in the tools they can use to compete electorally, especially in contexts where there is not a level playing field. Yet the type of low-intensity violence most common at election time is a strategy that is widely available to even relatively weak actors. In some cases the aim of perpetrators may be simply to disrupt the electoral process and depress participation, as is the case, for example, with the Taliban in Afghanistan (Condra et al. 2018; Weidmann and Callen 2013). But in as much as violence is risky and often attracts costly repression, it tends to be used sparingly and tends to be reserved for contexts in which a close race suggests that the opposition has a chance of victory, as demonstrated in the large-N analyses presented in the second section of the chapter. Combining violence with vote buying is another way of multiplying the electoral effectiveness of clientelism. Informal institutions are resources that can remain latent for considerable periods of time and be mobilized at opportune moments. It is thus not surprising that the use of nonstate violence should ebb and flow depending on the current political context.

Indeed, the examples discussed in this chapter show that the role of context is a very important determinant of patterns of electoral violence. So far this study has examined broad-brush patterns that can be found in a wide variety of settings. Having established these general patterns, we are now ready to turn in chapter 5 to an examination of how different social and political contexts structure the use of electoral violence.

5

Divergent Contexts and Patterns of Violent Elections

Chapters 3 and 4 have provided insight into general trends in electoral violence; the aim of this chapter is to explore variations in patterns across time and space. Three types of variation will be considered: temporal variations linked to the point in the electoral cycle at which violence takes place, temporal variations across elections, and geographic variations. As we shall see, the same basic dynamics of politicized states that account for broad patterns in electoral violence also go a considerable way toward explaining common patterns of variation.

One of the most obvious ways in which electoral violence can be broken down into its component parts is by point in the electoral cycle. Violence that takes place during the election campaign and on polling day is in many ways a distinct phenomenon from postelection violence. Though violent protests following an election can and often do have as their aim the alteration or reversal of electoral results, it is at this point no longer possible to employ force to influence the voting decision. By the same token, state and other actors have less motivation to seek to pander to voters after the votes have been counted, and they may see themselves as being freer to engage in retribution for voting decisions (Bhasin and Gandhi 2013). It is thus instructive to consider temporal patterns of electoral violence over the electoral cycle in order to deepen our understanding of the political dynamics involved. This will be the topic of the first section of this chapter.

The examples presented in previous chapters suggest that in addition to variation over time, there is also considerable contextual variation in patterns of electoral conflict. A distinction was made in chapter 2 between endemic, episodic, and rare violence, and it was posited that this distinction would be relevant in understanding the way in which incumbent and opposition actors reacted to violence. It is also possible to distinguish between contexts where conflict at election time is localized and settings where it is widespread. The second section of the chapter will employ selected case studies of the Philippines, Tanzania, Ukraine, and Jamaica to examine the different contexts in which violence affects elections. A final section concludes.

Violence before, during, and after Elections

Limited research has been carried out on the dynamics of conflict over the course of the electoral cycle. Moreover, there is contradictory evidence on the use of violence by different actors at various points in the electoral process. Studies by Burchard (2015) and Hafner-Burton, Hyde, and Jablonski (2014) both found there to be more violent acts committed before an election than after, whereas Bhasin and Gandhi (2013) showed the opposite. Straus and Taylor (2012) argued that the use of force by state actors is triggered by violent acts committed by the opposition, while Hafner-Burton, Hyde, and Jablonski (2014) argued that it is preelectoral state harassment that provokes postelectoral violence. In the African context, Van Ham and Lindberg (2015) found that government harassment and electoral violence by the opposition covary. Daxecker (2012, 2014) and Borzyskowski (2019) demonstrated that the presence of international observers mediates the use of violence, displacing violence from election day to the preelectoral period, and triggering postelectoral violence if observer reports are critical of electoral conduct. Harish and Toha (2017) found that in Indonesia, candidates are targeted with violence before elections, whereas state institutions (government agencies) are affected most heavily following the polls. Rich as it is, this literature has yet to uncover consistent patterns in the use of force by state and nonstate actors during the electoral period.

Monthly data on electoral violence from the Countries at Risk of Electoral Violence (CREV) data set (Birch and Muchlinski 2019) enables us to unravel the dynamics of electoral conflict with greater precision than has been the case in most previous studies. These data cover the period from 6 months before the election, through election month, and 3 months after the election, for a total time span of 10 months per election cycle. We find that

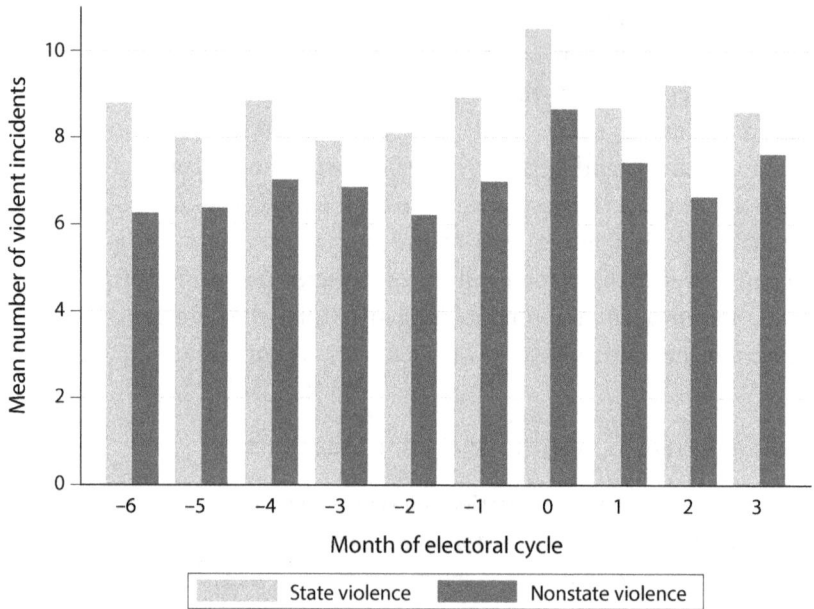

FIGURE 5.1. Electoral violence by point in the electoral cycle

violence by state actors at one point in time is met by violence by nonstate actors at a subsequent point in the electoral cycle; likewise, violence by nonstate actors is met by state violence. This suggests that electoral violence involves cycles of reinforcing aggression.

Figure 5.1 displays the overall means of violent incidents over the electoral period, broken down by actor type. These data show that election violence peaks during the month of the polls. Consistent with the argument put forward in chapter 4, there is a greater risk of nonstate violence in the wake of voting than is the case during the preelectoral period, though the likelihood of state-initiated violence remains high throughout the electoral cycle.

The overall patterns evident in figure 5.1 are informative, but there are nevertheless considerable variations from country to country and from election to election, depending on repertoires of violence specific to the local context, and also on election-specific events. From the point of view of understanding the dynamics of electoral violence, a relevant question is the extent to which violence is a reactive move, in the sense that attacks and other violent acts are undertaken in response to actions by other actors, as is often the case with other types of political violence (Balcells 2010; Fuiji 2009; Linke, Witmer, and O'Loughlin 2012). If this is true, it points to a danger that violence will breed violence, and that once triggered, electoral violence can exhibit escalating cycles of conflict. This would also indicate that there may be scope for implementing confidence-building mechanisms that help to resolve differences peacefully and defuse triggers of violence.

Case-study evidence demonstrates that this does indeed occur. There are frequent reports in the literature on electoral violence of revenge being one of the objectives of attacks. The horrific atrocities that took place in the wake of the Kenyan elections of 2007 is perhaps the best known example of retaliatory violence. Vengeance has historically motivated electoral conflict in that country (Bekoe and Burchard 2017), and the retaliatory nature of much of the violence that shook Kenya in 2007 and 2008 has been well documented (CIPEV 2008; Dercon and Gutiérrez-Romero 2012; Klaus and Mitchell 2015). The report of the official Commission of Inquiry into the Post Election Violence (CIPEV; the "Waki Commission") commented on the intentional and premeditated nature of much retaliation:

> The report concludes that the post-election violence was more than a mere juxtaposition of citizens-to-citizens opportunistic assaults. These were systematic attacks on Kenyans based on their ethnicity and their political leanings. Attackers organized along ethnic lines, assembled considerable logistical means and traveled long distances to burn houses, maim, kill and sexually assault their occupants because these were of particular ethnic groups and political persuasion. Guilty by association was the guiding force behind deadly "revenge" attacks, with victims being identified not for what they did but for their ethnic association to other perpetrators. (CIVEP 2008, viii)

In Nigeria also, a commission of inquiry (the Lemu Panel) implicated retaliatory attacks in the 2011 electoral violence that resulted in 938 deaths and 735 injuries (Fischer 2017a). Revenge as a motive for electoral violence has been identified in a wide range of contexts, including Timor-Leste (EU 2017; Fischer 2016), Zimbabwe (Creative Associates International 2010; Kriger 2005), and Sri Lanka (Höglund 2009). In a perceptive comment, Van Ham and Lindberg noted that:

> The willingness of the opposition to resort to violence does not necessarily appear to be a function of the government's superior capacity to use manipulation, as opposition violence is not significantly affected by the level of election administration manipulation or vote buying in African elections. Rather, it seems to be driven by tit-for-tat reasoning: if governments engage in intimidation, opposition actors are more likely to retaliate by resorting to violence. (2015, 545n22)

Van Ham and Lindberg's analysis accords broadly with that presented in chapter 4 of this volume and with H6 set out in chapter 2, which predicts strategic interaction in the use of violence by electoral contestants. Yet there has been virtually no cross-national analysis of retaliatory electoral violence or the extent of strategic interaction by actors in the electoral arena.

In order to examine more systematically the extent to which a threat or attack at one point in time triggers a reactive act at a subsequent point in time, we can again make use of the monthly electoral CREV data. As noted in chapter 1, this data set provides counts of threats and attacks committed by state and by nonstate actors against the other. Though violent acts can attract immediate retaliation, many forms of violence require planning. This suggests that there will often be a delay between the use of force by one actor and retaliation by another. As a rough measure of the propensity of acts of electoral violence to attract tit-for-tat reactions, we can thus examine the pattern of correlation coefficients between violence committed by one actor (state or nonstate) in a given month and the use of violence by the other actor the following month. Where such correlations are particularly strong, this suggests that the use of force is highly likely to attract retaliatory action.

Figure 5.2 plots the correlation coefficients between each type of state violence in a given month, and each type of nonstate violence the following month. Figure 5.3 does the same for the correlation coefficients between nonstate violence in a given month and state violence the following month. A total of nine time periods are represented here, from the use of force six months before the election and retaliation five months before the polls, to violence two months after election day and reaction in the third postelectoral month. If there were no strategic interaction between actors, we would still expect to see statistically significant positive coefficients, as elections with higher overall levels of violence generally have more violence of all kinds by all actors (and indeed, all the coefficients represented in these graphs are significant at the .01 level). But in as much as there are clear variations in the strength of the coefficients across type of violent act and across time, this suggests that patterns of violence are least in part reflective of reactive behavior.

The pattern of correlations evident in figures 5.2 and 5.3 points to the reactive use of force by both state and nonstate actors in the electoral arena, confirming Van Ham and Lindberg's (2015) evidence of covariation in the African context. The coefficients are all positive and range in magnitude from .116 to .805. By far the most noteworthy association is that between *attacks* by one actor in a given month and *attacks* by the other actor in the

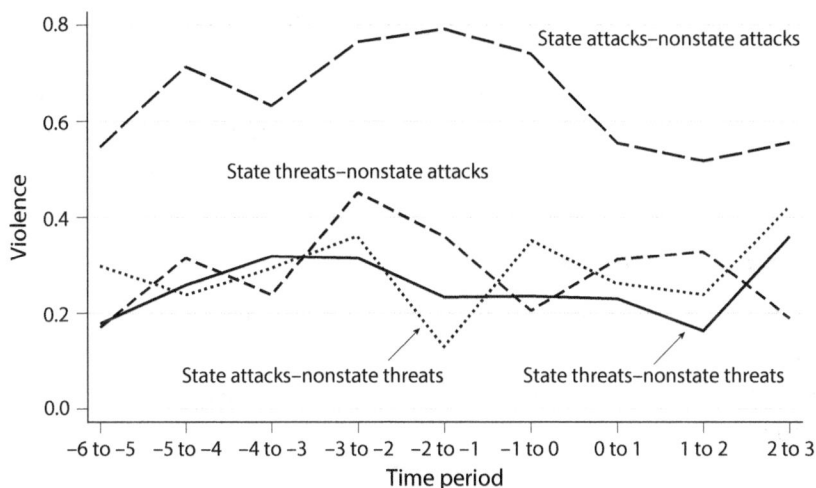

FIGURE 5.2. Reactive patterns of violence over the electoral period: state violence

NB: The data plotted in the graph represent correlation coefficients between violence committed by the first-named actor in the dyad in month *t* and the second-named actor in the dyad in month *t* − 1.

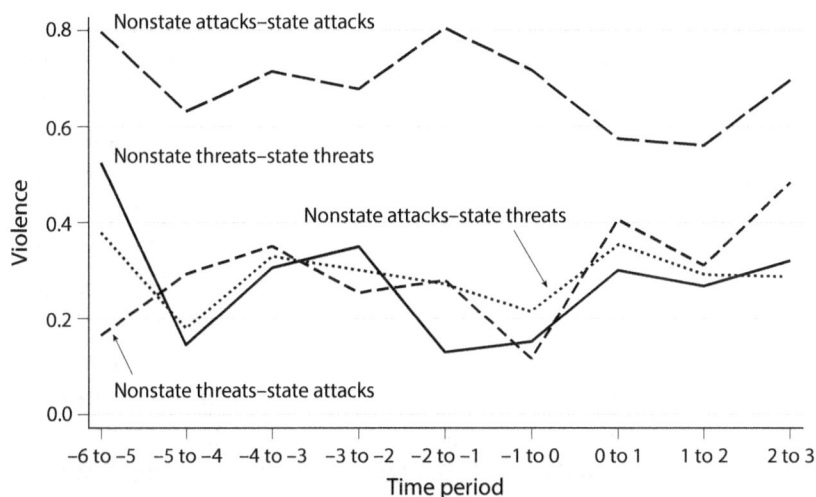

FIGURE 5.3. Reactive patterns of violence over the electoral period: nonstate violence

NB: The data plotted in the graph represent correlation coefficients between violence committed by the first-named actor in the dyad in month *t* and the second-named actor in the dyad in month *t* − 1.

following month: this holds true for both state and nonstate actors. This suggests that both types of actor engage in like-for-like retaliatory activity, and that they are particularly sensitive to physical assaults. The period of closest association for both state-initiated and nonstate-initiated retaliation is the two-month stretch prior to polling day, with the riskiest period of all being the month before the election. The patterns of correlations presented here indicate that it is in this month that both sides are most likely to undertake tit-for-tat attacks in response to physical violence committed the previous month by the other side. The run-up to voting is thus the phase of the electoral cycle where conflict-defusing strategies may be most useful.

Temporal and Geographic Patterns

So far in this book electoral violence has been considered largely in isolation from the political context in which it occurs. But, as noted in chapter 1, contextual factors will undoubtedly be important in shaping the strategies and expectations of those who perpetrate violence. In some settings, the use of force is endemic at election time and the anticipation of violence is built into the way in which people think about elections. Examples of countries with endemic electoral violence include the Kenyan and Nigerian cases mentioned in the previous section, as well as states such as Bangladesh, Honduras, and the Philippines. When, at the opposite extreme, elections are almost always peaceful, as is the case in most established democracies, electoral violence comes as a surprise when it erupts. In between these two polar opposites is a situation that is common in the contemporary world: widespread electoral violence is foreseen as a possibility, but not necessarily anticipated. The 2002 election in Kenya was largely peaceful, whereas the 1997 polls witnessed significant widespread violence (Brown 2011). The Iranian election of 2009 sparked a far greater amount of conflict than either the preceding contest of 2008 or the subsequent poll in 2012 (Hafner-Burton, Hyde, and Jablonski 2014). There have also been significant variations in the level of electoral violence in Thailand, with peaks in 2005 and 2014, but lower levels in the intervening contests (McCargo and Desatová 2016), and in Uganda, with notably higher levels of violence in the 2001, 2006, and 2016 elections than in those held in 1996 and 2011 (Sjögren 2018). When a state has a history of episodic violence at election time, the possibility of outbreaks is always on the horizon, but there is considerable uncertainty as to whether any given election will turn violent, the extent to which the electoral peace will be disrupted, and the point in the electoral cycle at which the use of force is likely to intervene. We can thus delineate a threefold typology of endemic, episodic, and rare violence, bearing in mind that these terms designate points along what is in fact a continuum. Rare violence tends to be highly idiosyncratic and difficult to conceptualize: the violence that broke out at the time of the 2019 European Parliament election campaign in the United Kingdom had little in common with the letter bombs that were sent to known partisan actors in the run-up to the 2018 US midterm elections. And when Spanish police used what was described by both Amnesty International and Human Rights Watch as "excessive force" to obstruct the conduct of an independence referendum in Catalonia that had been declared illegal by the Spanish Constitutional Court (Amnesty International 2017; Human Rights Watch 2017), the resulting injury of over 800 people shocked politicians and political commentators across Europe (Rodríguez and Congostrina 2017; Williams 2017). Such events are exceptional, however, and not part of a pattern in the Spanish policing of elections. Thus, while events such as this merit analysis in order to understand what caused them, it is difficult to say that they form part of a distinct category of violence that afflicts democracies. Episodes of this sort are best interpreted in the context of political developments in the country in question rather than considered within frameworks developed to study electoral violence. Endemic and episodic electoral conflicts are, on the other hand, worthy of analysis as discrete phenomena that are repeated across contexts.

Another contextual factor that varies across states is whether violence is localized or widespread. There is virtually always geographic variation in levels of electoral conflict, with capital cities very often experiencing relatively high numbers of incidents. Yet there are also contexts in which violence at election time takes on distinctive regional characteristics, generally reflecting historic and/or ethnic differences. Indonesia is an example of a state where electoral violence has a regionalized character, with different geographic patterns of pre- and postelectoral violence. Harish and Toha (2017) have shown that there is a concentration of preelectoral violence in former separatist areas, whereas postelectoral violence disproportionately affects regions with preexisting communal tension. Murray noted the geographically concentrated nature of electoral violence in Honduras, which is "worse in areas where 'big men' dominate politics" (2016, 178), a finding that is in keeping with this volume's argument about the link between electoral violence and informal institutions. Violence before and after the Kenyan elections of 2002, 2007, and 2013 was also highly regionalized, with the majority of deaths occurring in a relatively limited number of areas (Dercon and Gutiérrez-Romero 2012; Fjelde and Höglund 2018; Malik 2018). Borzyskowski and Wahman (2019) found electoral-violence hot spots in otherwise relatively peaceful Malawi and Zambia. In the Zambian context, Wahman and Goldring (2020) found considerable subnational variations in the strategic use of preelectoral violence, which varied with patterns of partisan control. Even established democracies may have regions that remain vulnerable to violence at election time, as Alesina, Piccolo, and Pinotti (2018) demonstrated in relation to contemporary Italy.

Implicit in the patterns set out here is the two-by-two matrix displayed in table 5.1. This typology establishes a set of stylized distinctions between levels of a priori uncertainty surrounding the likelihood of violence and levels of regional concentration of conflict. These two factors can also be expected to interact, in as much as violence is expected in some regions, unexpected in others, and uncertain in still other areas of a country. Another potential driver of interaction is the phenomenon of "authoritarian learning," whereby leaders of competitive democratic states learn over time from their own successes and failures, and also from the experience of leaders elsewhere, to develop strategies—including violent strategies—that can help them to achieve and retain power (Hall and Ambrosio 2017; Heydemann and Leenders 2011; Sjögren 2018; Vanderhill 2012).

Why might previously peaceful electoral institutions suddenly be affected by violence? And why might certain elections in a state be violent and others not? In some cases extraneous (nonelectoral) factors account for the sudden upsurge in attacks and threats. The Albanian parliamentary election of June 1997 is a good example of this. The election took place in the wake of a period of lawlessness precipitated by the collapse of a pyramid scheme earlier in the year and the looting of state munitions stores; not surprisingly, the electoral process was characterized by unusually high levels of intimidation and violent attacks (Mochtak 2018a). Temporal variation in the availability of firearms has also been credited with explaining violence in several other electoral contexts, such as Sri Lanka (Devotta 2003; EU 2001), Kenya (SAS 2012), and the Philippines (Patino and Velasco 2004). Changes in political tactics by leaders can likewise account for sudden sharp spikes in political contention in general, and electoral violence as a component of political tension. The rise to power of Thaksin Shinawatra discussed in chapter 1 is an example of this phenomenon, as are the election of Vladimir Putin in Russia and that of Hugo Chávez in Venezuela, both of which were followed by sharp upticks in levels of electoral violence.

In other cases, factors intrinsic to elections account for variation. Contested outcomes may spark a surge in postelectoral violent protest, as discussed in chapter 4. Examination of individual cases suggests that elections may also be at particular danger when the incumbent miscalculates in estimating the degree of genuine support enjoyed by opposition forces. For example, when a liberalization in electoral competition in advance of the

TABLE 5-1. Contextual Variations on Electoral Violence:
A Typology

	Localized	Widespread
Rare		
Episodic	Jamaica	Ukraine
Endemic	Tanzania	Philippines

For alternative typologies of electoral violence, see Burchard (2015),
Staniland (2014), and Straus and Taylor (2012).

2005 elections in Ethiopia led to an unexpected surge in opposition activity and popularity, the government responded by engaging in the abuse of state resources for incumbent campaigning purposes and the obstruction of opposition campaign activities, as well as the intimidation of opposition candidates and supporters, which then fueled the flames of opposition insurgent groups, particularly in the Muslim-inhabited East of the country (Carter Center 2009; EU 2005; Hagmann 2012; Lyons 2005: Pettersen and Salvesen 2006; Tronvoll and Hagmann 2012). Conversely, expectations of victory that emerge during the campaign can dampen incentives to resort to violence, as noted in chapter 4 in relation to Côte d'Ivoire. Akhter attributed the lower level of violence in Bangladeshi elections held in 1981 and 1994 to the fact that the incumbent looked set to win:

> The opposition was aware that during the presidential election of 1981 the ruling party candidate could win by using the image of Zia after his brutal death. . . . The major parties in the 1994 CC [City Corporation] poll were hopeful of success and this contributed to the low level of violence and intimidation. (Akhter 2001, 170)

Power-sharing arrangements have also been linked to lower levels of violence. Again in Bangladesh, Macdonald reported lower levels of violence in the 1991 elections, where there was a degree of cooperation between the two main parties, the Awami League and the Bangladesh Nationalist Party (2016). Power-sharing arrangements that vary from election to election and from region to region may also account for variations in patterns of violence. In Sri Lanka, elections have resulted in regular changes in control of the apparatus of state coercion, and in particular the police, who have been found in many cases to turn a blind eye to violence perpetrated by supporters of the party in power (Devotta 2003; EU 2001; Höglund and Piyarathne 2009). This was particularly pronounced in elections held in

2001, whereas in 2004 and 2005, when the president and the prime minister represented different parties, the pattern of violence was less partisan and the police behaved in a more neutral manner (EU 2004; Hickman 2009; Höglund and Piyarathne 2009). Wilkinson's detailed study of ethnic violence in India linked geographic variations in the severity of conflict to the incentives of ruling parties (and the security forces under their control) to protect ethnic minorities, which in turn varied with the need to include minorities in coalitions (Wilkinson 2004).

The specifically electoral causes of intracountry patterns in electoral violence are of particular relevance to the concerns of this study. These examples suggest that electoral violence varies according to the perceived need to resort to extreme measures to win elections, the resulting opposition backlash when extreme measures include blatant fraud, and also the willingness of electoral rivals to enter into power-sharing arrangements. The impact of electoral context on patterns of violence will be considered via four case studies. The Philippines will be taken as an example of widespread endemic violence, Tanzania (Zanzibar) as an example of localized endemic violence, Ukraine 2004 as an example of widespread episodic violence, and Jamaica as an example of localized episodic violence. Examination of these cases will demonstrate that political corruption of ostensibly impartial state institutions such as electoral management bodies and the security services is an important background factor in setting the scene for the contextual dynamics just mentioned. The weakness of highly politicized and corrupt states means that they find it difficult both to rule without resorting to force, and to regulate the use of force by others.

THE PHILIPPINES

Electoral violence has been endemic in the Philippines since the advent of modern multiparty competition, owing largely to state weakness, as will be shown in the paragraphs to follow. Ferdinand Marcos ruled the Philippines for 21 years. There had been a long tradition of clientelism, intimidation, and other forms of electoral abuse in the Philippines, but a relatively independent electoral commission had kept a check on wholesale vote rigging (Thompson 1998). Several years after Marcos came to power he declared martial law, and suspended democratic elections until the late 1970s. But by the early 1980s, Marcos was beginning to lose his grip on power, which was weakened by extreme personalism and intense elite rivalries (Brownlee 2007; Thompson 1998). Significant elements of the military had lost confidence in the dictator, who was himself suffering from a terminal form of lupus. At the same time, the communist party was gaining strength in rural areas and the economy was faltering. To address his political weakness, Marcos increased the use of electoral fraud and intimidation, and the 1978, 1980, and 1981 elections were all marred by significant abuse (Thompson 1998).

The unceremonious murder of opposition leader Benigno Aquino upon his return from exile in 1983 helped to galvanize popular opposition to the Marcos regime; significantly, the opposition movement had the support of the Catholic Church, including vocal Cardinal Jaime Sin. Heightened confrontation led to an estimated 2000 deaths at the time of the 1984 election, making this the bloodiest election in the country's history (Linantud 1998). The opposition eventually managed to unite around Aquino's widow Corazon, who contested the snap 1986 presidential elections. An effective and well-organized domestic election observer group, the National Citizens' Movement for Free Elections, had also been established prior to the 1984 parliamentary elections with the help of an American nongovernmental organization (NGO). Marcos made last-minute attempts at fraud as it became obvious that he had in fact lost the 1986 election in the face of the "People Power" revolution (Brownlee 2007; Case 2006; Hartmann, Hassall, and Santos 2001). The dictator also went on television and ordered the military to attack, demolish, and exterminate "the rebels" (quoted in Case 2006, 110). This is yet another example of the phenomenon discussed in chapter 2 of force being used in conjunction with electoral misconduct by an authoritarian leader facing a serious challenge.

However, the demise of Marcos's rule did not bring an end to electoral violence in the Philippines; on the contrary, the period of increased electoral competitiveness after 1986 ushered in a rise in conflictual polls. In the decade between 2001 and 2010 alone, the CREV data set records 8644 violent incidents over four electoral cycles, and there were an average of 1461 incidents per election over the 1995–2013 period.

Patino and Velasco noted that in the Philippines election-related violence takes numerous forms:

Election-related harassment and violence can range from intimidating and threatening persons with bodily harm, to kidnapping and murder, as well as arson and bombings of strategic locations. Victims and perpetrators are not limited to the candidates and their campaign staff. Hired goons, private armies, the police and military, as well as armed rebel groups, also figure prominently. (Patino and Velasco 2004, 3)

Several authors have maintained that such violence most commonly occurs during the campaign period where rivals target each other's candidates and voters (Creative Associates International 2012; Linantud 1998; Patino and Velasco 2004). Over the years, politicians have learned to develop repertoires that reappear in election after election. Preelectoral violence is often followed by fatal attacks on election day itself, typically triggered by allegations of fraud or efforts to obstruct voting and counting (Patino and Velasco 2004).

Patronage, the desire to plunder state coffers, state weakness, and clan rivalries have all been identified as factors that contribute to electoral violence in the Philippines. In the context of a weak state, the use of violence serves to legitimize the power of local bosses (Creative Associates International 2012; Linantud 1998; Patino and Velasco 2004; Quimpo 2009). Gaining public office is also a convenient way for warlords and gang leaders to protect illicit activities (Creative Associates International 2012; Patino and Velasco 2004; Quimpo 2009). In the southern Philippines, communist insurgents have been known to attack electoral candidates who have taken part in the state's counterinsurgency drives (Patino and Velasco 2004).

Thus the Filipino state is strong enough to make elected office a valuable asset, but weak enough that it is unable to control competition for such positions; violence is endemic as the central problems of state weakness and political corruption are inherent features of the way the country is governed, though it also exhibits geographic and temporal variations that correspond to patterns of clan rivalry, insurgent activity, and political support. In this sense the Philippines fits the central argument of this study almost perfectly.

TANZANIA

Tanzania—and in particular the offshore region of Zanzibar—is a case of localized violence, which can, as this section demonstrates, be attributed to a combination of structural and institutional factors. Tanzania was formed in 1964 as the union of the former British colonies of Tanganyika on the African mainland and the much smaller islands that make up Zanzibar (Pemba and Unguja). Following a period of single-party rule in which regular, peaceful, competitive, but nonpartisan elections were held (Samoff 1987), Tanzania initiated a protracted democratic transition in 1992. In the years that followed, the Revolutionary Party (Chama Cha Mapinduzi, CCM), which ruled the country during the authoritarian period, has not lost an election.

Since the early 1990s, elections in Tanzania have been largely peaceful on the mainland, and prone to violence in Zanzibar, thus exemplifying the phenomenon identified by Bekoe of "pockets of violence" (2012a, 9). Zanzibar is semiautonomous with its own president and assembly, which since 1980 has had its own electoral commission. The two parts of the country have different histories and different racial compositions, with mainland Tanzania inhabited mainly by people of African heritage, and Zanzibar home to people of both African and Arab descent. In recent years they have also exhibited political differences, in that the opposition is far stronger in Zanzibar than on the mainland. The Civic United Front (CUF), with strong support from people of Arabic heritage, frequently clashes with both the dominant CCM and the security services at election time (Bekoe 2012b). The island of Pemba, in particular, is a CUF stronghold.

Elections have been held in 1995, 2000, 2005, 2010, and 2015, with an average of 99 violent events recorded per election in the CREV data set. The contests with the most high-profile violence to date were those of 2000. After the closely fought 1995 elections in Zanzibar that were widely believed to have been marred by serious fraud, the Commonwealth-mediated Mufaka I accord was signed between the two main parties, calling for reforms to electoral administration, the judiciary, and the media (Pottie 2002). This accord went largely unimplemented, however (Bekoe 2012b). The result was an election in 2000 that was marked by serious conflict. The campaign period was affected by state harassment and intimidation. CUF supporters clashed with both supporters of the CCM and the police; 45 CUF supporters were detained during the preelection period (Pottie 2002). The vote counting process on election day raised considerable suspicions when it was suspended in a number of places and the electoral commission declared that the elections would be rerun in 16 constituencies. The period between the original election and the rerun was racked by violent clashes, which resulted in 150 CUF supporters being arrested (Pottie 2002). Following the election, the CUF protested against alleged electoral misconduct. The security forces responded to the protests by killing between 35 and 67 CUF supporters, causing an estimated 2000 Zanzibaris to flee to Kenya (Bekoe 2012b).

Following these fraught events, the Mufaka II accord was signed in 2001. This agreement committed the parties to bipartisan participation in the selection of members of the Zanzibar Electoral Commission and compensation for victims of past violence, as well as a range of electoral, security sector, and media reforms, to be overseen by a bipartisan supervisory body, which in theory afforded a degree of power sharing in the sphere of electoral conduct (Bekoe 2012b; Opitz, Fjelde, and Höglund 2013). However, the accord was never fully implemented, and the bipartisan oversight body soon became dysfunctional (Bekoe 2012b; Opitz, Fjelde, and Höglund 2013). Though less conflictual than the 2000 polls, subsequent elections in 2005 were marred by a number of violent incidents, including alleged intimidation by the government and the security sector during the registration process and the campaign, clashes during campaign rallies and at polling stations between supporters of rival parties), and the excessive use of force and voter intimidation by the security sector on polling day (Commonwealth 2005; EISA 2006; Mjåtvedt 2006). The reduction in severe violence between 2000 and 2005 has been attributed by Opitz, Fjelde, and Höglund (2013) to the power-sharing provisions built into the Mufaka II accord, though they also acknowledge the "limited" influence of institutional factors in the context of historic divisions.

In 2010 a more effective power-sharing arrangement came into existence when the CCM and the CUF agreed a government of national unity, an agreement that was approved by referendum in July of that year (Bekoe 2012b). This led to a significant reduction in violence at the 2010 elections (EU 2010). The run-up to the 2015 elections was relatively calm also, though there were a number of violent incidents following a decision by the Zanzibar Election Commission to annul the results of the election and rehold it (EU 2015). The CUF refused to take part in the rerun election, effectively ending the power-sharing arrangement.

The Tanzanian case demonstrates that geographic variations in structural patterns of ethnic and political support can lead to isolated areas of increased electoral tension and conflict that persist from election to election. The Zanzibari experience suggests that such conflicts can be managed at least temporarily through power-sharing arrangements, which mitigate tensions somewhat. However, in dominant-party Tanzania, violence has been a persistent feature of elections in Zanzibar since the advent of electoral competition in 1992, even if it has not been prominent in those held in mainland Tanzania. State institutions that on the mainland were capable of managing political competition relatively effectively proved unable to achieve this end peacefully in the more ethnically and politically heterogeneous context of Zanzibar.

UKRAINE 2004

Ukraine is a case of episodic electoral violence. The 2004 election was an instance of unusually high levels of conflict in a context where electoral competition was often affected by misconduct. The 2004 presidential contest—held over three rounds—was the only Ukrainian election to be coded 2 or higher on either of the two V-DEM electoral-violence ordinal scales; the CREV data set records 202 violent incidents in this electoral period, whereas the mean for other elections held since 1991, when Ukraine gained independence from the Soviet Union, is 36.

Early postindependence elections in the mid-1990s were relatively credible, but with the rise to power of President Leonid Kuchma in 1999, the conduct of elections began to deteriorate (Birch 2002b, 2010; Myagkov, Ordeshook, and Shakin 2009; Wilson 2005a). At this point other authoritarian tendencies also began to manifest themselves, most notably lack of rule of law and centralization of power in the presidential administration (Birch 2008; D'Anieri 2006; Wilson 2005a). The final years of Kuchma's administration were increasingly authoritarian; freedom of the press was seriously curtailed, corruption was rife, and a number of prominent public figures were murdered or died in suspicious circumstances (Copsey 2010; D'Anieri 2005). The 2004 contest was from the start affected by this heightened state of tension, and in the end the process was so contentious that the results were eventually overturned following street protests in what became known as the "Orange Revolution."

In the run-up to the 2004 election, the incumbent political grouping was under pressure. Kuchma was not able to run again owing to a term-limit rule; his anointed successor was Viktor Yanukovych, whose support was concentrated in the Russophone East of the country. The main opposition candidate was Viktor Yushchenko, a pro-Western liberal who was most popular in the Ukrainophone West of Ukraine. The race was very close, with a first-round difference of only 0.6 percent between the top two candidates, according to official results. From the outset of the campaign, there were allegations of serious fraud, intimidation, and violence (D'Anieri 2005; Hesli 2006; Myagkov, Ordeshook, and Shakin 2009; Wilson 2005a). The most egregious such incident was undoubtedly the near-fatal poisoning of Yushchenko, but there were many others, including a number of bombs and attacks by anonymous perpetrators (Wilson 2005a).

During the campaign period, seven journalists from television news channel 1+1 quit in protest against censorship. They were quoted by Interfax as saying: "We refuse to take part in the information war. The authorities unleashed this war against its own people, trying to win the presidential race through intimidation and the use of force."[1] Though it was not often clear

---

1. RadioFreeEurope/RadioLiberty, "Newsline—October 29, 2004," October 29, 2004, https://www.rferl.org/a/1143272.html.

who was responsible for attacks that took place, the electoral campaign was marked by frequent violent episodes. There was a series of mysterious bomb attacks in the run-up to the election for which both sides blamed the other.[2] Bomb-making materials were found in headquarters of a student opposition group, and authorities accused NGO Pora of terrorism, whereas the student group claimed the materials had been planted.[3]

Threats of violent disruption of the constitutional order were alleged by both sides. In the days following the release of the second-round results, Yanukovych repeatedly accused his opponent of attempting to stage a coup d'état.[4] Though mass-scale civil strife was probably never a real possibility in Ukraine, the Yushchenko camp did to some extent fuel the view that violent revolutionary action was a possibility by setting up a "Committee of National Salvation" following the release of the second-round results, harking back to establishment of a similar body in Romania at the time of the bloody 1989 events. But the opposition also claimed the moral upper hand, arguing that Yanukovych's support for abortive separatist moves in the eastern regions of Ukraine during this period threatened to break the country apart. Following a deal on the rerun of the second round, Yanukovych said he would bring his supporters to Kiev to avert possible "crisis" and that his supporters might challenge those of Yushchenko for control of the streets; Yushchenko claimed in response that "this is an attempt by the former premier to destabilize civil peace and the political situation in Ukraine."[5]

State bodies appear to have played a role in tipping this contest over into violence. The abuse of state resources—a concept that has entered popular parlance in Ukraine under the term *"adminresurs"*—had long been a problem in this post-Soviet state (Birch 2002b; 2003), but in 2004 this practice was extended to include widespread intimidation. One of the resources used to partisan ends was the state police. The OSCE's election observation report noted that police were present in 62 percent of polling stations for no clear reason. The same report also noted the presence of numerous

2. RadioFreeEurope/RadioLiberty, "Newsline—September 3, 2004," September 3, 2004, https://www.rferl.org/a/1143236.html.

3. RadioFreeEurope/RadioLiberty, "Newsline—October 18, 2004," October 18, 2004, https://www.rferl.org/a/1143264.html.

4. RadioFreeEurope/RadioLiberty, "Newsline—November 29, 2004," November 29, 2004, https://www.rferl.org/a/1143289.html; "Newsline—December 9, 2004," December 9, 2004, https://www.rferl.org/a/1143297.html; "Newsline—December 23, 2004," December 23, 2004, https://www.rferl.org/a/1143307.html.

5. RadioFreeEurope/RadioLiberty, "Newsline—December 17, 2004," December 17, 2004, https://www.rferl.org/a/1143303.html.

other "unauthorized persons," including armband-wearing "private security" guards who in some cases engaged in gross intimidation and interfered with the electoral process in other ways (OSCE-ODIHR 2005b, 26).

When the official result of the second round gave the victory to Yanukovych, the opposition took to the streets en masse. Though their protest was generally peaceful, it was a tense period when many expected the state to respond with force. The government in fact did attempt to mobilize the army to quell the protests, but the army refused, and some interior ministry forces defected to the opposition also (Wilson 2005a). The electoral impasse was eventually resolved when the Supreme Court ruled that the second round of the election should be rerun, and in the event, the rerun was won by Yushchenko.

Scholars have noted that the competitiveness of the 2004 race prompted contestants to use more extreme manipulative tactics than had heretofore been practiced (D'Anieri 2005; Wilson 2005a). Writing of the poisoning of Yushchenko, Andrew Wilson concluded:

> The Ukrainian authorities were used to fixing elections, having had some good practice in 1999 and 2002. This time, however, the stakes were much higher. The existence of a strong opposition and the prospect of real change produced a much dirtier fight. A decision had been taken that Yanukovych would win, whatever it took. (Wilson 2005a, 104)

Taras Kuzio agreed:

> The stakes in the 2004 election were always high. As early as December 2003 Kuchma warned that the October 2004 elections would be Ukraine's dirtiest, a prophecy that proved to be accurate. The attempted poisoning of Yushchenko during the campaign shows how far his opponents were willing to go to stop his election. (Kuzio 2005, 30)

The 2004 elections were more competitive than previous polls for two principal reasons: Yanukovych did not possess the gravitas or personal authority of outgoing Kuchma, and the months of anticorruption protests had enabled the opposition to mobilize to a degree that had been inconceivable in the context of previous elections.

The blatant politicization of electoral administration was also a major factor that contributed to the poor electoral conduct and galvanized protests. Thousands of local electoral officers were bribed to "deliver" desired electoral results (Wilson 2005a). And in what is perhaps one of the most egregious instances of political corruption in the history of modern electoral conduct, a team within the presidential administration intercepted and altered electoral results as they were being transferred electronically from localities to the Central Electoral Commission, via a procedure that was subsequently revealed in evidence given to the Ukrainian Supreme Court by one of those involved (Myagkov, Ordeshook, and Shakin 2009; Wilson 2005a). There were also numerous other electoral irregularities that it was possible for domestic and international observers to document in real time, including the removal of valid entries in the electoral register, multiple voting, ballot-box stuffing, and mistabulation (OSCE-ODIHR 2005b; Wilson 2005a).

Thus, a high-stakes election pitting a corrupt state apparatus against a newly invigorated opposition set the stage for both violent forms of electoral manipulation and a forceful opposition protest. Though subsequent elections—especially the presidential polls of 2012 and 2015—also witnessed problems of various kinds, including violence, the 2004 election was unique in the degree of united oppositional mobilization and the brazenness of electoral manipulation by the state.

JAMAICA

Jamaica is an example of a state where electoral violence is both localized and episodic, owing to the unusual sociopolitical characteristics of areas of the capital city, Kingston. The Caribbean island, which has since 1962 been an independent state, has high levels of crime, which has major impacts on elections in particular places and under particular circumstances. Jamaican politics is dominated by two main parties, the Jamaica Labour Party (JLP) and the People's National Party (PNP), which are organized along similar lines and have both historically relied on criminal gangs to help mobilize supporters and to disrupt the campaign activities of the opposing party (Clarke 2006; Edmonds 2016; Sives 2010). Most electoral violence in Jamaica is committed by rival groups linked to the main parties. The geographic aspect of electoral violence in Jamaica is a function of the existence of socially and politically closed "garrison" communities (mostly in the capital, Kingston) that are dominated by criminal gangs who deliver votes to the political party associated with the garrison in question. Akin to eighteenth-century "rotten boroughs" in Britain, these fiefdoms are under the direct control of gangs, and the writ of the state does not run in them. We saw that in the Philippines the geographic distribution of electoral violence is at least in part shaped by the location of criminal groups, but this is much more the case in Jamaica, and the geographic delineation of the "garrisons" is much more rigid. Thus in the four-fifths of Jamaica not affected by the garrison process, elections are relatively peaceful, whereas within the garrison areas, the intertwining of violence and vote buying discussed in chapter 4 is observed in stark form.

As Figueroa and Sives describe them, garrison communities are effectively totalitarian enclaves within a democratic state:

> A "garrison" community can be defined as one in which any individual/ group that seeks to oppose, raise opposition to or organise against the locally dominant party would be in physical danger, thus making continued residence in the area extremely difficult, if not impossible. Any significant social, political, economic or cultural development within the "garrison" can only take place with the tacit approval of the leadership (national and/or local) of the dominant party. The "garrison" is therefore, in its extreme form, a totalitarian social space in which the options of its residents are largely controlled. . . . In the core "garrisons" disputes have been settled, matters tried, offenders sentenced and punished, all without reference to the institutions of the Jamaican state. (Figueroa and Sives 2002, 85)

In these communities, turnout is often recorded as being 100 percent several hours before the polls officially close, and virtually all the votes at a given polling place go to the same party. Scholars have attributed garrison politics to the clientelism that pervades political life in Jamaica. Housing is one of the principal benefits distributed by political elites in exchange for votes. Large-scale social housing began to be built in the 1960s and 1970s, and units were allocated disproportionately to supporters of the party in power upon completion (Clarke 2006; Edmonds 2016; Figueroa and Sives 2002; Sives 2010). In as much as two main parties have alternated in power throughout Jamaica's recent history, the result was politically homogeneous clusters of residents supporting the party that had the power to allocate housing in that district. At election time, the effective purchase of votes with housing tenure is coupled with violence to enforce vote choice and to pressure supporters of the other party to move out of the area in question (Figueroa and Sives 2002; Sives 2010).

At the same time, electoral violence in Jamaica also exhibits temporal variation. On the binary NELDA electoral-violence variable (*Nelda33*), precisely every third election since independence has been labeled violent, including the polls of 1967, 1980, 1993, and 2007, suggesting that violence in Jamaica exhibits cyclic patterns. A particularly large spike in violence occurred at the time of the 1980 elections, which achieved the highest score on the V-DEM nonstate-violence-interval scale of any election in the data set employed in this study. Given that Jamaica is generally regarded as a democracy,[6] this is particularly shocking.

An estimated 500–800 people died in the 1980 elections (Clarke 2006; Edmonds 2016). This traumatic episode prompted politicians to undertake reforms designed to limit the practices that had resulted in such a high number of fatalities (Sives 2010). As in Zanzibar in 2000 and Kenya in 2007/8, a sudden intensification of violence led to a widespread recognition that the cost of using force was escalating out of control. The package of reforms, which had bipartisan support, included measures designed to increase confidence in the electoral authorities and the security sector, and penalties for violations of electoral law were stiffened (Sives 2010). However, violence flared once again, particularly in 1993. In 1997 a second wave of electoral and security-sector reforms took place, in the wake of the disturbances that had affected the preceding polls; bipartisan commitment to the reforms led to lower levels of conflict in elections held that year (Carter Center 1997; Figueroa and Sives 2002). Yet the closely fought 2007 elections were once again especially violent (OAS 2008), suggesting that reforms had not succeeded in breaking the cycle of violence that afflicts Jamaican electoral politics.

The foregoing analysis has shown that electoral violence in democratic Jamaica has many of the same characteristics as electoral violence in more authoritarian settings. The Jamaican case is another example of weak state capacity giving rise to localized alternative power structures that operate along corrupt and predatory rather than democratic lines, employing electoral violence in conjunction with vote buying and other clientelist practices. The episodic nature of the violence, which has exhibited a cyclic pattern over the course of the last five decades, can be attributed to processes internal to the garrison communities themselves, as well as to waves of reform to which actors are committed for a period, before they lose their purchase amid renewed political tensions.

Common to all four cases is the inability or unwillingness of those in charge of state institutions to rule via law and to regulate the use of force. State weakness is closely related to corruption and the capture of state institutions

---

6. Jamaica received a perfect score of 10 on the combined polity indicator of the Polity IV data set until 1992, and it has been awarded a score of 9 since that time (Marshall, Gurr, and Jaggers 2016).

by clientelist political machines in the Philippines, Tanzania, Ukraine, and Jamaica. The temporal and geographic variations in violence observed here can be understood in terms of variations in the challenges faced by weak and corrupted state institutions. In the Philippines and Jamaica, enclaves controlled by criminal structures are especially prone to violence at election time, with such enclaves being the only site of serious violence in the Jamaican context. Ethnic tensions in Zanzibar and Ukraine interact with varying levels of electoral need to explain levels of both electoral misconduct and violence. Close elections that were eventually annulled in Zanzibar and a hard-fought poll that generated suspicious second-round results in Ukraine are both situations where incumbents had incentives to ratchet up levels of electoral abuse—including violence—in order to achieve the outcome they desired. In the Zanzibari case, opposition protests against fraud have also regularly led to deadly clashes with state authorities. This suggests that heavily politicized states are often capable of managing peaceful electoral processes that deliver the results their political patrons require, but that when and where state structures are especially compromised or the delivery of electoral victory is particularly challenging, the stage is set for the use of force by state and nonstate actors alike. In the Tanzanian and Jamaican cases, troubling levels of violence led to temporary power-sharing arrangements between the opposing camps, but in both cases these broke down and violence once again erupted in the face of ongoing political and social tensions.

Conclusion

This chapter has considered temporal and geographic variations in electoral violence. Temporal variations have been examined both within and across electoral cycles. The examples considered here demonstrate the considerable heterogeneity in patterns of electoral violence in the contemporary world. In some contexts, conflict is highly localized and large areas of the country may be free of strife during the electoral period; in other settings there is considerable variation in the level of violence from one election to the next.

The analysis of within-cycle patterns shows evidence of strategic interaction between actors and suggests that reactive behavior is greatest when it comes to the use of physical force; there is less evidence of tit-for-tat responses to threats. The data also suggest that the two months leading up to the election is the time when there is the greatest risk of retaliatory attacks. This finding could be useful for electoral-violence-prevention practitioners, in that it could shape the timing of interventions designed to defuse crises and engender dialogue between political rivals. Somewhat less obviously, there may also be a lesson here for potential perpetrators of violence: attacks do not quell conflict; on the contrary, they attract retaliation. In as much as the use of force by state actors is commonly justified as a "pacifying" measure, the findings presented here show the hollowness of such rationales.

The analysis of cross-election and cross-region patterns in electoral violence presented in the second section of this chapter largely confirms the findings of chapters 3 and 4. The degree of politicization of state structures, which is closely tied to level of state capacity, accounts in large measure for observed temporal and geographic variations in the use of force at election time. The Filipino, Tanzanian, Ukrainian, and Jamaican examples all demonstrate that patterns in the distribution of violence across time and space result from temporal and geographic variations in the capacity of the state to defuse conflict, manage competition for resources, and regulate the use of force by nonstate actors. Weak and politicized state structures are vulnerable to shocks such as a sudden surge in the availability of firearms, the efforts of a new leader to consolidate power, or miscalculations of political support. They are also vulnerable to opposition backlash to their own use of fraud and other forms of electoral manipulation, which can precipitate protests and repressive countermeasures. In some contexts, temporary power-sharing arrangements may be effective in breaking cycles of violence, though the examples examined here suggest that such arrangements are fragile. The patterns observed can therefore be explained in large measure by the need of corrupt leaders to use force to rule, and their inability to regulate the use of force by others.

6

Strategies of Electoral-Violence Prevention

The foregoing chapters have delineated the factors that shape patterns of electoral violence in a variety of contexts. If analyses such as these have any practical relevance, it is in helping to understand not only what causes violence, but what can be done to prevent it. This chapter takes as its focus targeted efforts to reduce electoral violence. Such measures are undertaken by a wide variety of actors, most of them domestic. Electoral-management bodies (EMBs) often work with the police and political parties to keep elections peaceful. Civil-society organizations are also active in many contexts in seeking to prevent violence from erupting into the electoral process. Working with domestic actors, a range of different international organizations have been involved in delivering electoral-assistance projects whose aim is—in part if not in whole—to reduce the use of force in elections.

For over two decades following the post–Cold War rise in electoral assistance, electoral-violence prevention (EVP) was often not an explicit objective of programming, as "electoral security" was tied up in broader electoral-assistance activities designed to reform electoral-management institutions and to train those working in roles that touch on elections. Yet since the deadly violence that took place following the Kenyan elections of 2007 and the Ivorian elections of 2010, there has been a dramatic increase in programs or program elements designed specifically to prevent or mitigate electoral violence (Darnolf and Cyllah 2014; Fischer 2002; GCEDS 2012; International IDEA 2009). Organizations including the United Nations

Development Program (UNDP), the International Institute for Democracy and Electoral Assistance (International IDEA), the United States Agency for International Development (USAID), the International Foundation for Electoral Systems (IFES), and the United States Institute of Peace (USIP) have developed a range of EVP techniques that have been rolled out now in a variety of contexts (Bekoe 2018; Claes 2016; Creative Associates International 2009, 2013; Cyllah 2014; EC-UNDP 2011; Fischer 2002; International IDEA 2009, 2011; Kammerud 2011; UNDP 2009). Such programs are typically deployed in settings where violence is perceived to be a significant risk, though an overview of international EVP activities in the Electoral Violence Practice Database (preventelectoralviolence.org) reveals that such countries are many in number: the interventions listed in this database cover approximately four dozen states.

The questions that concern us in this chapter are: How successful are EVP initiatives? Which interventions are most likely to be successful? And under what conditions do EVP activities "work"? These questions will be addressed by means of cross-national analysis of quantitative data and the qualitative analysis of individual cases, drawing on EVP measures undertaken by domestic actors and to some extent also by international electoral-assistance providers. The chapter starts by providing a theoretical and practical analysis of EVP, followed in the second section by a review of existing research in this area, which has focused mainly on international interventions and has neglected the role of domestic electoral-justice institutions. The third section sets out to begin filling this gap by analyzing of the impact of the design of electoral-administrative and electoral-justice institutions on electoral violence. The impact of institutional governance on electoral violence is analyzed in the fourth section, while the fifth section presents case studies from Macedonia and Haiti. A final section concludes.

The overall finding from the investigations carried out in this chapter is that the design of state institutions that might potentially quell or contain electoral violence is less relevant than their functioning in practice, and the degree to which they are impartial. Good governance is the most important ingredient in an effective system for deterring and mitigating electoral violence.

Electoral-Violence Prevention in Theory and in Practice

The foregoing chapters have confirmed the supposition that electoral violence is not generally caused by ancient hatreds or spontaneous outbursts of anger, but it is rather a product of formal and informal power structures.

Informal political groups in corrupt states employ violence as a tool to manipulate political processes and to secure their grasp on resources (including populations), while the constraints built into formal democratic institutions work to curb the use of force at election time. These findings have implications for projects designed to prevent election-related violence, as they suggest that this phenomenon can be prevented through an increase in the cost of violence, which can in theory be achieved by bolstering those institutional structures that constrain the use of force as a tool. It may also be possible to reduce the benefits of violence by working with intermediary and victim groups to lessen the psychological effects of threats and attempts at coercion. These insights suggest a dual approach to EVP that focuses on deterrence and effectiveness.

The formal institutions of the state provide the most obvious ingredients with which to craft an electoral-violence deterrence strategy. The state structures most intimately connected with electoral-violence regulation include EMBs, the judiciary, and the security sector (police, military and paramilitary units, and other bodies whose job it is to prevent disorder and identify the perpetrators of violence). The effectiveness of these institutions in preventing the use of force depends in large measure on their willingness to do so, which is in turn commonly linked to their degree of politicization. As Wilkinson has persuasively demonstrated in the Indian context, the propensity of police units to intervene and stop communal violence varies considerably from region to region, and these variations correspond to political incentive structures, which shape security-sector behavior (Wilkinson 2004). The Macedonian example detailed below will show that the same is true in this Balkan state. Three aspects of institutions can be expected to affect their effectiveness in preventing violence: institutional design, institutional capacity, and institutional autonomy. In as much as institutional design can be altered, capacity can be strengthened, and autonomy can be enhanced, these dimensions of institutional performance are susceptible to concerted efforts to increase the ability of the state to control the use of force during elections.

A second type of democratic constraint is that provided by the documentation of illicit acts of violence and their dissemination to wide audiences. Increasing the information available about the use of conflict as a tool generates audience costs for perpetrators and would-be perpetrators, which can also, in theory, have a deterrent effect. Information received by national and international elites can discredit the groups identified as having committed violence, and information received by voters can potentially alter the decisions they make in the voting booth, thereby reducing the electoral benefit of violence (Bratton 2008; Gutiérrez-Romero and LeBas 2020; Rosenzweig 2016). Popular aversion to electoral violence following outbreaks of extreme conflict is a theme in the Tanzanian and Jamaican case studies in chapter 5, and leveraging citizen support for an end to violence is potentially a useful means of increasing the reputational costs of those who use force for electoral ends (cf. Young 2020).

A third strategy that can be employed to alter the cost-benefit calculus of those considering using force to achieve their electoral ends is the alteration of perceptions of and beliefs about violence on the part of intermediaries and victims. A noted in chapter 2, much of the effect of electoral violence works through psychological channels, as anger and fear condition peoples' attitudes toward coercive measures and the extent to which they are affected by them. If these groups' perceptions of the likelihood and impact of violence are altered, their orientations toward, and reactions to, intimidation and physical harm can potentially be changed as well.

These considerations suggest a fourfold typology of potential interventions that might be employed to prevent electoral violence: institutional reform, institutional capacity building, the documentation of violence, and the conditioning of beliefs and attitudes. EVP can also be classified according to the actors involved. Actors include state institutions, such as EMBs, the judiciary, and the security sector; nonstate institutions, such as political parties and politicians, the media, and civil society (including domestic observer groups, women's groups, and youth groups); voters; and international organizations, such as electoral-assistance providers and diplomatic agents. Table 6.1 sets out a typology of EVP, with examples of activities undertaken. It should be noted that this typology is intended to capture the range of common EVP activities, but is not designed to be exhaustive. It should also be borne in mind that some programs of activity simultaneously involve multiple actors; as, for example, when an international electoral-assistance provider implements a program designed to involve civil-society organizations and EMBs in undertaking voter education.

This is not of course the only possible typology, and other scholars have offered slightly different conceptualizations of EVP. Jonas Claes and colleagues categorize EVP into eight broad types: security-sector engagement, election management and administration, preventive diplomacy, peace messaging, civic and voter education, monitoring and mapping, voter consultations, and youth programming (Claes 2016). Inken von Borzyskowski (2019) classifies EVP according to election observation and technical assistance.

TABLE 6-1. A Typology of Electoral-Violence Prevention

Actor	Institutional Reform	Capacity Building	Documentation	Attitudinal Change
Electoral-management bodies (EMBs)	Electoral-process reforms; development of complaint-reporting systems	Training of electoral administrators in conflict prevention	Creation of platforms for monitoring incidents of electoral violence	Voter education
Security sector	Reforms to procedures for policing potentially violent situations	Security-sector training	Creation of platforms for monitoring incidents of electoral violence	Mediation between parties to disputes
Judiciary	Reforms to electoral-justice systems	Training of judges in electoral justice		
Political parties	Codes of conduct	Training of candidates and activists	Use of platforms for monitoring and mapping electoral violence	Preventive diplomacy; peace messaging
Media	Development of policy on hate speech	Media training in the avoidance of hate speech and incitement to violence	Media monitoring; development of platforms for monitoring electoral violence	
Civil society and voters	Development of victims' services	Training in election observation; voter education	Development of platforms for monitoring and mapping electoral violence	Peace messaging; mediation
International actors	Advice on reforms	Training of various actors	Development of platforms for monitoring and mapping electoral violence	Peace messaging

Other surveys of the topic have also identified engagement with the judiciary, youth programs, media training, and the prevention of electoral violence against women as common forms of EVP (Creative Associates International 2013; International IDEA 2009; UNDP 2009).

Concerted efforts to prevent electoral violence have a long history; many EVP activities were deployed by international organizations in the 1990s and the early years of the twenty-first century. The IFES Election Violence Education and Resolution (EVER) program and its successors are among the best known and longest-standing EVP initiatives, incorporating a variety of training and monitoring techniques (Kammerud 2011). International IDEA's Electoral Risk Management Tool is another widely used set of analytic instruments that can be employed by EMBs to identify and reduce electoral risks (International IDEA 2016). Many of the customized EVP programs undertaken by the UNDP and other assistance providers place considerable emphasis on training and other forms of technical capacity building, often with EMBs as their main beneficiaries. A range of activities focused on mediation, pacting, social enforcement, and messaging activities are also integrated into the program activities of all the main EVP providers, as well as the grassroots projects of local and smaller international organizations (Fischer 2017b).

The Impact of Electoral-Violence Prevention: Existing Evidence

A small body of literature has begun to study of impact of international EVP interventions. Smidt (2020) documented an impact of alternative-dispute-resolution workshops run by UN peacekeepers in Côte d'Ivoire in reducing election-related intercommunal violence. In a comparative study, Reeder and Goldring (2018) also showed that under certain conditions peacekeepers can deter electoral violence, especially in the postelection period. The positive impact of international election monitoring on electoral processes has been demonstrated in a number of studies (Hyde 2011; Kelley 2012; McCoy 1998). If potential perpetrators of violence have reasons to believe that their actions will be recorded and disseminated, they will be cautious in undertaking violent acts, for fear of punishment and/or retribution, as well as reputational damage that could entail electoral costs. However, international intervention is not always helpful in deterring electoral conflict. Daxecker has found evidence that the presence of monitors displaces violence from election day to the preelectoral period (Daxecker 2014), and that critical reports by international election monitors can trigger postelectoral violence (Daxecker 2012). In a study of the 2010 elections in Côte d'Ivoire, Bekoe (2018) has shown how even the more intensive tool of international certification can fail to staunch violence.

International support for domestic institutions is generally held to be a promising means of EVP. Several studies have found that technical assistance to EMBs and security-sector bodies can work to prevent electoral violence (Bekoe 2012b; Borzyskowski 2015, 2019; Borzyskowski and Claes 2018; Kammerud 2011; Kumar and Ottoway 1998; Lyons 1999). In a study of UN technical assistance to EMBs in Latin America and Africa, Borzyskowski found that such assistance can reduce postelectoral violence; her principal explanation is that technical assistance increases objective electoral quality, which sends a signal that the regime is prepared to commit to electoral integrity and allays the fears of election losers, who then refrain from undertaking violence (Borzyskowski 2019). In a wide-ranging collection of systematic case studies, Claes and colleagues likewise provided evidence that the most effective forms of international EVP are those that involve engagement with EMBs and security-sector organizations, as well as long-term voter education and monitoring activities (Claes 2016). In the cases they have analyzed, these authors identified little evidence for the success of the sorts of grassroots activities typically undertaken with civil-society organizations—peace messaging, voter consultations, and youth programming. In a global study of the effect of EVP activities, Birch and Muchlinski compared capacity-building forms of EVP with attitude-transforming activities, and found that the former reduced violence by nonstate actors—presumably through the confidence-enhancing channel posited by Borzyskowski—whereas the latter reduced violence by state actors (Birch and Muchlinski 2018).

Research has also been undertaken on initiatives that involve civil society and could in theory be carried out in the absence of international intervention. Some studies have focused on the role of messaging, mediation, pacting, and peace forums in transforming attitudes and expectations (Bekoe 2012b; Collier and Vicente 2014; Fischer 2017b; Oduro 2012; Zorbas and Tohbi 2011). In the Nigerian context, Collier and Vicente (2014) found that community activities—street theatre, town hall meetings—can reduce electoral violence by overcoming the collective action problem associated with efforts to resist intimidation and altering perceptions of how legitimate intimidatory tactics are. Less is known about the impact of domestic monitors on electoral abuse, including violence; there is some evidence that they can deter conflict and intimidation (Asunka et al. 2017; Burchard 2015;

Grömping 2017; Ichino and Schündeln 2012; López-Pintor 1998), though displacement effects have also been noted in this context (Asunka et al. 2017; Ichino and Schündeln 2012).

In sum, there is some evidence from research to date of the effectiveness of international EVP. Yet the international electoral-assistance agencies that work to curb this phenomenon typically rely on limited resources. They cannot hope to undertake large-scale EVP programs in all the contexts where these might be useful; they must pick and choose where they go. The process of picking and choosing has so far been carried out in a relatively ad hoc fashion, as there has been little evidence of the conditions under which EVP is most likely to be effective. There are reasons for believing that domestic EVP activities will have the greatest impact and will be most sustainable. Domestic institutions are the main ones that structure political arrangements and have direct control over the electoral administrative process. Domestic institutions are typically also those with the greatest legitimacy in society; moreover, they remain functional even after international missions depart and individual civil-society initiatives cease to function. If EVP is to have permanent traction, it is arguably best fostered by those structures in the state that are charged with overseeing the electoral process.

Electoral-Violence Prevention and Institutional Design

The architecture of electoral management incorporates a number of distinct state bodies that are involved in the delivery of elections and the adjudication of election-related disputes. These two administrative functions are by convention termed "electoral administration" and "electoral justice," and the analysis in this chapter will employ this terminology, while bearing in mind that there is some overlap between these two spheres, as for instance in the processing of complaints and measures to ensure security at the polls.

Electoral administration involves planning for elections, recruiting and training elections staff, overseeing voter and candidate registration, overseeing the electoral campaign and collating data on campaign spending, organizing and delivering the polling and vote-counting process, and publishing the results of the elections. Electoral administration is carried out by a variety of institutions, including government ministries, local government officials, and formally independent EMBs. While the range of electoral administrative arrangements is considerable, a basic distinction can be made between countries that have formally autonomous EMBs and those where EMBs form part of the government. A number of jurisdictions have mixed models, where some functions are carried out by governmental departments and others by independent electoral commissions or other bodies (Catt et al. 2014; López-Pintor 2000). For example, until 2001 the National Tax Agency was responsible for running elections in Sweden (Brogren 2014). Formal EMB independence has accompanied democratization in many "third-wave" states (Goodwin-Gill 1994; Hartlyn, McCoy, and Mustillo 2008; López-Pintor 2000; Mozaffar 2002). As Mozaffar and Schedler noted: "Removing electoral governance from executive control has turned into a rallying cry of democratizing forces all over the globe. Establishing an independent electoral commission, in fact, has become a compelling international norm, a *sine qua non* of electoral credibility" (2002, 15). Analysis of the impacts of de jure independent EMBs on electoral integrity is mixed, however. In the Latin American context, Hartlyn, McCoy, and Mustillo (2008) found that independent and mixed independent-governmental EMBs were associated with significantly higher levels of electoral integrity than EMBs run by a branch of the government. Yet in global studies, Birch and Van Ham (2017) and Norris (2015) identified no significant effect. There is far less systematic evidence of the impact of formal EMB independence on electoral violence. Norris (2015) noted that formally independent electoral commissions failed to stop outbreaks of large-scale violence in Nigeria in 2007, Ethiopia in 2005, and Kenya in 2007, but large-N tests of the role of de jure EMB independence in preventing electoral violence are lacking.

The functions collectively referred to as electoral justice are those that include the collection and adjudication of disputes between electoral contestants and complaints made about the conduct of elections. In most contexts, electoral justice involves different state bodies in different aspects and at different stages of the process. These bodies include EMBs, the judiciary, and in some cases other institutions such as the legislature (Orozco-Henriquez 2010; Solijonov 2016). For example, in Switzerland, cantonal governments have a formal role in electoral-dispute adjudication, and in Zimbabwe multiparty liaison committees play this role (International IDEA 2014).

The literature on the links between electoral conduct and electoral-justice-system design is very limited. International IDEA has published two useful volumes—*Electoral Justice: The International IDEA Handbook* (Orozco-Henriquez 2010) and *Electoral Justice Regulations around the World: Key Findings from International IDEA's Global Research on Electoral Dispute-Resolution Systems* (Solijonov 2016)—which contain analysis as well as descriptive information. Mexico's Federal Electoral Tribunal provides the best known example in the literature of a de facto independent judicial body whose establishment reduced postelectoral violent conflict (Eisenstadt 1999), and eventually paved the way for democratization (Magaloni 2006, 2010). There is also evidence from several former Soviet states that courts can work to make elections more credible (Herron 2009; Moraski 2009; Popova 2006), though these studies do not consider the impact of the judiciary on electoral violence. Sara Staino (2011) provided a rare and useful analysis of the role of electoral justice in preventing and mitigating election-related conflict. Drawing on International IDEA's experience of work in the area of electoral justice, Staino detailed how electoral-dispute-resolution systems can help to contain and deal with conflict, provided those systems are impartial and offer "effective and efficient" dispute resolution that is free of charge or low cost, is accessible to users, resolves disputes in a timely manner, and enforces rulings (Staino 2011, 181). The studies reviewed here are insightful and help considerably to develop understandings of the role of electoral-justice systems in quelling electoral violence, yet none of them includes a systematic comparative analysis of the effectiveness of electoral justice in this area. Elucidation of this relationship cross-nationally thus awaits empirical investigation.

In as much as one would expect institutions that safeguard electoral integrity to prevent violence, one might anticipate that states with formally independent EMBs might experience less electoral violence, all else equal. The IDEA data indicate that in the second decade of the twenty-first century, 62 percent of countries had independent EMBs, 21 percent had elections run by a branch of government, and 14 percent had mixed systems (International IDEA 2018). Formal EMB independence can be expected to engender confidence in the electorate and to increase the extent to which people perceive electoral processes to be credible. Both the objective and the subjective components of EMB independence can potentially contribute to maintaining peace at election time, the first by removing grounds for grievance, and the second by reducing perceptions of injustice on the part of electoral losers.

Electoral-justice systems are designed to enable people with legitimate grievances about the electoral process to seek redress. If electoral-justice institutions function well, the availability of redress ought in theory to go a considerable way toward addressing the legitimate concerns that citizens, candidates, and other electoral actors have about electoral results. The analyses presented in the previous chapters indicate that legitimate grievances about electoral misconduct are not by any means the most important drivers of electoral violence, but they certainly cannot be discounted, and in certain contexts such concerns may well be the trigger that unleashes conflict, turning a tense situation into an explosive one. The Kenyan election of 2007 and the Ivorian election of 2010 are examples of this phenomenon. A robust electoral-justice system should in theory go some way toward defusing anger generated by unwelcome electoral results and providing an alternative to violence for addressing complaints related to the outcome.

Several specific electoral-dispute-resolution design features can be expected to facilitate access to electoral justice. A system where any voter can lodge a complaint against the result of the election is more inclusive than one in which only political parties or other elite actors have the ability to avail themselves of dispute-resolution procedures. In the IDEA global sample, voters can lodge complaints of this sort in 47 percent of cases, and in a further 7 percent this option is open to any citizen (Solijonov 2016). Another inclusivity feature is the cost of lodging a complaint. Of the states in the IDEA database, 27 percent charge a fee or require a deposit to accompany a complaint related to the electoral outcome; in 43 percent, electoral justice is provided by the state free of charge; and in a further 31 percent of cases, the cost is not specified in law (Solijonov 2016). The absence of a fee lowers the barrier to entry into the system, and this inclusivity mechanism can be expected to be associated with lower levels of violence. There are two aspects of complaint processing that might also have a bearing on the propensity of electoral-justice systems to deter the use of force: the requirement to hold a hearing where concerns can be aired openly, and the right to appeal decisions made by the body that considers complaints in the first instance. Both institutions ought in theory to enhance confidence in the robustness of electoral-justice institutions. The IDEA data indicate that 55 percent of electoral-justice systems make provision for hearings related to complaints against electoral results, and 49 percent allow appeals (Solijonov 2016). In sum, we would expect to see more peaceful elections in contexts where any voter can lodge an appeal against the outcome of an election, where there is no fee for doing so, where the judicial process includes a formal hearing, and where there is a right of appeal against the outcome of the first-stage dispute-resolution process.

International IDEA maintains several useful databases of electoral-institution design that furnish cross-national data on aspects of electoral administration and electoral justice. The Electoral Management Design Database (www.idea.int/data-tools/data/electoral-management-design) and the Electoral Justice Database (www.idea.int/data-tools/data/electoral-justice) include between them key data on EMB type and electoral-justice-system features that might be expected to have an impact on electoral violence.

The IDEA data sets have both been collected since 2010. The Electoral Management Design Database was originally published in 2010, but it is updated periodically. The data that constitute the Electoral Justice Database were originally collected in 2013 and 2014, and the database is updated when new information reaches International IDEA. Electoral-governance institutions do change, but radical overhauls of institutional design are rare. It is thus safe to assume that in the vast majority of cases the data in these databases reflect the institutional designs that have been in force in the countries in question since the data-collection operation began, but it cannot necessarily be assumed that the same design features were in place for many elections prior to the most recent ones. Moreover, no longitudinal data are available on electoral-institution design that would make it possible to trace changes over time, which necessitates cross-sectional analysis. In order to assess the impact of electoral-institution design on electoral violence, an appropriate tool is analysis based on variable means. This approach reduces the number of cases in the resulting models substantially, but sufficient cases are available for it to be possible to have a relatively high degree of confidence in the results.

The first model to be considered here starts by including variables designating electoral administrative type alone, together with mean values over the 2009–16 period for the global data used in previous chapters. Two dummy variables are included for this purpose, one for formally independent EMBs and another for mixed EMBs, with governmental EMBs as the baseline category. Models 1 and 2 in table 6.2 display the results for state and nonstate violence respectively, with the transformed V-DEM indicators described in chapter 1 employed as dependent variables, and key controls identified from previous models.[1] As can be seen from these models, EMB design has no discernible impact on either state or nonstate violence. Once relevant controls are included, whether the EMB was a formally independent body, a branch of government under political control, or a hybrid of these two forms appears to have little or no bearing on the extent to which violence of any kind afflicts elections; neither of the EMB coefficients in either model is significant.

Models 3 and 4 add in electoral-justice variables, with dummy variables designating a fee requirement for lodging a complaint against the results of an election, the ability of a voter to lodge a complaint, the use of hearings, and

---

1. Owing to the restricted number of cases in these models and the undesirability of losing cases with missing data, only the core independent and control variables from previous models are included here, and the V-DEM electoral-violence data are used alone.

TABLE 6-2. Electoral Institutional Design and Electoral Violence

	Model 1: State Violence (V-DEM electoral intimidation— *v2elintim*)	Model 2: Nonstate violence (V-DEM electoral peace—*v2elpeace*)	Model 3: State Violence (V-DEM electoral intimidation— *v2elintim*)	Model 4: Nonstate violence (V-DEM electoral peace—*v2elpeace*)
Independent EMB	0.043 (0.170)	−0.109 (0.221)	−0.060 (0.205)	−0.076 (0.287)
Mixed EMB	0.107 (0.204)	−0.072 (0.266)	0.253 (0.231)	0.151 (0.323)
Fee to lodge complaint			−0.005 (0.144)	0.476[a] (0.201)
Voter can lodge complaint			0.271[a] (0.128)	0.014 (0.179)
Hearing			0.154 (0.135)	−0.235 (0.190)
Appeal			0.313[a] (0.122)	0.259 (0.170)
Corruption	0.879[c] (0.243)	1.132[c] (0.317)	1.119[c] (0.311)	1.294[c] (0.437)
Executive constraints	−0.292[c] (0.031)	0.658[b] (0.231)	−0.267[a] (0.038)	0.743[b] (0.270)
Executive constraints^2		−0.076[b] (0.025)		−0.089[b] (0.030)
Per capita GDP	−0.053 (0.056)	−0.150 (0.078)	−0.066 (0.069)	−0.155 (0.105)
Constant	2.390 (0.663)	0.555 (1.091)	1.835 (0.831)	0.400 (1.466)
N	125	125	87	87
Adjusted R^2	0.660	0.429	0.656	0.466
AIC	197.161	264.409	137.175	196.279
BIC	214.131	284.207	161.834	223.404

These are ordinary least squares models. Cell entries are coefficients (robust standard errors). AIC, Akaike information criterion; BIC, Bayesian information criterion.

[a] $p < .05$
[b] $p < .01$
[c] $p < .001$

the availability of an appeal option. The total number of cases is reduced in these models, yet despite the decline in statistical power, we see marginally more interesting results. No design feature is associated with a statistically significant reduction in state violence; the ability to lodge a complaint and the fact of having an appeal option both appear to increase it slightly, however (though these effects are only weakly significant). These are unexpected results, but may be due to the fact that the appeals process and complaints generate episodes of contentious politics (protests, demonstrations) that the state then represses. The requirement to pay a fee to lodge a complaint is associated with higher levels of nonstate violence, as anticipated, but this effect is only very weakly significant and of modest magnitude (accounting for 15.87 percent of the observed range of this variable), cautioning against attaching too much importance to this finding.

The results presented in this section indicate that, overall, the formal features of electoral-institution design have scant bearing on whether or not elections are violent. The formal independence of EMBs does not seem to be related to violence; nor do most mechanisms that one would expect to make the electoral-justice system more credible and inclusive, such as the ability of any voter to file a complaint against some aspect of the outcome of an election, or the right of appeal. Indeed, these devices actually seem to increase state-initiated electoral violence. If electoral institutions are to help prevent electoral violence, it does not seem to be via their formal design features, or at least not those assessed here, which on the face of it would seem to be most likely to work to keep elections peaceful. This raises the question of whether it might be the more informal governance aspects of electoral institutions that could be capable of doing the "work" necessary to maintain the electoral peace, and under what conditions they might be most effective in accomplishing this role.

Electoral-Violence Prevention and Electoral Governance

In addition to design features, electoral institutions have other dimensions that may potentially be relevant to the prevention of electoral violence. These other dimensions can be grouped under the broad heading of "governance," which refers to how institutions work in practice. Electoral governance is a topic that has received limited focused attention from academic scholars,[2] but is of intense concern to practitioners working in the areas of electoral administration and electoral assistance. Good electoral governance involves the delivery of elections and election-related services such as dispute adjudication in a professional and impartial manner. If elections are well governed, electoral institutions are more likely to command the confidence of the population, and election outcomes are less likely to be challenged. Well-governed elections are also processes that have effective inbuilt mechanisms for preventing electoral violence, such as joint liaison between electoral administrators, security-sector actors, and political parties; the training of polling officials and police in tactics designed to defuse confrontational situations; and efficient dispute resolution systems. When elections are poorly governed, by contrast, this can be because of lack of resources, or it can be because of intentional efforts to sway the outcome of the election to the benefit of one party or candidate or to otherwise manipulate the election for private benefit. Lack of resources generates capacity issues, whereas lack of impartiality leads to political manipulation (Birch 2011; Mozaffar and

---

2. For an early critical overview of research in this field, see Mozaffar and Schedler (2002). For more recent reviews of relevant literature, see Birch and Van Ham (2017) and Norris (2015).

Schedler 2002; Norris 2015). Both aspects of governance can be expected to impact on the effectiveness of electoral institutions in preventing and containing violence that erupts as part of the electoral process. It can thus be hypothesized that the quality of electoral governance plays a part in preventing electoral violence. There is fragmentary evidence from case studies of the role played by electoral governance in deterring electoral violence. Claes and Macdonald (2016) found that professional and well-functioning EMBs are linked to lower levels of electoral violence. In a comparison of elections held in Malawi, Ethiopia, and Zanzibar, Opitz, Fjelde, and Höglund (2013) demonstrated that inclusive EMBs incorporating the views of multiple political parties are more effective in containing violence than those under pressure from a single partisan actor. A recent cross-national study of democratizing regimes showed that electoral-authority autonomy promotes alternation in power, which in turn reduces state violence (Ruiz-Rufino and Birch 2020). That study only examined one aspect of electoral violence and only the democratizing context, however.

In order to test whether there a systematic link between electoral governance and electoral violence, it is necessary to operationalize the capacity and the impartiality of electoral-administrative and electoral-justice systems. The V-DEM database provides two ready-made indicators for the measurement of electoral administrative governance: *v2elembcap* and *v2elembaut*. Electoral-authority capacity is measured via *v2elembcap*, which reflects answers to the question "Does the Election Management Body (EMB) have sufficient staff and resources to administer a well-run national election?" The *v2elembaut* indicator is a measure of EMB autonomy coded in response to the question "Does the Election Management Body (EMB) have autonomy from government to apply election laws and administrative rules impartially in national elections?" (Coppedge et al. 2018a, 53–54). Answers to both questions range on 0–4 five-point scales, where higher scores represent higher levels of capacity and autonomy respectively. A V-DEM indicator for judicial independence *v2juhcind*, designating high-court independence, provides a convenient measure of the impartiality of the judiciary, and records responses to the question "When the high court in the judicial system is ruling in cases that are salient to the government, how often would you say that it makes decisions that merely reflect government wishes regardless of its sincere view of the legal record?" (153–54). Again, this indicator is coded on a 0–4 scale where higher scores correspond to greater levels of autonomy. Unfortunately there is no available judicial-capacity measure analogous to the *v2embcap* indicator that reflects EMB capacity. The dependent variables used in this analysis are those employed in the previous section, namely the

V-DEM-derived indicators for state and nonstate electoral violence. Because of high levels of multicollinearity between electoral-authority autonomy, electoral-authority capacity, and judicial independence, these variables are entered into separate equations.

Table 6.3 presents the results of these analyses. As expected, electoral-authority autonomy is effective in countering electoral violence, but only that perpetrated by the state. Electoral-authority capacity, by contrast, is associated with lower levels of nonstate violence, but has no discernible impact on violence initiated by state actors. Judicial independence has a modest and weakly significant effect in curbing state violence, but no evident influence on violence by nonstate actors. All three effects work both cross-sectionally and longitudinally. These results suggest that the substantive credibility of the institutions charged with delivering elections is the most important institutional factor in deterring and mitigating electoral violence. They also indicate that it is de facto rather than de jure electoral-authority independence that is the variable that really "counts" in this regard. This result mirrors Birch and Van Ham's (2017) finding with regard to the role of de facto electoral-authority autonomy in maintaining overall levels of electoral integrity, but with an important nuance. Whereas electoral-authority autonomy plays a major role in preventing violence initiated by state actors, is appears to have little impact in shaping levels of violence by nonstate actors. Interestingly, it is the capacity, not the de facto autonomy, of the electoral authority that has the greatest impact on nonstate violence. When EMBs have high levels of capacity, they evidently command sufficient respect from opposition and societal actors that violence is less likely to result from electoral contests.

The substantive impact of these effects is depicted in figures 6.1—6.3, which plot the predicted impact of over-time changes in levels of electoral-authority autonomy on state violence (figure 6.1), electoral-authority capacity on nonstate violence (figure 6.2), and judicial independence on state violence (figure 6.3). Figure 6.1 shows that the probability of state violence being at its lowest level increases from approximately 2 in 10 to 8 in 10 as electoral-authority autonomy increases from the lowest to the highest observed value. At the same time, the chances of an election witnessing the highest level of state violence decreases from just under half to near zero. Figure 6.2 shows a similar pattern in the relationship between electoral-authority capacity and nonstate violence. The chances of the lowest level of violence rise from approximately 35 percent to 75 percent as electoral-authority capacity increases from the bottom to the top of its observed

TABLE 6-3. Electoral Governance and Electoral Violence

	V-DEM state violence (v2elintim)			V-DEM nonstate violence (v2elpeace)		
	Model 1	Model 2	Model 3	Model 4	Model 5	Model 6
CROSS-NATIONAL "BETWEEN" EFFECTS						
Electoral-authority autonomy	−1.255c (0.285)			0.017 (0.384)		
Electoral-authority capacity		0.187 (0.191)			−0.965b (0.327)	
High-court independence			−0.596a (0.249)			0.414 (0.386)
Corruption	4.231c (1.021)	5.752c (1.078)	4.844c (1.095)	5.318c (1.307)	4.202c (1.101)	5.977c (1.604)
Executive constraints	−0.251 (0.218)	−0.946c (0.163)	−0.673c (0.192)	2.163a (0.999)	2.237a (0.985)	2.043a (1.024)
Executive constraints²	−0.553 (0.304)			−0.266a (0.121)	−0.247a (0.113)	−0.266a (0.117)
Per capita GDP (log)	−0.481a (0.236)	−0.425 (0.260)	−0.377 (0.238)	−1.566c (0.334)	−1.170b (0.372)	−1.586c (0.338)
LONGITUDINAL ("WITHIN") EFFECTS						
Electoral-authority autonomy	−1.121c (0.179)			0.075 (0.205)		
Electoral-authority capacity		−0.151 (0.261)			−0.903c (0.272)	
High-court independence			−0.595c (0.168)			0.107 (0.181)
Corruption	3.838c (1.140)	4.337c (1.259)	4.135c (1.103)	6.261c (1.287)	4.703c (1.217)	6.221c (1.275)
Executive constraints	−0.434c (0.085)	−0.725c (0.106)	−0.625c (0.094)	0.274 (0.338)	0.366 (0.319)	0.321 (0.331)
Executive constraints²	−0.553 (0.304)			−0.059 (0.041)	−0.056 (0.038)	−0.066 (0.041)
Per capita GDP (log)	−0.553 (0.304)	−0.705a (0.335)	−0.519 (0.325)	−0.913b (0.329)	−0.895b (0.342)	−0.902b (0.325)
N	2116	2116	2115	2116	2116	2115
Log pseudolikelihood	−1491.539	−1567.473	−1543.100	−1442.013	−1412.812	−1436.703
AIC	3149.078	3300.947	3253.999	3056.027	2997.624	3045.407
BIC	3618.633	3770.501	3723.514	3542.553	3484.150	3531.892

The models in this table are random effects ordered logit models; cut points not shown. Cell entries are coefficients (robust standard errors). All models include year fixed effects (not shown). See chapters 3 and 4 for details of variable creation. AIC, Akaike information criterion; BIC, Bayesian information criterion.

[a] p < .05
[b] p < .01
[c] p < .001

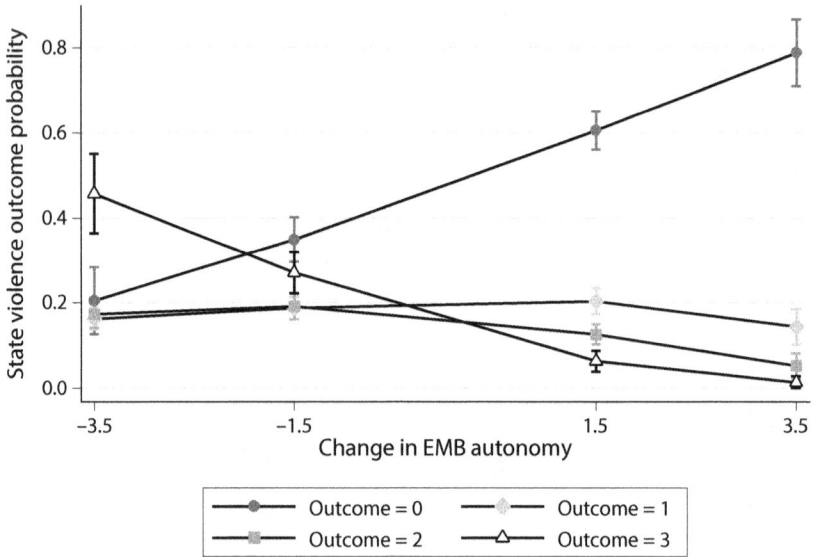

FIGURE 6.1. Electoral-authority autonomy and state violence

NB: Figure shows predictive margins with 95% confidence intervals.

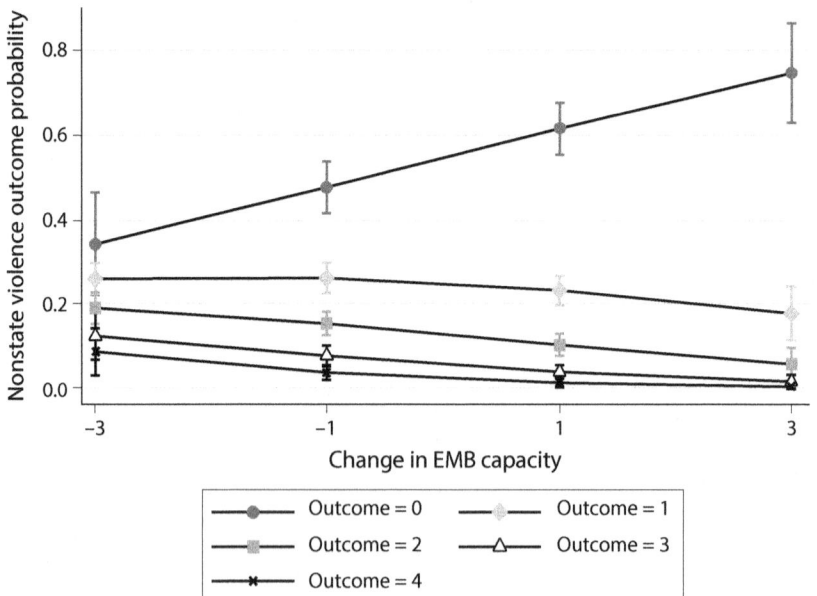

FIGURE 6.2. Electoral-authority capacity and nonstate violence

NB: Figure shows predictive margins with 95% confidence intervals.

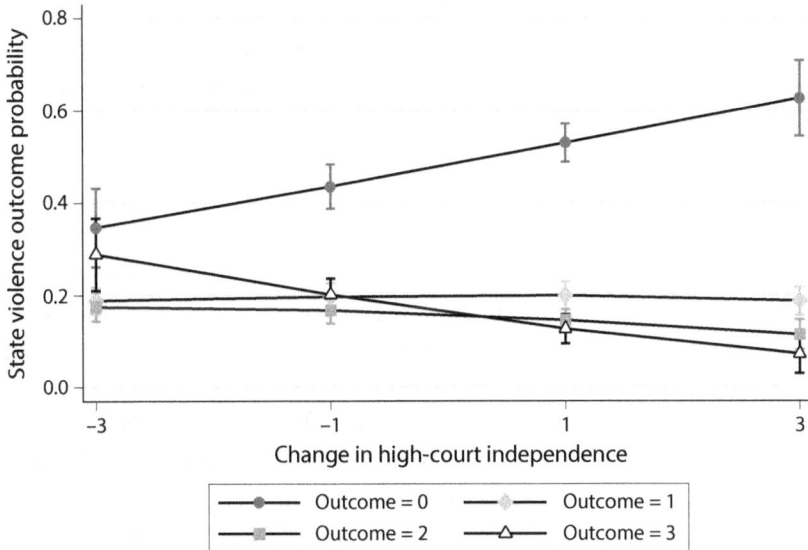

FIGURE 6.3. High-court independence and state violence

NB: Figure shows predictive margins with 95% confidence intervals.

range. The likelihood of the highest level of violence is low already and therefore has limited scope to fall, but it also exhibits a substantive decline to almost zero with increasing electoral-authority capacity. Figure 6.3 shows the more modest impact of judicial independence on state violence, where the chances of the lowest level of violence fall by approximately a quarter and the chances of the highest level of violence increase by a similar amount as high-court independence increases from the bottom to the top of the observed range of this variable.

All in all, we can therefore conclude that electoral governance has substantively important effects on levels of electoral violence. This conclusion chimes with the analyses of Borzyskowski, who found that international technical assistance delivered to EMBs had the effect of reducing violence by boosting the credibility of these bodies (Borzyskowski 2015, 2019). Case studies of Macedonia and Haiti serve to tease out how these effects operate in practice.

Case Studies

Macedonia and Haiti both provide imperfect but realistic examples of how improvements in electoral governance over time have curbed electoral violence. In neither case has the governance of elections achieved ideal levels, and in neither case has the prospect of violence been removed from the electoral process. However, both cases demonstrate how in real-world contexts modest gains in the quality of governance can yield tangible results.

MACEDONIA

The role of EMB reform in preventing electoral violence is exemplified by the case of Macedonia (whose official name was previously the Former Yugoslav Republic of Macedonia and is now North Macedonia). Developments in electoral administration in this Balkan state provide a good example of how improvements in EMB autonomy and capacity can bolster the ability of electoral administrators to oversee peaceful polls and build confidence in the electoral process. At the same time, this case also highlights limits in the extent to which administrative change can address electoral violence in the absence of a reduction in the role of informal institutions in structuring power.

Macedonia gained independence in 1991 in the wake of the collapse of Yugoslavia. The small landlocked state of two million struggled during the initial years of its life to build effective state institutions. Disputes over the country's official name with its southern neighbor Greece, over the status of the Macedonian language with Bulgaria to the east, over its northern border with Serbia, and over the language rights of Macedonia's large Albanian population caused diplomatic, economic, and social turbulence over the course of the 1990s. This turbulence culminated in an episode of ethnic strife in 2001, resolved via the internationally mediated Ohrid Agreement, which mandated elements of power sharing and a more secure role for ethnic Albanians in Macedonian social and political life. Tensions flared again in 2015–16 following the release of audio recordings that appeared to document official involvement in electoral misconduct and other wrongdoing by incumbent political leaders and officials. The resulting political turmoil, involving a boycott of parliament by the opposition, was resolved only following the intervention of the European Union, which negotiated the 2015 Pržino Agreement. The agreement called for, among other things, early parliamentary elections, which were planned for June 2016 but postponed when the opposition declared its intention to boycott the polls. Following further negotiations, peaceful elections were eventually held in December 2016.

Amid these recurrent crises, electoral violence has generally fallen, aided in no small part by several waves of electoral reform. According to the V-DEM data, state violence in Macedonia rose from 1 to 2 in 1999 before falling back to 1, where it remained virtually unchanged through 2016. Nonstate violence rose from 0 to 1 in 1999, 2002, 2008, and 2011, though it remained at 0 during the 2014–16 crisis. Though these numbers are fairly low by global standards they are high for a European state, where anything other than peaceful elections is a rarity. The CREV data confirm this interpretation, identifying an excess of electoral-violence incidents in 1999 and 2002 alone, with 12 events (3 state and 9 nonstate) in 1999 and 51 incidents (15 state and 36 nonstate) in 2002. Thus violence has fallen overall in recent years, but tensions remain.

Problems noted by international observer reports include frequent inter-party clashes during election campaign periods, as well as the persistent intimidation by party activists and partisan officials of rival candidates, activists, poll workers, and voters (OSCE-ODIHR 2000b, 2002, 2004a, 2006a, 2008, 2011, 2014, 2016). There have also been problems with the partisan application of electoral justice. The 2002 parliamentary elections, held in the wake of the 2001 civil disturbances, were fraught with clashes between adherents of rival parties and attacks on media outlets; the OSCE election observation report commented that "apparently selective application of law enforcement proceedings against candidates have no place in the democratic process" (OSCE-ODIHR 2002, 1–2). The early 2008 parliamentary elections were also affected by numerous incidents of party-on-party violence, which resulted in contests in a number of areas having to be rerun (OSCE-ODIHR 2008). In its report on these elections, the same observation organization expressed concerns with state neutrality even more forcefully:

> Numerous violent incidents in predominantly ethnic Albanian areas before and during the official campaign period produced an environment of intimidation. Failure to take effective preventive action was attributed by many interlocutors to senior police officials in the north and west of the country openly supporting one ethnic Albanian party. The fact that such acts remained unaddressed by the responsible local and national authorities contributed to a culture of impunity during the 1 June elections. (OSCE-ODIHR 2008, 2)

Yet, over the course of this period, electoral-authority autonomy and capacity have improved overall, following several waves of reforms precipitated by crises. In the country's first elections as an independent state, in 1994, electoral-authority autonomy was at the midpoint of 2 on the 0–3 V-DEM scale, improving to 3 after 1999 in parallel with the decline in state violence that occurred at the same time. This is in keeping with the findings of the quantitative analysis, which show state violence to be inversely related to the impartiality of electoral-management authorities. Electoral-authority capacity remained at 3 during the entire period on the ordinal measure for this indicator, but improved slightly on the more nuanced interval variant of the measure from 0.84 in 1999 to 1.26 in 2009, only to fall back to 0.80 in the fraught 2011 polls. These movements also accord with the results of the quantitative analysis, which suggests that improvements in electoral-authority capacity should be associated with reductions in nonstate violence, and vice versa.

Several waves of reforms to electoral legislation gradually provided the framework for improved electoral administration. There was a major overhaul of electoral infrastructure in 1998, when an 11-member electoral commission was created and administrative procedures were redesigned (Lopez-Pintor 2000). Yet international observers noted lack of clarity in the electoral law and poor electoral registration practices (OSCE-ODIHR 1998); ethnic Albanians in particular voiced grievances about electoral procedures, especially about the bloated electoral register and gerrymandering (Szajkowski 1999). Further electoral reforms that followed in 2002 partially addressed ethnic Albanian concerns (OSCE-ODIHR 2002; Reka 2008), and the OSCE's election observation report noted approvingly that "the State Election Commission (SEC) in particular operated transparently and in a collegial way," and praised its "professionalism" (OSCE-ODIHR 2002, 1–2). However, the report also noted that "undue pressure was brought on the SEC after election day by the Minister of the Interior and other representatives of his Ministry and of the governing party VMRO-DPMNE" (2), indicating ongoing limits to electoral-authority autonomy. A new law enacted in advance of the 2006 parliamentary election increased sanctions for election-related criminal offences and clarified several aspects of the law that had previously been criticized by international observers (OSCE-ODIHR 2006a). Following the violent episodes that had affected ethnic Albanian areas at the time of the 2008 parliamentary elections, greater attention was given to the development of electoral security plans involving electoral authorities and the police; this arrangement resulted in far more peaceful polls in 2009, 2011, 2014, and 2016 (OSCE-ODIHR 2009, 2011, 2014, 2016). In the wake of the 2015–16 political crisis, further measures to improve the quality of the voter register and to clarify aspects of electoral law also appear to have gone some way toward addressing concerns with the quality of electoral administration (OSCE-ODIHR 2016).

Macedonia's trade ties with western Europe, its European values, and aspirations to join the European Union (with candidacy status achieved in 2005) mean that leaders have usually been willing to cede to the demands of regional democratic-standard-setting bodies such as the OSCE and the European Union, and have undertaken electoral reforms that have been recommended to them. In Levitsky and Way's (2010) terminology, Macedonia is a case of both high "linkage" and high "leverage," so normative influence has been more straightforward than in some other contexts. Yet the state has remained dominated by clientelist partisan networks and corruption is rife. A European Commission memo on the 2016 crisis noted that "democracy and rule of law have been constantly challenged, in particular due to state capture affecting the functioning of democratic institutions and key areas of society" (EC 2016, 1). In this context the reform process has been subject to fits and starts, as the political will to create genuinely impartial electoral administration appears to be lacking. The result has been a context in which tensions periodically rise to the surface. This is not to discount the positive impact of electoral administrative reforms, but rather to note that without political will to back them up, tensions remain under the surface of otherwise calm polls.

Thus there has been a gradual professionalization of Macedonian electoral administration, and reforms have gone some way toward addressing concerns about inbuilt bias in electoral provisions. At the same time, commitments on paper have not always translated into reality. The highly partisan nature of state administration in Macedonia appears to be one of the main obstacles to meaningful change, and ethnicized political parties have been identified as the engines of both violence and misconduct (EC 2016; Mochtak 2018a; Willemsen 2006). Mochtak's analysis showed that:

> The source of violence was mainly political rivalry, which has recently been increasingly accompanied by ethnic contestation between the Macedonian majority and the Albanian minority. . . . The majority of these events occurred in the pre-election period and were linked to the organization of election campaigns as a part of broader political competition. Victims and organizers predominantly line up according to political camps and/or ethnically-based groups." (2018a, 92)

It is telling that here have been repeated codes of conduct committing parties to refrain from electoral misconduct and intimidation, with eight signed between 2002 and 2011 alone (NDI 2011), yet partisan manipulation in electoral processes persists.

The Macedonian example shows the benefits of, but also the limits to, efforts to improve electoral administration with a view to preventing violence from disrupting the electoral process. Western powers and intergovernmental organizations have long pressed the country to address problems with electoral conduct, and the country has been relatively amenable to undertaking reforms. Macedonia is in this sense an ideal context in which to target efforts to engineer electoral integrity and electoral peace. Yet even in this most propitious context, the underlying drivers of violence—informal institutions of patronage and state capture—have hampered these efforts. The Balkan state has in recent polls been spared the level of lethal attacks that affect many of the other countries studied in this book, but intimidation remains an ongoing problem that technical reforms do not appear to have solved.

HAITI

Haiti provides a second but very different example of growing electoral-authority autonomy and capacity being associated with a reduction in nonstate violence. Between 1987 and 1995 Haiti experienced an especially fraught transition from authoritarian rule, and when it emerged as a fragile democratic regime, its electoral-authority capacity was severely lacking. The change of regime resulted eventually in a substantial reduction in state violence, from a high of 3 on the V-DEM ordinal scale prior to the transition to 1 for most elections from 1995 onwards; nonstate violence remains a problem in Haiti, with scores of 1 or 2 recorded for most of the post-1995 period, but the overall level of conflict has subsided considerably from the highly contentious transitional polls. At the election of 1987–88, both state and nonstate violence in Haiti had been recorded at the highest levels on the ordinal scales for the V-DEM measures for these variables—3 and 4 respectively. In 1990, state violence fell one point on the V-DEM 0–3 ordinal scale, and nonstate violence also fell a point on the corresponding 0–4 scale. Both types of violence experienced a further point reduction at the time of the 1995 election. Thus by 1995 electoral violence had not been eliminated in Haiti, but it had been significantly reduced from the level experienced in the late 1980s, despite widespread social and political disorder at several points in the country's posttransition history.

Haiti has been a sovereign state since 1804, when it gained independence from France, yet it was nearly two centuries before it experienced anything approaching democracy. A democratic transition was launched following the ouster of Jean-Claude "Baby Doc" Duvalier in 1986. The Duvalier regime (1957–86) has been described by Chehabi and Linz (1998) as "sultanistic" for the extreme concentration of political, economic, and social power in the hands of the ruling family. Duvalier and his wife ran a brutal dictatorship where violence was routinely used as a tool of rule; they also gradually gained control of a large proportion of private-sector enterprise, and they shaped cultural perceptions of the regime by selectively appealing to superstition and widely held cultural values (Nicholls 1998; O'Neill 1993). The couple's excesses eventually turned against them the domestic population as well as key guarantors of the Duvaliers' authority: the army, the church, sections of the media, and the United States, on whose patronage the impoverished state depended (Nicholls 1998). A new constitution was introduced in 1987 following approval by referendum, and a general election was held in November 1987 and January 1988. The dismantling of the paramilitary Tontons Macoutes, which had been Duvalier's principal means of maintaining order, left Haiti lawless and violent (Levitsky and Way 2010; Maingot 1992). This situation had a major impact on the 1987–88 election, which was marred by high levels of strife. Two presidential candidates were assassinated in the run-up to the polls and election staff were attacked. On election day (November 29, 1987), troops massacred several dozen voters waiting to vote and intimidated many more (O'Neill 1993). The election was promptly cancelled and reheld in January1988, but a boycott ensued and turnout was only 4 percent (Carter 1990).

In the years that followed, elections in Haiti were run by a series of temporary electoral authorities—provision electoral councils. Though a permanent election council was enshrined in the constitution in 1987, it struggled to obtain the requisite number of members. There followed two coups in 1988, and a third in 1991. Amid this unrest and weak administration, the 1990 presidential elections—which saw the election of former Catholic priest and left-wing populist Jean Bertrand Aristide—were judged free and fair by commentators (Ulloa 2001), and they marked a step change in electoral quality that was to launch Haiti on the rocky path toward less-authoritarian rule. In 1993 the UN sent a peacekeeping mission that remained in Haiti until 1996, and a US force invaded in 1994 in the aim of defending democracy, but abandoned Aristide after 2000 when he began exhibiting strongly patrimonial behavior. The result was widespread civil unrest, only halted with the arrival of UN peacekeepers who remained in the country from 2004 to 2006. The 2010 earthquake and a series of destructive hurricanes in 1994, 1998, 2004, and 2016 have led to further distress, yet the country has throughout most of the post-1987 period remained more democratic than authoritarian, with Polity scores ranging from −2 to 7.

The generally high level of political turbulence in the Haiti has made EVP a challenging prospect. There have remained numerous problems with the conduct of elections since the 1990s—lack of resources, poor organization, disregard for the law, and fraud (Levitsky and Way 2010; Lopez-Pintor 2000; Ulloa 2001). Popular confidence in the electoral process has been low and boycotts common. But the worst forms of violence have been avoided. Commenting in 2000, Lopez-Pintor noted that:

> several elections have taken place in a peaceful manner since 1988, and some political problems at a basic level have been successfully handled through the intervention of electoral politics: demilitarization, one transfer of power among civilians, and a reduction of violence. Some credit should be given to those who managed the electoral machinery, independent of the many serious problems that they helped to create or were unable to handle in a more effective manner. (Lopez-Pintor 2000, 230).

Low-level violence has remained widespread at election time; intimidation by armed thugs has been commonplace following 1995, and especially problematic polls in 2000 caused the United States to withdraw its support (Levitsky and Way 2010; OAS 2000). Elections held in 2006 under the supervision of UN peacekeepers were more peaceful, but violence has since returned. At the time of the 2015 elections voters attending polling stations were attacked with rocks and bottles, and intimidation was rife (Norris 2017).

Serious though these problems are, they pale in comparison to the violent chaos of the early transition years when electoral-authority capacity was lowest. International involvement indisputably played a major role in Haitian electoral administration during this period, with an estimated 96 percent of the budget for the 1995 elections being paid for by donors (Lopez-Pintor 2000). But factors internal to the transition to democracy, including gradual improvements in electoral-authority capacity, also played a considerable part in quelling unrest at election time. While democratic institutional constraints were slow in taking hold in the posttransition period, electoral capacity was gradually built up from very low initial levels, and the worst forms of arbitrary violence were held in check.

Conclusion

As we have seen in the foregoing chapters, electoral violence is ubiquitous in the contemporary world, affecting every continent and most types of state. Keeping the use of force from conditioning electoral processes and outcomes is a major challenge in many contexts. Though there are a range of international organizations that have sought to address this challenge, it is ultimately the responsibility of domestic actors and state institutions to maintain the electoral peace in the territories under their control. The analyses carried out in this chapter have gone some way toward delineating the characteristics of institutions that reduce electoral violence. The main result of these analyses is that it is governance rather than institutional design that matters most in this connection. Numerous institutional-design features that might be expected to be associated with reduced levels of violence have limited impact, whereas governance characteristics of electoral authorities do appear to have a relatively substantial effect on electoral violence. The de facto autonomy of electoral authorities from political control is associated with lower levels of state violence, whereas high-capacity EMBs that deliver elections professionally and efficaciously are linked to lower levels of nonstate violence. These findings have important implications for electoral assistance, as they suggest that fiddling with the details of institutional design is in most cases not worthwhile; attention should instead be focused on building professional and genuinely autonomous EMBs that can withstand political pressure and oversee well-run elections.

The analysis in this chapter has been restricted to things that can "be done" to electoral institutions; in other words, specific reforms that might be introduced by those in charge of running and overseeing electoral processes. It therefore ignores the myriad instances of exceptional individuals and citizen-led campaigns that have succeed against the odds in reducing violence in specific contexts. The Jamaican and Tanzanian examples cited above offer examples of concerted action that was successful, for a time, in making elections more peaceful. More incremental change in Macedonia and Jamaica was also helped along by individual leaders who recognized the importance of peaceful polls. Dramatic reduction in corruption or increases in the quality of democracy as, for example, occur when a country undergoes a regime change can also alter the balance of factors that contribute to violent elections. As we have seen throughout this book, electoral violence is a complex phenomenon that is often woven into the fabric of societies affected by it. The concluding chapter seeks to draw together the strands in this analysis and sum up the findings of the study.

7

Conclusion

IMPLICATIONS FOR THEORY, POLICY, AND PRACTICE

From one perspective, elections are designed as alternatives to violence, peaceful means of deciding who will rule; so the basic theoretical question one has to ask in studying electoral violence is what goes wrong in violent polls. From another perspective, it is virtually inevitable in all but the best-established democracies with the most impeccable pedigrees of rule of law that in any high-stakes event where the outcome is important, people should at least contemplate using force in order to ensure that they obtain their desired result. From this point of view, one must wonder why all elections are not racked by violence. Which perspective is the correct one? The answer, as this book has shown, is "both" and "neither." Violence is always an option, but its use is promoted and constrained by a host of other factors.

Research has recognized that manipulated elections often play a key role in maintaining authoritarian regimes (Birch 2011; Cox 2009; Gandhi and Przeworski 2007; Geddes 1999; Lust-Okar 2005; Magaloni 2006, 2010; Schedler 2002b, 2006). In such cases, we can talk of alternative political orders that differ markedly from the order of accountability and interest aggregation that is the stuff of democratic theory and which subtends most writing on elections in established democracies. In order to understand these alternative political orders, and to understand the way elections are institutionalized in such states, it is therefore necessary not simply to consider electoral practices in terms of their deficiencies, but to seek to understand the role they play in reproducing power relations. In such cases, electoral violence and other forms of manipulation become functional systems of practices that can exhibit considerable internal coherence.

Over the past decade, comparative political scientists have begun to devote greater attention to the link between political violence and elections. Much valuable research has been carried out in this area on the basis of case studies and region-specific analyses, highlighting the role of factors such as grievance, constraints, and uncertainty in augmenting or reducing the chances that elections will turn violent. This book builds on and extends work in this burgeoning field. The main argument advanced here is that actors' incentives to use violence as part of the electoral process will be strongly conditioned by the material benefits of office and the disadvantages of being out of office. In "open access orders" (North, Wallis, and Weingast 2009) where power holders have limited opportunities to plunder state coffers for the benefit of themselves and their allies and limited ability to use state resources to restrict the activities of their rivals, the risks associated with violence will typically be deemed too high, and elections will remain largely peaceful. Yet in sociopolitical contexts characterized by corruption, where control over the state enables power holders to extract significant resources and to punish their rivals, the stakes of elections will be extremely high, and all actors will have an incentive to use any means at their disposal to win electoral contests, including force.

Though previous scholars have noted the role of informal institutions in shaping electoral conflict (Boone 2011; Boone and Kriger 2012; Burchard 2015; Fjelde and Höglund 2016; Höglund 2009; LeBas 2006; Mueller 2011, 2012; Sisk 2012), such institutions have generally been interpreted in terms of ethnic grievance, owing to the geographic context in which much of the literature on electoral violence has developed. The analyses presented in the preceding chapters broaden and extend such arguments by tying them to the well-known dynamics of corruption (Acemoglu and Robinson 2012; Mungiu-Pippidi 2015; Rothstein and Varraich 2017). In the terminology of corruption literature, electoral violence can be seen as a tool of illicit rent seeking, whereby leaders treat the state as a source of private benefits for themselves and their allies, to the detriment of the public benefit. These considerations suggest an approach to explaining electoral violence that is relevant in a variety of contexts: when the material rewards of victory are high enough, force is likely to be used to secure that end.

This concluding chapter will summarize the main findings of the volume and draw out the implications of the investigation for political science, institutional design, electoral administration, and electoral assistance. In so doing, the chapter will consider the circumstances under which different strategies of EVP are likely to be successful, and it will provide a series of lessons and recommendations for the academic, policy, and practitioner communities.

Summary of Findings

This study has sought to provide a global descriptive overview and explanatory account of electoral violence, assessing variations in this phenomenon across both space and time. The first chapter set the conceptual and descriptive scene for the analyses to follow. It showed that electoral violence is a truly global problem, and one that is especially likely to afflict states at intermediary levels of democracy. It also provided evidence that the bulk of electoral violence is perpetrated by state actors, though their nonstate counterparts are responsible for a larger number of violent attacks.

The main explanatory message of the book, as detailed in chapter 2, is that electoral violence is driven by the corruption that is characteristic of states lacking in rule of law and democratic constraints. Before reviewing the specific empirical results of the investigation, it is worth pausing to summarize the main argument in some detail and revisit some of the examples that have been discussed in previous chapters. In rule-governed democracies, the power to be gained through assuming electoral office may be considerable, but it is political power constrained by a raft of legal institutions, including courts, other branches of power, and the press, which prevent or severely restrain opportunities for illicit rent seeking. In many "competitive authoritarian" states where rule of law is less well entrenched and corruption is rife, however, the political and economic realms are fused in clientelist networks of dependence that dictate who has access to state resources, who has opportunities to pursue private business ventures, and who benefits from protection under the law (Mungiu-Pippidi 2015; North, Wallis, and Weingast 2009; Rothstein and Varraich 2017). In such systems, rent seeking is typically the primary objective of those aspiring to office, and losing office means not just loss of control over the making of laws and policies, but also loss of access to economic benefits for oneself and one's social group, loss of legal protection, and potentially even imprisonment, exile, or loss of life. Though to a lesser extent this phenomenon is observed even in many democracies that are ridden with patronage and corruption, it is starkest in hybrid and authoritarian states. These considerations have two important implications for the viability of using violence to secure political ends: First, in many contexts, electoral defeat results in negative outcomes that are political, economic, and legal. Likewise, the material benefits that accrue to those who win office are considerable: these include the opportunity to steal state resources for personal enrichment and the benefit of one's social group, and the opportunity to dispossess, imprison, or kill one's enemies or business rivals (Bayart, Ellis, and Hibou 1999; Bratton 2008; Fjelde and Höglund 2016; North, Wallis, and Weingast 2009). The material benefits of electoral violence are thus far higher in corrupt than in uncorrupt states, all else equal. Second, the political interference in state institutions characteristic of corrupt and clientelist states means that those who control the state benefit from relative legal impunity, which vastly reduces the cost of violence. This combination of great benefits and low costs creates the ideal setting for the use of force: when there is so much riding on an election, contestants can be expected to resort to every possible means of winning, especially in contexts where the legal system is sufficiently weak that winners have little need to fear legal sanction for illicit behavior.

A number of scholars of African politics have remarked on the connection between clientelist practices and electoral violence. Catherine Boone, Susanne Mueller, and Adrienne LeBas have all analyzed the violent state redistribution of land to client groups as a technique of electoral manipulation in the African context (Boone 2011; Boone and Kriger 2012; LeBas 2006; Mueller 2011, 2012). Boone commented on the state supporters' "perception and expectation that land seizure and reallocation was the ruler's prerogative" (2011, 134). Other researchers have noted the role of informal institutions in increasing the stakes of elections in the African context (Bratton 2008; Fjelde and Höglund 2016; Höglund 2009; Sisk 2012). As Sisk put it:

> A common cause of election violence is that in many situations, especially in conditions of high scarcity and underdevelopment, the stakes of winning or losing valued political posts are incredibly high. When winning a state office is key to the livelihood not just for an individual but for the entire clan, faction, or even ethnic group, the stakes for prevailing in electoral competition are dangerously high. (2012, 44–45).

The 2007 Nigerian election is one of the examples provided by Sisk to illustrate this point. More recent events in Nigeria serve further to support the same argument. Following the violence that occurred at the time of the 2011 election, Nigeria set up the Panel on Election Violence and Civil Disturbances, commonly known as the "Lemu Panel" after its chairperson, Sheikh Ahmed Lemu. The report of this commission identified as one of the most important causes of the 2011 violence "a history of impunity by previous regimes on prosecutions of perpetrators guilty of fomenting widespread violence," together with "the financial incentives associated with holding public office" and the fact that "elected officials 'lucritised' their offices for financial gain" (Fischer 2017a).

This book demonstrates that this dynamic is not evident just in Africa but can be observed elsewhere as well. Wilkinson (2004) documented the factors shaping electoral violence in India, noting how the complex interplay of party factionalization, electoral-system design, and the ethnic composition of constituencies generates ethnic violence in some areas but not others. Though many of these factors, such as ethnic rivalry, are context specific, Wilkinson emphasized that violence is enabled by two aspects of Indian political culture that are highly salient to the argument advanced here: the politicization of the state, and in particular of the police, who typically await orders from political leaders prior to quelling unrest, and the impunity of power holders. As the author remarked in a telling passage: "perhaps it is a sign of how many politicians feel themselves to be immune from the law that many are quite open about the relationship between communal violence and an improvement in their electoral prospects" (47).

A third example of this dynamic is Thailand, with which this volume opened. In his study of electoral violence in this state, Kongkirati tracked the decline of violence as programmatic competition increased and patronage politics declined in Thai elections over the course of the 2000s. With the replacement of localized patronage-based competition by ideologically driven contests, so the use of violent coercive techniques by local political bosses subsided as their power declined: "The exercise of private violence by the provincial bosses was a remnant of the political and economic order established in the 1980s. This unsettling phenomenon will not entirely disappear until the patrimonial structure of the state is radically transformed and personalistic fighting over government spoils and rent-distribution are substantially reduced" (Kongkirati 2014, 386).

At the same time, we observe many contexts where the state commands considerable economic power but we do not observe excessive violence during the electoral period. This is in most cases due to the fact that despite the presence of rent-seeking motives, there are sufficient institutional constraints on the activities of actors that it would be too risky to use force in the pursuit of their electoral ends. These constraints include the formal sanctions of the courts and the electoral authorities, as well as the informal constraints of the media and monitors (Burchard 2015; Fjelde and Höglund 2016; Hafner-Burton, Hyde, and Jablonski 2014; Klaus and Mitchell 2015).

In short, the more corrupt a state, the more vulnerable are its elections to violence, but this relationship is mediated by democratic constraints. This argument was elaborated in chapter 2, which also theorized the likely connections between the use of electoral violence and other strategies of electoral manipulation. The argument advanced was that violence is rarely used in isolation, but is commonly part of a set of strategies for winning elections that reflect the resources available to actors. In states where informal institutions are strong, incumbent parties and candidates typically have the advantage of being able to manipulate the conduct of elections by putting pressure on electoral authorities. Such pressure is a relatively "cheap" and efficient means of manipulating elections, though there may be limits to the number of votes that can reasonably be shifted in this way without fatally compromising the international and domestic credibility of the process. Violence and intimidation are thus often used to back up fraud, both to ensure that efforts to manipulate elections are successful by deterring scrutiny, and as additional measures that can be employed when misconduct alone is insufficient. Nonstate actors, for their part, are more likely to resort to purchasing votes as well as using violence, as fraud is typically not available to them but they can often rely on clientelist networks to facilitate vote buying.

Encapsulating these arguments, chapter 2 presented six hypotheses, all of which have been largely confirmed by the analyses in subsequent chapters:

H1: Corruption tends to promote electoral violence.

H2: Democratic institutions tend to curb electoral violence.

H3: Significant electoral misconduct often necessitates and is accompanied by state-initiated electoral violence.

H4: Significant vote buying often necessitates and is accompanied by nonstate-initiated electoral violence.

H5: Nonstate actors in opposition can be expected to favor forms of violence associated with mass mobilization, including protest violence, which will typically lead to countermeasures by state actors.

H6: Actors' use of electoral violence will increase when they are the object of violent acts by their electoral opponents.

The evidence presented in chapter 3 confirmed that violence initiated by actors associated with the state is facilitated by corruption, and constrained by the formal institutions of democracy and the informal constraints exercised by freedom of expression. The analyses presented in this chapter also support the association between violence and electoral misconduct, strategies often used in conjunction by incumbents to ensure reelection. The cases of Zimbabwe, Syria, Belarus, and Paraguay showed in detail how state-initiated violence is used as an adjunct to other forms of electoral manipulation. These cases demonstrated that leaders often fall back on violence, or the threat of violence, as a means of ensuring that strategies for electoral misconduct work as planned.

The cross-national analyses and case studies in chapter 4 demonstrated that nonstate violence is strongly conditioned by corruption, though less so by formal and informal democratic constraints. Unlike state violence, its nonstate counterpart is inversely correlated with per capita GDP, suggesting that deprivation plays a role in making the use of force a viable strategy. It is also clear from the evidence presented here that nonstate actors frequently employ violence together with vote buying in a "carrot-and-stick" approach. Scrutiny of election-related protest activity—election boycotts and postelectoral protests—indicated that these are commonly accompanied by violence, and that force can be used as a mobilizing device by nonstate actors. Examination of the Pakistani and Ghanaian cases demonstrated how violence is used by nonstate actors as a means of enforcing vote buying. Analyses of the dynamics of nonstate violence in Kyrgyzstan and Côte d'Ivoire showed how violence is often used by nonstate actors in conjunction with mobilizational strategies such as protest to pressure leaders to yield power.

It is interesting to note that democratic institutions are more important in conditioning state-initiated violence, whereas level of economic development is more closely associated with a nonstate violence. Corruption, on the other hand, is closely linked to both phenomena. This suggests that while corruption—and the potential rewards of corrupt exchange—provides a powerful motive for both state and nonstate actors to secure electoral victory even at the cost of violence, the incentives for those already part of the state machinery to resort to the use of force are curbed by robust political constraints, whereas economic opportunities dampen the desire for those outside the state to seek access to state resources through violent means.

With broad-brush cross-national patterns in the occurrence of electoral violence established, chapter 5 went on to probe temporal and geographic variations in the distribution of this phenomenon. The analysis of trends within electoral cycles suggested strategic interaction between rival actors in the use of physical force, though less reactive activity vis-à-vis threats. Examination of geographic patterns in the Philippines, Tanzania, and Jamaica indicated considerable spatial variation in the distribution of electoral violence, with pockets of state weakness frequently associated with heightened risk of disturbances at election time. The Ukrainian, Tanzanian, and Jamaican cases also showed how electoral violence varies over time, with episodes of political crisis sparking violence, and subsequent popular backlashes against the deadly use of force quelling electoral unrest temporarily.

The focus in chapter 6 turned to strategies for reducing electoral violence. The analyses found the design of formal institutions to be far less influential than the quality of electoral governance in shaping incentives to commit violent acts. Elections run by professional, well-resourced, and politically neutral EMBs are less likely to be afflicted by conflict than those managed by politicized and/or incompetent electoral administrators. In comparison to electoral governance, the details of electoral-management and electoral-justice design systems appear to be of minor significance in preventing violence from occurring. This suggests that in preference to sweeping reforms and redesigns, those seeking to make elections more peaceful should focus instead on bolstering the capacity and de facto autonomy of electoral authorities. As the cases of Macedonia and Haiti suggest, this project can be halting and slow owing to lack of political will and underdevelopment, but gradually efforts to strengthen and professionalize EMBs can help promote more orderly and peaceful elections.

Implications for Political Science

This study most obviously carries implications for the study of elections, the study of political violence, and the study of informal institutions. Political science has traditionally viewed elections as opportunities for citizens to assess the policies and track records of competitors for power and to select, individually and collectively, the leaders whom they believe will do the best job of running their state in the years to come. The stylized democratic electoral contest is one in which all citizens have access to accurate information about the parties and/or candidates seeking their vote, and make their choices on the basis of a reasoned assessment of the options. Though they may use heuristic devices to help them cut cognitive corners (Downs 1957; Lupia and McCubbins 1998), they nevertheless gather a sufficient quantity of information of a sufficient quality that they generally do a reasonably good job of navigating the electoral terrain and making collective choices that roughly reflect their collective preferences (Powell 2000; Soroka and Wleizen 2010). As such, democratic elections are institutions that establish a means of gaining power and legitimacy. They are also peaceful means of determining the leadership of a country.

But there are many ways in which elections can be won. They can be won through open competition in which parties (or other political forces) present their achievements and proposals for the future of the country, and voters select parties on this basis. Yet in recent years the use of force has beset elections in many parts of the world. Although electoral violence is still the exception rather than the norm in most countries, this phenomenon is coming to be a significant global challenge and a threat to democratic institutions. If this volume has accomplished nothing else, it will hopefully have brought to the attention of students of elections a set of practices that have received little systematic treatment in most studies but which affect elections across the globe in sometimes very severe ways. In so doing the investigation contributes to the growing body of research that disaggregates electoral malpractice and focuses on the determinants of specific violations of electoral integrity. Indeed, there is a striking continuity in the suite of variables found to be significant in these pages and those known to drive electoral misconduct in general: informal institutions and democracy are well-established determinants of violations of electoral integrity as well as being shapers of electoral violence (e.g. Birch 2011; Norris 2015; Schedler 2013).

The implications of the findings presented in this volume for the study of political violence are multiple. Most commonly studied forms of political violence are extra-institutional in that they operate outside of the formal structures of the state. These include terrorism and violence linked to organized criminal groups. Electoral violence, by contrast, takes place in the interstices of the formal institution of elections and it is typically designed to alter the functioning of that institution. It is thus fundamentally different from most types of political violence or conflict, even if other types of violence in and between states often condition electoral violence (Harish and Toha 2018). The way in which force is used to alter the internal workings of democracy is an understudied topic, but recognition that this can happen may alert scholars to similar manifestations of violence in other democratic domains.

Those who study corruption and informal institutions are already well aware of the manifold ways in which violence ban be blended with particularism to reshape and redirect the structure of the state, privatizing functions designed to be public and hijacking state institutions to serve personal ends. Though the link between electoral violence and corruption has been adumbrated in a number of case studies, the extended treatment of this topic in this book has hopefully gone some way toward further clarifying the role of elections in reproducing power structures that exist beyond and within those formally mandated by constitutional practices.

Implications for Institutional Design

Several previous studies, mainly based on regional data sets, have posited that formal institutions have a bearing on a state's propensity to experience electoral violence (Alesina, Piccolo, and Pinotti 2018; Burchard 2015; Claes 2016; Daxecker 2020; Fjelde 2020; Fjelde and Höglund 2016; Höglund 2009; Malik 2018; Reilly 2001; Wilkinson 2004). Yet electoral-system variables proved insignificant in most of the analyses carried out in chapters 3 and 4. The models presented in chapter 6 likewise indicated that formal administrative institutional design is less effective in shaping electoral violence than good electoral governance. The major exception is the important role played by the constraints that democratic institutions place on executives. Democracy does make a difference for levels of state-initiated violence, but though this is partly a question of institutional design, it is also partly a matter of practice.

These findings corroborate the experience of imposing institutional change in a variety of contexts. As recent experience with forcible "regime change" indicates, removing dictators and rewriting constitutions is insufficient fundamentally to alter authoritarian systems, which are typically based on the collusion of millions of citizens in clientelist regimes based on violence and rent seeking (North, Wallis, and Weingast 2009). In such contexts, democratic institutions such as elections are reshaped for the purposes of these networks. Clientelist networks are innovative and resourceful—they use what is available to them. This suggests that the design of formal electoral institutions is typically endogenous, driven by the needs of informal institutions (Birch 2011; Boone 2003). Thus, recommending change in formal institutions is unlikely to be effective if such a change would not be consistent with the needs of informal institutions. This is not to say that the blatant manipulation of institutional design never matters for conditioning electoral violence, only that it is the manipulation that tends to matter more than the specific design features of the institution in question.

Implications for Electoral Administration

Electoral administrators are those most directly responsible for preventing violence from erupting at election time. In as much as electoral institutions have the confidence of all parties and of the citizenry, and democratic structures are free from capture by networks of cronyism and corruption, elections ought by and large to be peaceful. The analyses presented in chapters 3, 4, 5, and 6 suggest as much, and there are few cases where this is not true. Violence may occasionally afflict free, fair, and credible elections in established democracies, as in the cases of terrorist attacks or assassinations, but this is very rare. Vote buying and electoral misconduct are, by contrast, frequent companions of electoral violence. Poorly conducted elections can trigger violent electoral protests, but very often electoral violence is used strategically together with other forms of electoral malpractice. The analyses presented in chapter 5 suggest, moreover, that the two months leading up to election day are the period when violent retaliations against the actions of rivals is most common, which indicates that this period is the one that would benefit most from measures to defuse tension. As the models shown in chapter 6 indicate, electoral-authority autonomy from political control is very closely linked to state violence, and electoral-authority technical capacity is strongly associated with nonstate violence. These findings add to existing evidence that strengthening EMBs should be a priority for those wishing to quell electoral violence (Birch and Muchlinski 2018; Borzyskowski 2015, 2019; Borzyskowski and Claes 2018; Claes 2016). Together, these considerations suggest that rather than seeking to undertake wholesale redesigns of the electoral apparatus, those in charge of managing elections would do better to focus on building capacity and signaling autonomy from political control.

Implications for International Electoral Assistance

The desirability of strengthening EMB autonomy and capacity is also a lesson for providers of international electoral assistance, as this is one of the main activities undertaken by such bodies. The empirical results set out in the foregoing pages should be welcome to electoral-assistance practitioners in that they confirm the value of their activities. Yet there are other lessons that can be drawn from these results as well. Perhaps the most obvious of these is the need for closer integration between good governance and electoral-assistance programs, as electoral integrity and electoral peace are closely bound up with rule of law. Corruption control is typically undertaken by international-development professionals with economic goals in mind, yet the political science literature is rich with evidence of the nefarious effects of corruption on political processes such as representation and participation (Della Porta and Vannucci 1997; Rose-Ackerman 1999; Rothstein 2011; Rothstein and Uslaner 2005; Stockemer, LaMontagne, and Scruggs 2013). The research carried out here suggests that electoral integrity will only definitively be improved and electoral violence reduced when states are governed by rule of law and informal structures no longer shape power relations in a society. Closer systematic linkages between election- and governance-assistance programs could go some way toward locking in cycles of good governance and peaceful democratic elections.

Somewhat paradoxically, the findings of this study may also cause policy experts to reevaluate vote buying and fraud. The analyses in chapters 3 and 4 show that these strategies are often used in conjunction with violence, but under certain circumstances they may also replace violence. Alonso wrote of late-nineteenth- and early-twentieth-century Argentina:

> The absence of violence in the elections did not mean that the vote had become "clean". It only meant that more ingenious tricks had gradually replaced the electoral violence of the past. The list of complaints drawn up by the parties after the elections provide endless examples of electoral manipulations: false registrations, false voters, men voting several times. In the first years of the twentieth century, particularly after the election of 1904, a market of votes developed in the city, particularly in the poorer neighborhoods. Many had thought that the absence of violence in elections was a significant step forward: they also thought that the development of a market for votes was a further sign of the gradual pacification of the country's electoral practices. If people could sell their vote, that meant they could not be intimidated. (Alonso 1996, 194)

In the Argentine context, the political parties grew so adept at employing strategies of vote buying and manipulation that they were no longer required to rely on violent means to achieve their ends. Problematic as vote buying and fraud are, they are undoubtedly superior to violence, as violence directly impairs the welfare of those who suffer it. The main negative impact of vote buying and fraud is the harm done to democracy; less democratic political systems may well also negatively affect citizen welfare, though this relationship is not as certain or direct. It follows from these considerations that any intervention that led to the replacement of fraud or vote buying with violence (including intimidation) would be normatively undesirable. In some contexts election observation has been found to have precisely this effect when not all polling stations are observed (Asunka et al. 2017), which raises questions of how observation techniques might be improved so as to prevent this from happening, possibly by ensuring universal observation.

Directions for Future Research

This investigation has set out some of the core determinants of electoral violence and has suggested several ways in which the use of force could be prevented from affecting elections, yet there remain many questions unanswered in the emerging subfield of electoral violence studies. Some of these avenues represent more detailed scrutiny of the themes elaborated here, whereas others involve linking the results of this research to other relevant topics.

Future research could usefully examine the effect of different interventions in altering the incentives of electoral actors and preventing violence in the contexts where it is most likely to occur. It would also be interesting in future work to examine the role of information sources such as opinion polls and the media in conditioning perceptions of unpredictability, as well as the strategic interactions between state and nonstate perpetrators of violence within individual electoral cycles. Despite a recent upsurge in interest from scholars in electoral violence, the detailed study of this phenomenon remains underdeveloped, and there is considerable scope for fine-tuning our understanding of conflictual elections.

The global longitudinal data examined here enable a delineation of empirical regularities that is not possible through examination of individual cases alone, where an N of one precludes general comparative causal inferences from being drawn. That said, case studies can play an important role in probing causal pathways and exploring dynamics that are difficult to study comparatively. For example, future research on individual cases could help to enhance our understanding of the strategic calculus of leaders who opt to use violence. Insights from behavioral psychology could be especially useful in developing this line of inquiry. Prospect theory, as developed by Daniel Kahneman and Amos Tversky (Kahneman and Tversky 2000; Tversky and Kahneman 2000), is a theory of decision making under risk, which predicts that people are "loss averse" in the sense that when they face the prospect of losing (when they are in "the domain of loss"), they will seek to minimize their losses by engaging in behavior that is riskier than what purely "rational" considerations based on classical expected utility theory would dictate. Work on prospect theory suggests that the tendency it describes has its origins in the evolution of survival strategies, and that it may be particularly difficult to overcome for those whose survival is threatened, including dictators (McDermott, Fowler, and Smirnov 2008). The analysis presented here has hinted that the overuse of violence may also result from loss aversion associated with the psychological tendency to overvalue assets held and engage in excessively risky behavior to protect them. When leaders perceive that they are losing legitimacy, they tend to increase the amount of violence they employ. If violence is too blatant, the leader risks provoking a legitimacy crisis and being faced with protests that could potentially unseat him or her. Loss averse leaders will, however, be prepared to take such risks in order to avoid power slipping away. Research designs that are able to capture psychological phenomena would be welcome means of developing this line of investigation.

It would also be instructive to investigate further the types of subnational variations in patterns of electoral violence that were explored briefly in chapter 5, and to extend the analyses carried out here to local and regional elections. The cross-national data currently available focus mainly on national-level electoral contests, which have been the empirical object of this study, but it would be interesting to examine variations across regions in patterns of violence in local and regional elections, and how they relate to national-level power structures. For example, are subnational elections more or less violent than national elections? And do we observe more violence in regions controlled by parties that are in opposition at national level?

Another fruitful area of inquiry is the consequences of electoral violence for political, social, and economic development. If violence is most likely to be used to sway outcomes in corrupt states with weak accountability institutions, a relevant question is to what extent it is successful. In a perceptive review article, Staniland (2014) noted that electoral violence needs to be recast as an independent variable. Hafner-Burton, Hyde, and Jablonski (2018) have already found that state-initiated violence increases the chance of incumbent victory. Violence can be used to suppress turnout among the perpetrators' opponents in the electorate (Burchard 2015; Collier and Vicente 2014; Condra et al. 2018; Höglund and Piyarathne 2009; Sisk 2012; S. Taylor 2009), and to induce sectors of the electorate to vote in favor of the perpetrator's preferred electoral option. Though there are cases where the use of violence has been found to generate an electoral backlash (Bratton 2008; Rosenzweig 2016), there is considerable evidence from previous research that electoral violence is successful in achieving these ends (Hafner-Burton, Hyde, and Jablonski 2018; Wilkinson 2004; Wilkinson and Haid 2009). Those who use violence often target it selectively so as to minimize electoral backlash and to impose maximum damage on those actively involved in the campaigns of their opponents (Bhasin and Gandhi 2013) or on swing voters (Bangura and Söderberg Kovacs 2018; Robinson and Torvik 2009). Violence or the threat of violence can also weaken accountability institutions by deterring revelations of misconduct by monitors and other observers (Daxecker 2012; Kelley 2012). Further research might usefully explore whether violence is a more effective tool for governments or oppositions, how electoral violence affects citizen attitudes toward the state, and how it affects economic performance. It would also be useful to explore how involvement in electoral violence influences the life trajectories of the young men who are typically employed to carry out attacks.

The effectiveness of violent postelectoral protests in improving electoral integrity and/or removing governments is also a promising avenue for future research. Anyone with a television will have noticed that mass protests following the announcement of election results are increasingly occupying the screen. Though many have undoubtedly remarked on this fact in passing, there has been little work on the extent to which violent protest against electoral fraud is effective in achieving its ends. A number of scholars have noted that protest activity has been the principal motor of electoral reform in many states (Beaulieu 2014; Beissinger 2007; Bratton and Van de Walle 1997; Bunce and Wolchick 2009, 2010, 2011; Levtisky and Way 2010; Little, Tucker, and LaGatta 2015; Norris 2014; Schedler 2013; Thompson and Kuntz 2004, 2006; Tucker 2007; Van de Walle 2006). The way in which popular protests against electoral fraud play out has also been the subject of several macrolevel analyses (Beaulieu 2014; Bunce and Wolchik 2011; Case 2006; Cox 2009; Donno 2013; Howard and Roessler 2006; Lehoucq 1995; Magaloni 2006, 2010; Schedler 2002b, 2013; Thompson and Kuntz 2006). Yet most previous work has framed postelectoral protest as the *result* of electoral fraud (e.g. Kuntz and Thompson 2009; Norris 2014; Svolik and Chernyk 2012; Tucker 2007). This is undoubtedly true in many contexts, but it is of both academic and practical relevance to consider violent protest as an independent variable and to assess the extent to which it prompts leaders to address flaws in electoral conduct and improve electoral integrity.

Patterns in the occurrence of electoral violence could also be studied more systematically in connection with varieties of informal institutions. The unavailability of suitable large-N indicators hampered my ability to probe in detail differences between, for example, contexts of state capture by oligarchs, penetration of the state by drug cartels, or networks of cronyism. It is likely that variations such as these do have considerable bearing on the way in which violence inflects electoral processes. Case studies and more granular analyses would be useful in refining the overarching regularities established here and deepening our understanding of the linkages between elections, violence, and corruption in different contexts across the globe.

Finally, the gender dimension of electoral violence is an area in which there are currently very limited comparative data but one that merits further analysis, given the evidence from case studies of women playing distinctive roles both as perpetrators and as victims of violence connected to electoral processes (Bardall 2011; Krause 2018; Linantud 1998; Zvobgo 2018).

Though the foregoing pages have sought to shed more systematic comparative light on electoral violence than has been available in previous work, the study of conflictual elections remains a relatively new area of research; much exciting work will undoubtedly be carried out on this topic in the years to come. This emerging field may prove particularly relevant in the era of democratic backsliding that the world appears to be entering, and the role of violence in electoral processes throughout the modern history of democratic voting practices is a subject whose detailed analysis is long overdue.

REFERENCES

Acemoglu, Daron, and James A. Robinson. 2012. *Why Nations Fail: The Origins of Power, Prosperity and Poverty*. London: Profile Books.

Aidt, Toke. 2019. "Corruption." In *The Oxford Handbook of Public Choice*, vol. 1, edited by Roger D. Congleton, Bernard Grofman, and Stefan Voigt, 604–27. Oxford: Oxford University Press.

Akhter, Muhammad Yeahia. 2001. *Electoral Corruption in Bangladesh*. Aldershot, UK: Ashgate.

Alesina, Alberto, Salvatore Piccolo, and Paolo Pinotti. 2018. "Organized Crime, Violence, and Politics." *Review of Economic Studies* 86, no. 2: 457–99.

Alihodzic, Sead. 2012. "Electoral Violence Early Warning and Infrastructures for Peace." *Journal of Peacebuilding and Development* 7, no. 3: 54–69.

Alonso, Paula. 1996. "Voting in Buenos Aires before 1912." In *Elections before Democracy: The History of Elections in Europe and Latin America*, edited by Eduardo Posada-Carbó, 181–99. Basingstoke, UK: Macmillan.

Amnesty International. 2017. "Spain: Recent Developments in Catalonia from 1 October." Public statement, AI index: EUR 41/7473/2017. London: Amnesty International. https://www.amnesty.org/en/documents/eur41/7473/2017/en/.

Askoy, Deniz. 2014. "Elections and the Timing of Terrorist Attacks." *Journal of Politics* 76, no. 4: 899–913.

Asunka, Joseph, Sarah Brierley, Miriam Golden, Eric Kramon, and George Ofosu. 2017. "Electoral Fraud or Violence: The Effect of Observers on Party Manipulation Strategies." *British Journal of Political Science* 49, no. 1: 129–51. Published online ahead of print. doi:10.1017/S0007123416000491.

Bakke, Kristin, and Erik Wibbels. 2006. "Diversity, Disparity, and Civil Conflict in Federal States." *World Politics* 59, no. 1: 1–50.

Balcells, L. 2010. "Rivalry and Revenge: Violence against Civilians in Conventional Civil Wars." *International Studies Quarterly* 54: 291–313.

Bangura, Ibrahim, and Mimmi Söderberg Kovacs. 2018. "Competition, Uncertainty and Violence in Sierra Leone's Swing District." In *Violence in African Elections: Between Democracy and Big Man Politics*, edited by Söderberg Kovacs and Jesper Bjarnesen, 114–34. Uppsala: Nordic Africa Institute.

Bardall, Gabrielle. 2011. "Breaking the Mold: Understanding Gender and Electoral Violence." International Foundation for Electoral Systems (IFES) White Paper. Washington, DC: IFES. https://ifes.org/sites/default/files/gender_and_electoral_violence_2011.pdf.

Barker, Memphis. 2018. "Pakistanis Vote after Bitterly Contested and Violent Campaign." *Guardian*, July 25, 2018. https://www.theguardian.com/world/2018/jul/25/pakistanis-vote-after-bitterly-contested-yet-low-energy-campaign.

Bayart, Jean-François, Stephen Ellis, and Béatrice Hibou. 1999. "From Kleptocracy to the Felonious State?" In *The Criminalization of the State in Africa*, by Bayart, Ellis, and Hibou, 1–31. Oxford: James Currey.

BBC. 2013a. "Imran Khan's PTI 'Wins Revote' in Tense Karachi." *BBC News*, May 20, 2013. https://www.bbc.co.uk/news/world-asia-22593284.

———. 2013b. "PTI's Zahra Shahid Hussain is Buried in Karachi." *BBC News*, May 19, 2013. https://www.bbc.co.uk/news/world-asia-22587895.

———. 2015a. "Burundi Court Backs President Nkurunziza on Third-Term." *BBC News*, May 5, 2015. http://www.bbc.co.uk/news/world-africa-32588658.

———. 2015b. "Pakistan Soldiers Raid MQM's Karachi Headquarters." *BBC News*, March 11, 2015. https://www.bbc.co.uk/news/world-asia-31828474.

Beaulieu, Emily. 2014. *Electoral Protests and Democracy in the Developing World*. Cambridge: Cambridge University Press.

Beaulieu, Emily, and Susan D. Hyde. 2009. "In the Shadow of Democracy Promotion: Strategic Manipulation, International Observers and Election Boycotts." *Comparative Political Studies* 42, no. 3: 392–415.

Beissinger, Mark R. 2007. "Structure and Example in Modular Political Phenomena: The Diffusion of Bulldozer/Rose/Orange/Tulip Revolutions." *Perspectives on Politics* 5, no. 2: 259–76.

Bekoe, Dorina. 2012a. "Introduction: The Scope, Nature and Pattern of Electoral Violence in Sub-Saharan Africa." In *Voting in Fear: Electoral Violence in Sub-Saharan Africa*, edited by Bekoe, 1–13. Washington, DC: United States Institute of Peace.

———. 2012b. "Postelectoral Political Agreements in Togo and Zanzibar: Temporary Measures for Stopping Electoral Violence?" In *Voting in Fear: Electoral Violence in Sub-Saharan Africa*, edited by Bekoe, 117–44. Washington, DC: United States Institute of Peace.

———. 2018. "The United Nations Operation in Côte d'Ivoire: How a Certified Election Still Turned Violent." *International Peacekeeping* 25, no. 1: 128–53.

Bekoe, Dorina A., and Stephanie M. Burchard. 2017. "The Contradictions of Pre-election Violence: The Effects of Violence on Voter Turnout in Sub-Saharan Africa." *African Studies Review* 60, no. 2: 73–92.

Bell, Andrew, and Kelvyn Jones. 2015. "Explaining Fixed Effects: Random Effects Modeling of Time-Series Cross-Sectional and Panel Data." *Political Science Research and Methods* 3, no. 1: 133–53.

Berenschot, Ward. 2018a. "Patterned Pogroms: Patronage Networks as Infrastructure for Communal Violence in India and Indonesia." Paper presented at the Electoral Violence Workshop, University of Amsterdam, February 15–16, 2018.

———. 2018b. "The Political Economy of Clientelism: A Comparative Study of Indonesia's Patronage Democracy." *Comparative Political Studies* 51, no. 12: 1563–93.

Bhasin, Tavishi, and Jennifer Gandhi. 2013. "Timing and Targeting of State Repression in Authoritarian Elections." *Electoral Studies* 32: 620–31.

Birch, Sarah. 2002a. "The 2000 Elections in Yugoslavia: The 'Bulldozer Revolution.'" *Electoral Studies* 21: 499–510.

———. 2002b. "The Presidential Election in Ukraine, October 1999." *Electoral Studies* 21: 339–63.

———. 2003. "The Parliamentary Elections in Ukraine, March 2002." *Electoral Studies* 22: 503–59.

———. 2008. "Ukraine: Presidential Power, Veto Strategies and Democratisation." In *Semi-Presidentialism in Central and Eastern Europe*, edited by Robert Elgie and Sophia Moestrup, 220–38. Manchester: Manchester University Press.

———. 2010. "Ukraine." In *Elections in Europe*, edited by Dieter Nohlen and Philip Stoever, 1967–99. Baden Baden: Nomos.

———. 2011. *Electoral Malpractice*. Oxford: Oxford University Press.

Birch, Sarah, and David Muchlinski. 2018. "Electoral Violence Prevention: What Works?" *Democratization* 25, no. 3: 385–403.

———. 2019. "The Dataset of Countries at Risk of Electoral Violence." *Terrorism and Political Violence.* doi:10.1080/09546553.2017.1364636.

Birch, Sarah, and Carolien van Ham. 2017. "Getting Away with Foul Play?: The Importance of Formal and Informal Oversight Institutions for Electoral Integrity." *European Journal of Political Research* 56, no. 3: 487–511.

Birnir, Jóhanna K., and Anita Gohdes. 2018. "Voting in the Shadow of Violence: Electoral Politics and Conflict in Peru." *Journal of Global Security Studies* 3, no. 2: 181–97.

Blaydes, Lisa. 2011. *Elections and Distributive Politics in Mubarak's Egypt.* Cambridge: Cambridge University Press.

Bob-Milliar, George M. 2012. "Political Party Activism in Ghana: Factors Influencing the Decision of the Politically Active to Join a Political Party." *Democratization* 19, no. 4: 668–89.

———. 2014. "Party Youth Activists and Low-Intensity Electoral Violence in Ghana: A Qualitative Study of Party Foot Soldiers' Activism." *African Studies Quarterly* 15, no. 1: 125–52.

Bolt, J., and J. L. van Zanden. 2014. "The Maddison Project: Collaborative Research on Historical National Accounts." *Economic History Review*, 67, no. 3: 627–51.

Boone, Catharine. 2003. *Political Topographies of the African State: Territorial Authority and Institutional Choice.* Cambridge: Cambridge University Press.

———. 2011. "Politically Allocated Land Rights and the Geography of Electoral Violence: The Case of Kenya in the 1990s." *Comparative Political Studies* 44, no. 10: 1311–42.

Boone, Catherine, and Norma Kriger. 2010. "Multiparty Elections and Land Patronage: Zimbabwe and Côte d'Ivoire." *Commonwealth and Comparative Politics* 48, no. 2: 173–202.

———. 2012. "Land Patronage and Elections: Winners and Losers in Zimbabwe and Cote d'Ivoire." In *Voting in Fear: Electoral Violence in Sub-Saharan Africa*, edited by Dorina A. Bekoe, 75–115. Washington, DC: United States Institute for Peace.

Borzyskowski, Inken von. 2015. "Peacebuilding beyond Civil Wars: UN Election Assistance and Election Violence." Working paper. https://www.semanticscholar.org/paper/Peacebuilding -Beyond-Civil-Wars-%3A-UN-Election-and-Borzyskowski/9307e2844ba687948a9f27daf63 33651d65e445e.

———. 2019. *The Credibility Challenge: How Democracy Aid Influences Election Violence.* Ithaca, NY: Cornell University Press.

Borzyskowski, Inken von, and Jonas Claes. 2018. "What Works in Preventing Election Violence?: Evidence from Liberia and Kenya." Paper presented at the European Consortium for Political Research General Conference, Hamburg, August 22–25, 2018.

Borzyskowski, Inken von, and Michael Wahman. 2019. "Systematic Measurement Error in Election Violence Data: Causes and Consequences." *British Journal of Political Science.* doi:10.1017/ S0007123418000509.

Boschee, Elizabeth, Jennifer Lautenschlager, Sean O'Brien, Steve Shellman, James Starz, and Michael Ward. 2015. "ICEWS Coded Event Data." Harvard Dataverse, V25, UNF:6:PfMdeEpJsWznQePYYEcZSQ== [fileUNF]. doi:10.7910/DVN/28075.

Boschee, Elizabeth, Premkumar Natarajan, and Ralph Weischedel. 2013. "Automatic Extraction of Events from Open Source Text for Predictive Forecasting." In *Handbook of Computational Approaches to Counterterrorism*, edited by V.S. Subrahamanian, 51–67. New York: Springer.

Bozeman, Barry, Angel Luis Molina Jr., and Wesley Kaufmann. 2018. "Angling for Sharks, Not Pilot Fish: Deep Corruption, Venal Corruption, and Public Values Failure." *Perspectives on Public Management and Governance* 1, no. 1: 5–27.

Brancati, Dawn. 2016. *Democracy Protests: Origins, Features and Significance.* Cambridge: Cambridge University Press.

Brancati, Dawn, and Jack L. Snyder. 2012. "Time to Kill: The Impact of Election Timing on Post-conflict Stability." *Journal of Conflict Resolution* 57, no. 5: 822–53.

Bratton, Michael. 2008. "Vote Buying and Violence in Nigerian Election Campaigns." *Electoral Studies* 27: 621–32.

Bratton, Michael, and Nicolas van de Walle. 1997. *Democratic Experiments in Africa: Regime Transitions in Comparative Perspective.* Cambridge: Cambridge University Press.

Brogren, Helena. 2014. "Sweden: Governmental in Form, Independent in Practice: A Decentralized Election Management System." Ace Project, n.d., accessed October 18, 2019. http://aceproject.org/ace-en/topics/em/annex/electoral-management-case-studies/sweden-governmental-in-form-independent-in.

Brosché, Johan, Hanne Fjelde, and Kristine Höglund. 2020. "Electoral Violence, Political Legacies and Multipartyism in Kenya and Zambia." *Journal of Peace Research* 57, no. 1: 111–125.

Brown, Stephen. 2011. "Lessons Learned and Forgotten: The International Community and Electoral Conflict Management in Kenya." In *Elections in Dangerous Places: Democracy and the Paradoxes of Peacebuilding,* edited by David Gillies, 127–43. Montreal: McGill-Queens University Press.

Brownlee, Jason. 2005. "Political Crisis and Restabilization: Iraq, Libya, Syria, and Tunisia." In *Authoritarianism in the Middle East: Regimes and Resistance,* edited by Marsha Pripstein Posusney and Michele Penner Angrist, 59–86. Boulder, CO: Lynne Rienner.

———. 2007. *Authoritarianism in an Age of Democratization,* Cambridge: Cambridge University Press.

Bryce, Iñigo Garcia. 1986. "Signs of Change in Paraguay. *Harvard International Review* 8, no. 6: 30–31.

Bueno de Mesquita, Bruce, and Alastair Smith. 2010. "Leader Survival, Revolutions, and the Nature of Government Finance." *American Journal of Political Science* 54, no. 4: 936–50.

Bunce, Valerie J., and Sharon L. Wolchik. 2009. "Oppositions versus Dictators: Explaining Divergent Electoral Outcomes in Post-Communist Europe and Eurasia." In *Democratization by Elections: A New Mode of Transition?* edited by Staffan I. Lindberg, 246–68. Baltimore: Johns Hopkins University Press.

———. 2010. "Defeating Dictators: Electoral Change and Stability in Competitive Authoritarian Regimes." *World Politics* 62, no. 1: 43–86.

———. 2011. *Defeating Authoritarian Leaders in Post-Communist Countries.* Cambridge: Cambridge University Press.

Burchard, Stephanie M. 2015. *Electoral Violence in Sub-Saharan Africa.* Boulder, CO: Lynne Rienner.

———. 2018. "Get Out the Vote—or Else: How Effective Is Election Violence as a Campaign Strategy?" Paper presented at the European Consortium for Political Research General Conference, Hamburg, August 22–25, 2018.

Callahan, William A. 2000. *Pollwatching: Election and Civil Society in Southeast Asia.* Aldershot, UK: Ashgate.

Callahan, William A., and Duncan McCargo. 1996. "Vote Buying in Thailand's Northeast: The July 1995 General Election." *Asian Survey* 36, no. 4: 376–92.

Carter, Jimmy. 1990. "Haiti's Election Needs Help." *New York Times,* October 1, 1990.

Carter Center. 1997. *The Observation of the 1997 Jamaican Elections.* Atlanta, GA: Carter Center.

———. 2009. *Observing the 2005 Ethiopia National Elections.* Atlanta, GA: Carter Center.

Case, William. 2006. "Manipulative Skills: How Do Rulers Control the Electoral Arena?" In *Electoral Authoritarianism: The Dynamics of Unfree Competition,* edited by Andreas Schedler, 95–112. Boulder, CO: Lynne Rienner.

Catt, Helena, Andrew Ellis, Michael Maley, Alan Wall, and Peter Wolf. 2014. *Electoral Management Design.* Rev. ed. Stockholm: International IDEA.

Cederman, Lars-Erik, Kristian Skrede Gleditsch, and Simon Hug. 2012. "Elections and Ethnic Civil War." *Comparative Political Studies* 46, no. 3: 387–417.

———. 2013. *Inequality, Grievances and Civil War*. Cambridge: Cambridge University Press.

Chacón, Mario, James A. Robinson, and Ragnar Torvik. 2011. "When Is Democracy an Equilibrium? Theory and Evidence from Colombia's La Violencia." *Journal of Conflict Resolution* 55, no. 3: 366–96.

Chang, E., and M. Golden. 2010. "Sources of Corruption in Authoritarian Regimes." *Social Science Quarterly* 91, no. 1: 1–20.

Chaturvedi, Ashish. 2005. "Rigging Elections with Violence." *Public Choice* 125, no. 1/2: 189–202.

Cheeseman, Nic, and Brian Klaas. 2018. *How to Rig an Election*. New Haven, CT: Yale University Press.

Chehabi, H. E., and Juan J. Linz, eds. 1998. *Sultanistic Regimes*. Baltimore: Johns Hopkins University Press.

Cheibub, José A., and June C. Hayes. 2017. "Elections and Civil War in Africa." *Political Science Research and Methods* 5, no. 1: 81–102.

Christensen, Maya, and Mats Utas. 2008. "Mercenaries of Democracy: The 'Politricks' of Remobilized Combatants in the 2007 General Elections, Sierra Leone." *African Affairs* 107, no. 429: 515–39.

CIPEV (Commission of Inquiry into the Post Election Violence). 2008. *Commission of Inquiry into the Post Election Violence (CIPEV) final report*. Nairobi: Government of Kenya. https:// reliefweb.int/report/kenya/kenya-commission-inquiry-post-election-violence-cipev-final -report.

Claes, Jonas, ed. 2016. *Electing Peace: Violence Prevention and Impact at the Polls*. Washington, DC: United States Institute of Peace.

Claes, Jonas, and Geoffrey Macdonald. 2016. "Evaluation Findings and Conclusion." In *Electing Peace: Violence Prevention and Impact at the Polls*, edited by Jonas, 195–220. Washington, DC: United States Institute of Peace.

Claes, Jonas, and Maria Stephan. 2018. "Banging Pots for Peace: Strategies to Prevent Electoral Violence." Explaining and Mitigating Electoral Violence (blog), January 4, 2018. http://www .electoralviolenceproject.com/bangingposts-peace-strategies-prevent-electoral-violence.

Clarke, Colin. 2006. "Politics, Violence and Drugs in Kingston, Jamaica." *Bulletin of Latin American Research* 25, no. 3: 420–40.

Collier, Paul. 2009. *Wars, Guns and Votes: Democracy in Dangerous Places*. New York: HarperCollins.

Collier, Paul, and Dominic Rohner. 2008. "Democracy, Development and Conflict." *Journal of the European Economic Association* 6, no. 2/3: 531–40.

Collier, Paul, and Pedro C. Vicente. 2012. "Violence, Bribery, and Fraud: The Political Economy of Elections in Sub-Saharan Africa." *Public Choice* 153, no. 1/2: 117–47.

———. 2014. "Votes and Violence: Evidence from a Field Experiment in Nigeria." *Economic Journal* 124, no. 574: F327–55.

Commonwealth. 2005. *The Elections in Zanzibar, United Republic of Tanzania*. London: Commonwealth Secretariat.

Condra, Luke N., James D. Long, Andrew C. Shaver, and Austin L. Wright. 2018. "The Logic of Insurgent Electoral Violence." *American Economic Review* 108, no. 11: 3199–231.

Coppedge, Michael, John Gerring, Carl Henrik Knutsen, Staffan I. Lindberg, Svend-Erik Skaaning, Jan Teorell, David Altman, et al. 2018a. "V-Dem Codebook v8." Varieties of Democracy (V-Dem) Project. https://doi.org/10.23696/vdemcy18.

———. 2018b. "V-Dem [Country-Year/Country-Date] Dataset v8." Varieties of Democracy (V-Dem) Project. https://doi.org/10.23696/vdemcy18.

Copsey, Nathaniel. 2010. "Ukraine." In *The Colour Revolutions in the Former Soviet Union*, edited by Donnacha Ó Beachain and Abel Polese, 30–44. New York: Routledge.

Cox, Gary. 2009. "Authoritarian Elections and Leadership Succession, 1975–2004." Paper presented at the Annual Meeting of the American Political Science Association, Toronto, September 3–6, 2009.

Creative Associates International. 2009. "Technical Guidance for Election Security: Handbook and Implementation Framework First Draft." Unpublished report. Washington, DC: Creative Associates International.

———. 2010. *Electoral Security Assessments: Bangladesh, Zimbabwe and Colombia.* Washington, DC: USAID.

———. 2012. *Electoral Security Assessment: Philippines.* Washington, DC: USAID.

———. 2013. *Best Practices in Electoral Security: A Guide for Democracy, Human Rights and Governance Programming.* Washington, DC: USAID.

Cyllah, Almami, ed. 2014. *Elections Worth Dying For?: A Selection of Case Studies from Africa.* Washington, DC: IFES.

Dal Bó, E., P. Dal Bó, and R. di Tella. 2006. "'Plata o Plomo?': Bribe and Punishment in a Theory of Political Influence." *American Political Science Review* 100, no. 1: 41–53.

D'Anieri, Paul. 2005. "The Last Hurrah: The 2004 Ukrainian Presidential Elections and the Limits of Machine Politics." *Communist and Post-Communist Studies* 38: 231–49.

———. 2006. "Explaining the Success and Failure of Post-Communist Revolutions." *Communist and Post-Communist Studies* 39: 331–50.

Darnolf, Staffan, and Almami Cyllah. 2014. "EMBs and Electoral Violence." In *Elections Worth Dying For?: A Selection of Case Studies from Africa,* edited by Cyllah, 11–27. Washington, DC: IFES.

Davenport, Christian. 1997. "From Ballots to Bullets: An Empirical Assessment of How National Elections Influence State Uses of Political Repression." *Electoral Studies* 16, no. 4: 517–40.

Daxecker, Ursula. 2012. "The Cost of Exposing Cheating: International Election Monitoring, Fraud, and Post-Election Violence in Africa." *Journal of Peace Research* 49, no. 4: 503–16.

———. 2014. "All Quiet on Election Day?: International Election Observation and Incentives for Pre-election Violence in African Elections." *Electoral Studies* 34: 232–43.

———. 2020. "The Institutional Origins of Election Violence: Evidence from India." *Journal of Peace Research* 57, no. 1: 156–170.

Daxecker, Ursula, Elio Amicarelli, and Alexander Jung. 2019. "Electoral Contention and Violence (ECAV): A New Dataset." *Journal of Peace Research* 56, no. 5: 714–23.

Debrah, Emmanuel. 2011. "Measuring Governance Institutions' Success in Ghana: The Case of the Electoral Commission, 1993–2008." *African Studies* 70, no. 1: 25–45.

Della Porta, Donatella, and Alberto Vannucci. 1997. "The 'Perverse Effects' of Political Corruption." *Political Studies* 45, no. 3 (special issue): 516–38.

———. 1999. *Corrupt Exchanges: Actors, Resources, and Mechanisms of Political Corruption.* New York: Aldine de Gruyter.

Democracy Watch. 2010. "The 'Foot-Soldier' Phenomenon Revisited: Rewarding the Party versus Rewarding Ghanaians." *Democracy Watch* 8, no. 4: 6–8.

Dercon, Stefan, and Roxana Gutiérrez-Romero. 2012. "Triggers and Characteristics of the 2007 Kenyan Electoral Violence." *World Development* 40, no. 4: 731–44.

Devotta, Neil. 2003. "Sri Lanka's Political Decay: Analysing the October 2000 and December 2001 Parliamentary Elections." *Commonwealth and Comparative Politics* 41, no. 2: 115–42.

Diamond, Larry Jay. 2002. "Thinking about Hybrid Regimes." *Journal of Democracy* 13, no. 2: 21–35.

Dochev, Dilyan, and Gergely Ujhelyi. 2014. "What Do Corruption Indices Measure?" *Economics and Politics* 26, no. 2: 310–31.

Donno, Daniela. 2013. *Defending Democratic Norms: International Actors and the Politics of Electoral Misconduct.* New York: Oxford University Press.

Downs, Anthony. 1957. *An Economic Theory of Democracy*. New York: Harper and Row.

EC (European Commission). 2016. "Key Findings of the 2016 Report on the Former Yugoslav Republic of Macedonia." EC fact sheet, November 9, 2016. Brussels: EC. http://europa.eu /rapid/press-release_MEMO-16-3634_en.pdf.

EC-UNDP (European Commission–United Nations Development Programme) Joint Task Force on Electoral Assistance. 2011. *Thematic Workshop on Elections, Violence and Conflict Prevention*. 2nd ed. Brussels: Joint Task Force on Electoral Assistance. https://www.ec-undp -electoralassistance.org/wp-content/uploads/2018/08/ec-undp-jtf-04-our-trainings-2011 -barcelona-day-1-2-teresa-polara.pdf.

Edmonds, Kevin. 2016. "Guns, Gangs and Garrison Communities in the Politics of Jamaica." *Race and Class* 57, no. 4: 54–74.

Egorov, Georgy, Sergei Guriev, and Konstantin Sonin. 2009. "Why Resource-Poor Dictators Allow Freer Media: A Theory and Evidence from Panel Data." *American Political Science Review* 103, no. 4: 645–68.

EISA (Electoral Institute of South Africa). 2006. *EISA Election Observer Mission Report No 22: Zanzibar Presidential, House of Representatives and Local Government Elections 30 October 2005*. Johannesburg: EISA.

Eisenstadt, Todd A. 1999. "Off the Street and into the Courtrooms: Resolving Postelectoral Conflicts in Mexico." In *The Self-Restraining State: Power and Accountability in New Democracies*, edited by Andreas Schedler, Larry Diamond, and Marc F. Plattner, 83–104. Boulder, CO: Lynne Rienner.

———. 2006. "Mexico's Postelectoral Concertacesiones: The Rise and Demise of a Substitutive Informal Institution." In *Informal Institutions and Democracy: Lessons from Latin America*, edited by Gretchen Helmke and Steven Levitsky, 227–48. Baltimore: Johns Hopkins University Press.

EU (European Union). 2001. *EU Election Observation Mission to Sri Lanka: Final Report of the European Union's Observation Mission to Sri Lanka's December 5, 2001 Parliamentary Election*. Brussels: EU.

———. 2002. *Pakistan National and Provincial Assembly Election 10 October 2002: European Union Election Observation Mission Final Report*. Brussels: EU.

———. 2004. *Sri Lanka Parliamentary Elections 2 April 2004: European Union Election Observation Mission*. Brussels: EU.

———. 2005. *Ethiopia Legislative Elections 2005: European Union Election Observation Mission Final Report*. Brussels: EU.

———. 2008. *Islamic Republic of Pakistan Final Report: National and Provincial Assembly Elections 18 February 2008*. Brussels: EU.

———. 2010. *European Union Election Observation Mission to Tanzania General Elections October 2010: Final Report*. Brussels: EU.

———. 2013. *European Union Election Observation Mission: Islamic Republic of Pakistan Final Report: General Elections 11 May 2013*. Brussels: EU.

———. 2015. *European Union Election Observation Mission: Republic of Tanzania: Final Report General Elections of 2015*. Brussels: EU.

———. 2017. *Presidential and Legislative Elections 2017: European Union Election Observation Mission to Timor-Leste 2017*. Brussels: EU.

———. 2018. *Final Report: European Union Election Observation Mission Islamic Republic of Pakistan: General Elections 25 July 2018*. Brussels: EU.

Fearon, James D. 1995. "Rationalist Explanations for War." *International Organization* 49, no. 3: 379–414.

———. 2011. "Self-Enforcing Democracy." *Quarterly Journal of Economics* 126: 1661–708.

Fein, Helen. 1995. "More Murder in the Middle: Life-Integrity Violations and Democracy in the World, 1987." *Human Rights Quarterly* 17, no. 1: 170–91.

Figueroa, M., and A. Sives. 2002. "Homogenous Voting, Electoral Manipulation and the 'Garrison' Process in Post-Independence Jamaica." *Commonwealth and Comparative Politics* 40, no. 1: 81–108.

Fischer, Jeffrey. 2002. *Electoral Conflict and Violence: A Strategy for Study and Prevention*. Washington, DC: IFES. https://www.ifes.org/publications/electoral-conflict-and-violence-strategy-study-and-prevention.

———. 2016. "Getting away with Murder: When Electoral Violence Becomes a Crime against Humanity." Working paper, Project on Explaining and Mitigating Electoral Violence. http://www.electoralviolenceproject.com/pubviolence/.

———. 2017a. "National Commissions of Inquiry into Electoral Violence: A Study of Practices and Outcomes." Working paper, Project on Explaining and Mitigating Electoral Violence. http://www.electoralviolenceproject.com/pubviolence/.

———. 2017b. "Social Enforcement of Electoral Security." Working paper, Project on Explaining and Mitigating Electoral Violence. http://www.electoralviolenceproject.com/pubviolence/.

Fisman, Ray, and Miriam A. Golden. 2017. *Corruption: What Everyone Needs to Know*. Oxford: Oxford University Press.

Fjelde, Hanne. 2020. "Political Party Strength and Electoral Violence." *Journal of Peace Research* 57, no. 1: 140–155

Fjelde, Hanne, and Kristine Höglund. 2016. "Electoral Institutions and Electoral Violence in Sub-Saharan Africa." *British Journal of Political Science* 46, no. 2: 297–320.

———. 2018. "Ethnic Politics and Elite Competition: The Roots of Electoral Violence in Kenya." In *Violence in African Elections: Between Democracy and Big Man Politics*, edited by Mimmi Söderberg Kovacs and Jesper Bjarnesen, 27–46. Uppsala: Nordic Africa Institute.

Fleischhacker, H. 1999. "Congo (Brazzaville)." In *Elections in Africa: A Data Handbook*, edited by D. Nohlen, M. Krennerich and B. Thibaut, 259–80. Oxford: Oxford University Press.

Flores, Thomas, and Irfan Nooruddin. 2012. "The Effect of Elections on Postconflict Peace and Reconstruction." *Journal of Politics* 74, no. 2: 558–70.

———. 2016. *Elections in Hard Times: Building Stronger Democracies in the 21st Century*. Cambridge: Cambridge University Press.

———. 2018. "Elections in War and Peace." Paper presented at the Electoral Violence Workshop, University of Amsterdam, February 15–16, 2018.

Frantz, Erika, and Andrea Kendall-Taylor. 2014. "A Dictator's Toolkit: Understanding How Co-optation Affects Repression in Autocracies." *Journal of Peace Research* 51, no. 3: 332–46.

Frye, Timothy, Ora John Reuter, and David Szakonyi. 2014. "Political Machines at Work: Voter Mobilization and Electoral Subversion in the Workplace." *World Politics* 66, no. 2: 195–228.

———. 2018. "Hitting Them with Carrots: Voter Intimidation and Vote Buying in Russia." *British Journal of Political Science* 49, no. 3: 857–81. Published online ahead of print. doi:10.1017/S0007123416000752.

Fuiji, Lee A. 2009. *Killing Neighbors: Webs of Violence in Rwanda*. Ithaca, NY: Cornell University Press.

Gandhi, Jennifer. 2008. *Political Institutions under Dictatorships*. Cambridge: Cambridge University Press.

Gandhi, Jennifer, and Ellen Lust-Okar. 2009. "Elections under Authoritarianism." *Annual Review of Political Science* 12: 403–22.

Gandhi, Jennifer, and Adam Przeworski. 2007. "Authoritarian Institutions and the Survival of Autocrats." *Comparative Political Studies* 40, no. 11: 1279–301.

Gazdar, Haris, and Hussain Bux Mallah. 2013. "Informality and Political Violence in Karachi." *Urban Studies* 50, no. 15: 3099–115.

GCEDS (Global Commission on Elections, Democracy and Security). 2012. *Deepening Democracy: A Strategy for Improving the Integrity of Elections Worldwide*. Stockholm: International IDEA. https://www.idea.int/publications/catalogue/deepening-democracy-strategy-improving -integrity-elections-worldwide.

Geddes, Barbara. 1999. "What Do We Know about Democratization after Twenty Years?" *Annual Review of Political Science* 2: 115–44.

George, Alan. 2003. *Syria: Neither Bread nor Freedom*. London: Zed Books.

Goldring, Edward, and Michael Wahman. 2018. "Fighting for a Name on the Ballot: Constituency-Level Analysis of Nomination Violence in Zambia." *Democratization* 25, no. 6: 996–1015.

Goldsmith, A. J. 2015. "Electoral Violence in Africa Revisited." *Terrorism and Political Violence* 27, no. 5: 818–37.

González-Ocantos, Ezequiel, Chad P. Kiewiet de Jonge, Carlos Meléndez, David Nickerson, and Javier Osorio. 2020. "Carrots and Sticks: Experimental Evidence of Vote Buying and Voter Intimidation in Guatemala." *Journal of Peace Research* 57, no. 1: 46–61.

Goodwin-Gill, Guy S. 1994. *Free and Fair Elections*. Geneva: Inter-Parliamentary Union.

———. 1998. *Codes of Conduct for Elections*. Geneva: Inter-Parliamentary Union.

Grömping, Max. 2017. "Transparent Elections: Domestic Election Monitors, Agenda-building, and Electoral Integrity." PhD thesis, University of Sydney.

Gutiérrez-Romero, Roxana. 2014. "An Inquiry into the Use of Illegal Electoral Practices and Effects of Political Violence and Vote Buying." *Journal of Conflict Resolution* 58, no. 8: 1500–1527.

Gutiérrez-Romero, Roxana, and Adrienne LeBas. 2020. "Does Electoral Violence Affect Voting Choice and Willingness to Vote?: Evidence from a Vignette Experiment." *Journal of Peace Research* 57, no. 1: 77–92.

Gyimah-Boadi, Emmanuel. 1998. "Managing Electoral Conflicts: Lessons from Ghana." In *Elections and Conflict Management in Africa*, edited by Timothy D. Sisk and Andrew Reynolds, 101–17. Washington, DC: United States Institute of Peace.

———. 1999. "Institutionalizing Credible Elections in Ghana." In *The Self-Restraining State: Power and Accountability in New Democracies*, edited by Andreas Schedler, Larry Diamond, and Marc F. Plattner, 105–21. Boulder, CO: Lynne Rienner.

Gyimah-Boadi, Emmanuel, and H. Kwasi Pempel. 2012. "Oil, Politics and Ghana's Democracy." *Journal of Democracy* 23, no. 3: 94–108.

Hafner-Burton, Emilie, Susan D. Hyde, and Ryan S. Jablonski. 2014. "When Do Governments Resort to Election Violence?" *British Journal of Political Science* 44, no. 1: 149–79.

———. 2018. "Surviving Elections: Election Violence, Incumbent Victory, and Post-Election Repercussions." *British Journal of Political Science*, 48, no. 2: 459–88.

Hagmann, Tobias. 2012. "Fishing for Votes in the Somali Region: Clan Elders, Bureaucrats and Party Politics." In *Contested Power in Ethiopia: Traditional Authorities and Multi-Party Elections*, edited by Kjetil Tronvoll and Hagmann, 61–88. Leiden: Brill.

Hale, Henry E. 2005. "Regime Cycles: Democracy and Autocracy and Revolution in Post-Soviet Eurasia." *World Politics* 58, no. 1: 133–65.

———. 2006. "Democracy or Autocracy on the March?: The Colored Revolutions as Normal Dynamics of Patronal Presidentialism." *Communist and Post-Communist Studies* 39: 305–29.

Hall, Stephen G. F., and Thomas Ambrosio. 2017. "Authoritarian Learning: A Conceptual Overview." *East European Politics* 33, no. 2: 143–61.

Harish, S. P., and Andrew L. Little. 2017. "The Political Violence Cycle." *American Political Science Review* 111, no. 2: 237–55.

Harish, S. P., and Risa Toha. 2017. "A New Typology of Electoral Violence: Insights from Indonesia." *Terrorism and Political Violence* 31, no. 4: 687–711. Published online ahead of print. doi :10.1080/09546553.2016.1277208.

———.2018. "Bundled Violence: Evidence from Sub-Saharan Africa." Paper presented at the Electoral Violence Workshop, University of Amsterdam, February 15–16, 2018.

Hartlyn, J., J. McCoy, and T.M. Mustillo. 2008. "Electoral Governance Matters: Explaining Electoral Outcomes in Contemporary Latin America." *Comparative Political Studies* 41, no. 1: 73–98.

Hartmann, Christoph. 1999. "Côte d'Ivoire." In *Elections in Africa: A Data Handbook*, edited by Dieter Nohlen, Michael Krennerich and Bernhard Thibaut, 302–14. Oxford: Oxford University Press.

Hartmann, Christof, Graham Hassall, and Soliman M. Santos Jr. 2001. "Philippines." In *Elections in Asia and the Pacific: A Handbook*, vol. 2, *South East Asia, East Asia and the South Pacific*, edited by Dieter Nohlen, Florian Grotz, and Christof Hartmann, 186–238. Oxford: Oxford University Press.

Hayward, Fred M., and Siba N. Grovogui. 1987. "Persistence and Change in the Senegalese Electoral Process." In *Elections in Independent Africa*, edited by Hayward, 239–70. Boulder, CO: Westview.

Hegre, Håvard, Tanja Ellingsen, Scott Gates, and Nils Petter Gleditsch. 2001. "Towards a Democratic Civil Peace?" *American Political Science Review* 95, no. 1: 33–48.

Helmke, Gretchen, and Steven Levitsky. 2004. "Informal Institutions: A Comparative Politics Research Agenda." *Perspectives on Politics* 2, no. 4: 725–40.

———. 2006. Introduction to *Informal Institutions and Democracy: Lessons from Latin America*, edited by Helmke and Levitsky, 1–30. Baltimore: Johns Hopkins University Press.

Herron, Erik S. 2009. *Elections and Democracy after Communism?* Basingstoke, UK: Palgrave-Macmillan.

Hesli, Vicki L. 2006. "The Orange Revolution: 2004 Presidential Election(s) in Ukraine." *Electoral Studies* 25: 147–91.

Heydemann, Steven, and Reinoud Leenders. 2011. "Authoritarian Learning and Authoritarian Resilience: Regime Responses to the 'Arab Awakening.'" *Globalizations* 8, no. 5: 647–53.

Hickman, John. 2009. "Is Electoral Violence Effective?: Evidence from Sri Lanka's 2005 Presidential Election." *Contemporary South Asia* 17, no. 4: 429–35.

Hidalgo, F. Daniel, and Simeon Nichter. 2016. "Voter Buying: Shaping the Electorate through Clientelism." *American Journal of Political Science* 60, no. 2: 436–55.

Hirschman, Albert O. 1970. *Exit, Voice and Loyalty*. Cambridge, MA: Harvard University Press.

Höglund, Kristine. 2009. "Electoral Violence in Conflict-Ridden Societies: Concepts, Causes, and Consequences." *Terrorism and Political Violence* 21: 412–27.

Höglund, Kristine, Anna K. Jarstad, and Mimmi Söderberg Kovacs. 2009. "The Predicament of Elections in War-Torn Societies." *Democratization* 16, no. 3: 530–57.

Höglund, Kristine, and Anton Piyarathne. 2009. "Paying the Price for Patronage: Electoral Violence in Sri Lanka." *Commonwealth and Comparative Politics* 47, no. 3: 287–307.

Hoppen, K. Theodore. 1996. "Priests at the Hustings: Ecclesiastical Electioneering in Nineteenth Century Ireland." In *Elections before Democracy: The History of Elections in Europe and Latin America*, edited by Eduardo Posada-Carbó, 117–38. Basingstoke, UK: Macmillan.

Howard, Marc M., and Phillip G. Roessler. 2006. "Liberalizing Electoral Outcomes in Competitive Authoritarian Regimes." *American Journal of Political Science* 50, no. 2: 365–81.

Human Rights Watch. 2017. "Spain: Police Used Excessive Force in Catalonia." Human Rights Watch, October 12, 2017. https://www.hrw.org/news/2017/10/12/spain-police-used-excessive-force-catalonia.

Huntington, Samuel. 1991. *The Third Wave: Democratization in the Late Twentieth Century* Norman: University of Oklahoma Press.

Hyde, Susan. 2011. *The Pseudo-Democrat's Dilemma: Why Election Observation Became an International Norm*. Ithaca, NY: Cornell University Press.

Hyde, Susan, and Nikolai Marinov. 2012. "Which Elections Can Be Lost?" *Political Analysis* 20, no. 2: 191–210.

———. 2015. "NELDA 4.0: National Elections across Democracy and Autocracy Dataset Codebook for Version 4." http://hyde.research.yale.edu/nelda/.

ICG (International Crisis Group). 2011. *A Critical Period for Ensuring Stability in Côte d'Ivoire.* Africa Report no. 176. Brussels: ICG. https://www.crisisgroup.org/africa/west-africa /c%C3%B4te-divoire/critical-period-ensuring-stability-cote-d-ivoire.

Ichino, Nahomi, and Matthias Schündeln. 2012. "Deterring or Displacing Electoral Irregularities?: Spillover Effects of Observers in a Randomized Field Experiment in Ghana." *Journal of Politics* 74, no. 1: 292–307.

Inglehart, R., C. Haerpfer, A. Moreno, C. Welzel, K. Kizilova, J. Diez-Medrano, M. Lagos, et al., eds. 2014. *World Values Survey: Round Six—Country-Pooled Datafile Version: http://www .worldvaluessurvey.org/WVSDocumentationWV6.jsp.* Madrid: JD Systems Institute.

International IDEA (International Institute for Democracy and Electoral Assistance). 2009. *Towards a Global Framework for Managing and Mitigating Election-Related Conflict and Violence.* Stockholm: International IDEA. http://aceproject.org/ero-en/misc/towards-a-global -framework-for-managing-and.

———. 2011. *Guide on Internal Factors: The Guide on Factors of Election-Related Violence Internal to Electoral Processes.* Stockholm: International IDEA.

———. 2014. "Electoral Justice Database." International IDEA. Accessed October 18, 2019. https:// www.idea.int/data-tools/data/electoral-justice.

———. 2016. *Electoral Risk Management Tool.* Stockholm: International IDEA.

———. 2018. "Electoral Management Design Database." International IDEA. Accessed October 18, 2019. https://www.idea.int/data-tools/data/electoral-management-design.

Ishiyama, John, Amalia Pulido Gomez, and Brandon Stewart. 2016. "Does Conflict Lead to Ethnic Particularism?: Electoral Violence and Ethnicity in Kenya 2005–2008." *Nationalism and Ethnic Politics* 22, no. 3: 300–321.

Johnston, Michael. 2005. *Syndromes of Corruption: Wealth, Power and Democracy.* Cambridge: Cambridge University Press.

———. 2014. *Corruption, Contention and Reform: The Power of Deep Democratization.* Cambridge: Cambridge University Press.

Kahneman, Daniel, and Amos Tversky. 2000. "Prospect Theory: An Analysis of Decision under Risk." In *Choices, Values, and Frames*, edited by Kahneman and Tversky, 17–43. Cambridge: Russell Sage Foundation and Cambridge University Press.

Kalandadze, Katya, and Mitchell A. Orenstein. 2009. "Electoral Protests and Democratization: Beyond the Color Revolutions." *Comparative Political Studies* 42, no. 11: 1403–25.

Kalyvas, Stathis N. 2006. *The Logic of Violence in Civil War.* Cambridge: Cambridge University Press.

Kammerud, Lisa. 2011. "Merging Conflict Management with Electoral Practice: The IFES Experience." In *Elections in Dangerous Places: Democracy and the Paradoxes of Peacebuilding*, edited by David Gillies, 147–70. Montreal: McGill-Queen's University Press.

Kaufmann, Daniel, and Aart Kraay. 2016. "Worldwide Governance Indicators." World Bank. Accessed October 18, 2019. http://www.govindicators.org.

Kelley, Judith G. 2012. *Monitoring Democracy: When International Election Observation Works, and Why It Often Fails.* Princeton, NJ: Princeton University Press.

Khan, Faraz. 2015. "MQM Workers Attack PTI's Election Camp in Karachi." *Express Tribune* (Pakistan), April 4, 2015. https://tribune.com.pk/story/864111/mqm-attacks-ptis-election -camp-in-karachi/.

Kitschelt, Herbert, and Steven I. Wilkinson. 2007. "Citizen-Politician Linkages: An Introduction." In *Patrons, Clients and Policies: Patterns of Democratic Accountability and*

Political Competition, edited by Kitschelt and Wilkinson, 1–49. Cambridge: Cambridge University Press.

Klaus, Kathleen, and Matthew I. Mitchell. 2015. "Land Grievances and the Mobilization of Electoral Violence: Evidence from Cote d'Ivoire and Kenya." *Journal of Peace Research* 52, no. 5: 622–35.

Kongkirati, Prajak. 2014. "The Rise and Fall of Electoral Violence in Thailand: Changing Rules, Structures and Power Landscapes, 1997–2011." *Contemporary Southeast Asia* 36, no. 3: 386–416.

Krause, Jana. 2018. "Patterns of Sexual Violence in Election-Related Communal Conflict: A Comparison of Kenya and Nigeria." Paper presented at the Electoral Violence Workshop, University of Amsterdam, February 15–16, 2018.

Kriger, Norma. 2005. "ZANU(PF) Strategies in General Elections, 1980–2000: Discourse and Coercion." *African Affairs* 104, no. 414: 1–34.

Kuhn, Patrick. 2015: "Do Contentious Elections Trigger Violence?" In *Contentious Elections: From Ballots to Barricades*, edited by Pippa Norris, Richard Frank, and Ferran Martínez i Coma, 89–110. New York: Routledge.

Kuhn, Patrick, and Inken von Borzyskowski. 2020. "Dangerously Informed: Voter Information and Pre-electoral Violence in Africa." *Journal of Peace Research* 57, no. 1: 15–29.

Kumar, Krishna, and Marina Ottoway. 1998. "General Conclusions and Priorities for Policy Research." In *Postconflict Elections, Democratization and International Assistance*, edited by Kumar, 229–37. Boulder, CO: Lynne Rienner.

Kuntz, Philipp, and Mark R. Thompson. 2009. "More than Just the Final Straw: Stolen Elections as Revolutionary Triggers." *Comparative Politics* 41, no. 3: 253–72.

Kuzio, Taras. 2005. "From Kuchma to Yushchenko: Ukraine's 2004 Presidential Elections and the Orange Revolution." *Problems of Post-Communism* 52, no. 2: 29–44.

Lambert, Peter. 2000. "A Decade of Electoral Democracy: Continuity, Change and Crisis in Paraguay." *Bulletin of Latin American Research* 19: 379–96.

Larreguy, Horacio, John Marshall, and Pablo Querubín. 2016. "Parties, Brokers, and Voter Mobilization: How Turnout Buying Depends upon the Party's Capacity to Monitor Brokers." *American Political Science Review* 110, no. 1: 160–79.

Latif, Omayma Abdel. 2007. "Syria: Elections without Politics." *Arab Reform Bulletin* 5, no. 3. https://carnegieendowment.org/publications/index.cfm?fa=view&id=19113#latif.

LeBas, Adrienne. 2006. "Polarization as Craft: Party Formation and State Violence in Zimbabwe." *Comparative Politics* 39, no. 4: 419–48.

Ledeneva, Alena. 2006. *How Russia Really Works: The Informal Practices that Shaped Post-Soviet Politics and Business*. Ithaca, NY: Cornell University Press.

Lehoucq, Fabrice Edouard. 1995. "Institutional Change and Political Conflict: Evaluating Alternative Explanations of Electoral Reform in Costa Rica." *Electoral Studies* 14, no. 1: 23–45.

———. 2004. "Costa Rica: Modifying Majoritarianism with 40 Per Cent Threshold." In *Handbook of Electoral System Choice*, edited by Josep M. Colomer, 133–44. Basingstoke, UK: Palgrave-Macmillan.

Levitsky, Steven, and Lucan Way. 2010. *Competitive Authoritarianism: Hybrid Regimes after the Cold War*. Cambridge: Cambridge University Press.

Lewis, David. 2010. "Kyrgyzstan." In *The Colour Revolutions in the Former Soviet Republics: Successes and Failures*, edited by Donnacha Ó Beachain and Abel Polese, 45–61. New York: Routledge.

Linantud, John L. 1998. "Whither Guns, Goons, and Gold?: The Decline of Factional Election Violence in the Philippines." *Contemporary Southeast Asia* 20, no. 3: 298–318.

Lindberg, Staffan I. 2006. *Democracy and Elections in Africa*. Baltimore: Johns Hopkins University Press.

———. 2009. "A Theory of Elections as a Mode of Transition." In Staffan Lindberg (ed.). *Democratization by Elections: A New Mode of Transition?* edited by Lindberg, 314–41. Baltimore: Johns Hopkins University Press.

Linke, Andrew M., Frank D. W. Witmer, and John O'Loughlin. 2012. "Space-Time Granger Analysis of the War in Iraq: A Study of Coalition and Insurgent Action-Reaction." *International Interactions: Empirical and Theoretical Research in International Relations* 38, no. 4: 402–25.

Little, Andrew T., Joshua A. Tucker, and Tom LaGatta. 2015. "Elections, Protest, and Alternation of Power." *Journal of Politics* 77, no. 4: 1142–56.

López-Pintor, Rafael. 1998. "Nicaragua's Measured Move to Democracy." In *Postconflict Elections, Democratization and International Assistance*, edited by Krishna Kumar, 39–55. Boulder, CO: Lynne Rienner.

———. 2000. *Electoral Management Bodies as Institutions of Governance*. New York: Bureau for Development Policy, United Nations Development Programme.

Lupia, Arthur, and Mathew D. McCubbins. 1998. *The Democratic Dilemma: Can Citizens Learn What They Need to Know?* Cambridge: Cambridge University Press.

Lust-Okar, Ellen. 2005. *Structuring Conflict in the Arab World: Incumbents, Opponents, and Institutions*. Cambridge: Cambridge University Press.

Lyons, Terrence. 1999. *Voting for Peace: Postconflict Elections in Liberia*. Washington, DC: Brookings Institution.

———. 2005. *Ethiopia: Implications of the May 2005 Elections for Future Democratization Programs*. Washington, DC: IFES.

Macdonald, Geoffrey. 2016. "The Drivers of Election Violence in Bangladesh: Political Intransigence and Prevention Weakness." In *Electing Peace: Violence Prevention and Impact at the Polls*, edited by Jonas Claes, 31–62. Washington, DC: United States Institute of Peace.

Mac Giollabhui, Shane. 2018. "Battleground: Candidate Selection and Violence in Africa's Dominant Political Parties." *Democratization* 25, no. 6: 978–95.

Magaloni, Beatriz. 2006. *Voting for Autocracy: Hegemonic Party Survival and Its Demise in Mexico*. Cambridge: Cambridge University Press.

———. 2010. "The Game of Electoral Fraud and the Ousting of Authoritarian Rule." *American Journal of Political Science* 54, no. 3: 751–65.

Maingot, Anthony P. 1992. "Haiti and Aristide: The Legacy of History." *Current History* 91: 65–69.

Malesky, Edmund, and Paul Schuler. 2011. "The Single-Party Dictator's Dilemma: Information in Elections without Opposition." *Legislative Studies Quarterly* 36, no. 4: 491–530.

Malik, Aditi. 2018. "Constitutional Reform and New Patterns of Electoral Violence: Evidence from Kenya's 2013 Elections." *Commonwealth and Comparative Politics* 56, no. 3: 340–59.

Mansfield, Edward D., and Jack Snyder. 2005. *Electing to Fight: Why Emerging Democracies Go to War*. Cambridge, MA: MIT Press.

Mares, Isabela. 2015. *From Open Secrets to Secret Votes: Democratic Electoral Reforms and Voter Autonomy*. Cambridge: Cambridge University Press.

Mares, Isabela, and Lauren Young. 2016. "Buying, Expropriating, and Stealing Votes." *Annual Review of Political Science* 19: 267–88.

Marshall, Monty G., Ted Robert Gurr, and Keith Jaggers. 2016. "POLITY IV Project Political Regime Characteristics and Transitions, 1800–2015 Dataset Users' Manual." Center for Systemic Peace. Accessed August 22, 2016. http://www.systemicpeace.org/inscr/p4manualv2015.pdf.

Matanock, Aila. M. 2017a. "Bullets for Ballots: Examining the Effect of Electoral Participation on Conflict Recurrence." *International Security* 41, no. 4: 93–132.

———. 2017b. *Electing Peace: From Civil Conflict to Political Participation.* Cambridge: Cambridge University Press.

McCargo, Duncan, and Petra Desatová. 2016. "Thailand: Electoral Intimidation." In *Electing Peace: Violence Prevention and Impact at the Polls,* edited by Jonas Claes, 63–96. Washington, DC: United States Institute of Peace.

McCoy, Jennifer. 1998. "Monitoring and Mediating Elections during Latin American Democratization." In *Electoral Observation and Democratic Transitions in Latin America,* edited by Kevin J. Middlebrook, 53–90. La Jolla, CA: Center for US–Mexican Studies and University of California, San Diego.

McDermott, Rose, James H. Fowler, and Oleg Smirnov. 2008. "On the Evolutionary Origin of Prospect Theory Preferences." *Journal of Politics* 70, no. 2: 335–50.

McDonald, Laughlin. 2003. *A Voting Rights Odyssey: Black Enfranchisement in Georgia.* Cambridge: Cambridge University Press.

Meier, Patrick, Doug Bond, and Joe Bond. 2007. "Environmental Influences on Pastoral Conflict in the Horn of Africa." *Political Geography* 26: 716–35.

Mignozzetti, Umberto, and Renard Sexton. 2018. "Predatory Elections: How Norms of Democracy and the Rural Economy Incentivize Electoral Violence and Fraud." Working paper. Accessed October 18, 2019. https://www.dropbox.com/s/5rwea4e3z2a8dm8/state_formation_federalism.pdf?dl=0.

Min, Brian. 2015. *Power and the Vote: Elections and Electricity in the Developing World.* Cambridge: Cambridge University Press.

Mitchell, Neil J., and James M. McCormick. 1988. "Economic and Political Explanations of Human Rights Violations." *World Politics* 40, no. 4: 476–98.

Mjåtvedt, Annie-Lise. 2006. *Zanzibar Presidential and House of Representative Elections October 2005.* Nordem Report 5/2006. Oslo: Nordem.

Mochtak, Michal. 2018a. *Electoral Violence in the Western Balkans.* New York: Routledge.

———. 2018b. "Fighting and Voting: Mapping Electoral Violence in the Region of Post-Communist Europe." *Terrorism and Political Violence* 30, no. 4: 589–615.

Montinola, Gabriella, and Robert Jackman. 2002. "Sources of Corruption: A Cross-Country Study." *British Journal of Political Science* 32, no. 1: 147–70.

Moraski, Byron. 2009. "Judicial Complexity Empowering Opposition?: Critical Elections in Armenia and Georgia." In *Democratization by Elections: A New Mode of Transition,* edited by Staffan I. Lindberg, 269–88. Baltimore: Johns Hopkins University Press.

Mozaffar, Shaheen. 2002. "Patterns of Electoral Governance in Africa's Emerging Democracies." *International Political Science Review* 23, no. 1: 85–101.

Mozaffar, Shaheen, and Andreas Schedler. 2002. "The Comparative Study of Electoral Governance: An Introduction." *International Political Science Review* 23, no. 2: 5–27.

Mueller, Susanne D. 2011. "Dying to Win: Elections, Political Violence, and Institutional Decay in Kenya". *Journal of Contemporary African Studies* 29, no. 1: 99–117.

———. 2012. "The Political Economy of Kenya's Crisis." In *Voting in Fear: Electoral Violence in Sub-Saharan Africa,* edited by Dorina A. Bekoe, 145–80. Washington, DC: United States Institute of Peace.

Mundlack, Yair. 1978. "On the Pooling of Time Series and Cross Section Data." *Econometrica* 46, no. 1: 69–85.

Mungiu-Pippidi, Alina. 2015. "Good Governance Powers Innovation." *Nature* 518: 295–97.

Murray, Elizabeth. 2016. "Honduras: Unrealized Fears, Ordinary Violence." In *Electing Peace: Violence Prevention and Impact at the Polls,* edited by Jonas Claes, 165–94. Washington, DC: United States Institute of Peace.

Myagkov, Mikhail, Peter C. Ordeshook, and Dimitri Shakin. 2009. *The Forensics of Election Fraud: Russia and Ukraine.* Cambridge: Cambridge University Press.

Nagel, Beverly Y. 1999. "'Unleashing the Fury': The Cultural Discourse of Rural Violence and Land Rights in Paraguay." *Comparative Studies in Society and History* 41, no. 1: 148–81.

NDI (National Democratic Institute). 2011. "Macedonian Code of Conduct Asks 'What Mark Will We Leave?'" NDI website; published May 24, 2011; last updated May 26, 2011. http://www.ndi.org/macedonia-2011-code-of-conduct.

Nellis, Gareth, and Niloufer Siddiqui. 2018. "Secular Party Rule and Religious Violence in Pakistan." *American Political Science Review* 112, no. 1: 49–67.

Nicholls, David. 1998. "The Duvalier Regime in Haiti." In *Sultanistic Regimes*, edited by H. E. Chehabi and Juan J. Linz, 153–81. Baltimore: Johns Hopkins University Press.

Nickson, R. Andrew. 1988. "Tyranny and Longevity: Stroessner's Paraguay." *Third World Quarterly* 10, no. 1: 237–59.

———. 2009. "The General Election in Paraguay, April 2008." *Electoral Studies* 28: 141–73.

Nindorera, Willy, and Jesper Bjarnesen 2018. "The Geography of Violence in Burundi's 2015 Elections." In *Violence in African Elections: Between Democracy and Big Man Politics*, edited by Mimmi Söderberg Kovacs and Bjarnesen, 87–113. Uppsala: Nordic Africa Institute.

Norris, Pippa. 2014. *Why Electoral Integrity Matters*. Cambridge: Cambridge University Press.

———. 2015. *Why Elections Fail*. Cambridge: Cambridge University Press.

———. 2017. *Strengthening Electoral Integrity*. Cambridge: Cambridge University Press.

Norris, Pippa, Richard Frank, and Ferran Martínez i Coma. 2014. "Measuring Electoral Integrity around the World: A New Dataset." *PS: Political Science and Politics* 47, no. 4: 798–98.

———. 2015. "The Risks of Contentious Elections." In *Contentious Elections: From Ballots to Barricades*, edited by Norris, Frank, and Martínez i Coma, 133–49. New York: Routledge.

North, Douglass C., John Joseph Wallis, and Barry R. Weingast. 2009. *Violence and Social Orders: A Conceptual Framework for Interpreting Recorded Human History*. Cambridge: Cambridge University Press.

OAS (Organization of American States). 2000. *Electoral Observation in Haiti: Legislative, Municipal, and Local Elections February to July 2000*. Washington, DC: OAS.

———. 2008. *Final Report of the Electoral Observation Mission in Jamaica General Election 2007*. Washington, DC: OAS.

Ó Beachain, Donnacha. 2010. "Roses and Tulips: Dynamics of Regime Change in Georgia and Kyrgyzstan." In *Rethinking the "Coloured Revolutions,"* edited by David Lane and Stephen White, 87–114. London: Routledge.

Ó Beachain, Donnacha, and Abel Polese. 2010. "Introduction." In *The Colour Revolutions in the Former Soviet Republics*, edited by Ó Beachain and Polese, 1–12. New York: Routledge.

Oduro, Franklin. 2012. "Preventing Electoral Violence: Lesson from Ghana." In *Voting in Fear: Electoral Violence in Sub-Saharan Africa*, edited by Dorina A. Bekoe, 209–42. Washington, DC: United States Institute of Peace.

O'Neill, William G. 1993. "The Roots of Human Rights Violations in Haiti." *Georgetown Immigration Law Journal* 87, no. 7: 87–117.

Opitz, Christian, Hanne Fjelde, and Kristine Höglund. 2013. "Including Peace: The Influence of Electoral Management Bodies on Electoral Violence." *Journal of Eastern African Studies* 7, no. 4: 713–31.

Orozco-Henriquez, Jesus. 2010. *Electoral Justice: The International IDEA Handbook*. Stockholm: International IDEA.

OSCE-ODIHR (Organization for Security and Cooperation in Europe, Office for Democratic Institutions and Human Rights). 1998. *Parliamentary Elections in the Former Yugoslav Republic of Macedonia 18 October and 1 November*. Warsaw: OSCE.

———. 2000a. *Belarus Parliamentary Elections 15 and 29 October 2000: Technical Assessment Mission Final Report*. Warsaw: OSCE.

————. 2000b. *Former Yugoslav Republic of Macedonia Presidential Elections 31 October and 14 November: Final Report.* Warsaw: OSCE.

————. 2001. *Republic of Belarus Presidential Election 9 September 2001: OSCE/ODIHR Limited Election Observation Mission Final Report.* Warsaw: OSCE.

————. 2002. *Former Yugoslav Republic of Macedonia Parliamentary Elections 15 September 2002: OSCE/ODIHR Election Observation Mission Final Report.* Warsaw: OSCE.

————. 2004a. *Former Yugoslav Republic of Macedonia: Presidential Election 14 & 28 April 2004: OSCE/ODIHR Election Observation Mission Final Report.* Warsaw: OSCE.

————. 2004b. *Republic of Belarus Parliamentary Elections 17 October 2004: OSCE/ODIHR Election Observation Mission Final Report.* Warsaw: OSCE.

————. 2005a. *Kyrgyz Republic Presidential Election 10 July 2005: OSCE/ODIHR Election Observation Mission Final Report.* Warsaw: OSCE.

————. 2005b. *Ukraine Presidential Election 31 October, 21 November and 26 December 2004: OSCE/ODIHR Election Observation Mission Final Report.* Warsaw: OSCE.

————. 2006a. *Former Yugoslav Republic of Macedonia Parliamentary Elections 5 July 2006: OSCE/ODIHR Election Observation Mission Final Report.* Warsaw: OSCE.

————. 2006b. *Republic of Belarus Presidential Election 19 March 2006: OSCE/ODIHR Election Observation Mission Report.* Warsaw: OSCE.

————. 2008. *Former Yugoslav Republic of Macedonia Early Parliamentary Elections 1 June 2008: OSCE/ODIHR Election Observation Mission Final Report.* Warsaw: OSCE.

————. 2009. *Former Yugoslav Republic of Macedonia Presidential and Municipal Elections 22 March and 5 April 2009: OSCE/ODIHR Election Observation Mission Final Report.* Warsaw: OSCE.

————. 2011. *Former Yugoslav Republic of Macedonia Early Parliamentary Elections 5 June 2011: OSCE/ODIHR Election Observation Mission Final Report.* Warsaw: OSCE.

————. 2014. *Former Yugoslav Republic of Macedonia Presidential and Early Parliamentary Elections 13 and 27 April 2014: OSCE/ODIHR Election Observation Mission Final Report.* Warsaw: OSCE.

————. 2016. *Former Yugoslav Republic of Macedonia Early Parliamentary Elections 11 December 2016: OSCE/ODIHR Election Observation Mission Final Report.* Warsaw: OSCE.

Pak Institute for Peace Studies. 2013. *Parties, Candidates and Voters.* Islamabad: Pak Institute for Peace Studies.

Patino, Patrick, and Djorina Velasco. 2004. *Election Violence in the Philippines.* Manila: Friedrich Ebert Stiftung Philippine Office.

Perthes, Volker. 1992. "Syria's Parliamentary Elections: Remodeling Asad's Political Base." *Middle East Report* 174: 15–18, 35.

Pettersen, Espen, and Elisabeth Salvesen. 2006. *Ethiopia Parliamentary Election May 2005.* Nordem Report 9/2006. Oslo: Nordem.

Piccolino, Giulia. 2016. "One Step Forward, Two Steps Back? Côte d'Ivoire's 2015 Presidential Polls." *Africa Spectrum* 51, no. 1: 97–110.

Poe, Steven C., and C. Neal Tate. 1994. "Repression of Human Rights to Personal Integrity in the 1980s: A Global Analysis." *American Political Science Review* 88, no. 4: 853–72.

Pop-Eleches, Grigore, and Graeme B. Robertson. 2010. "Elections, Information and Political Change in the Post-Cold War Era." Working paper. Accessed October 18, 2019. https://www.princeton.edu/~gpop/Elections%20Info%20Pol%20Chg%20GPE%20GBR%20Dec%202010.pdf.

Popova, Maria. 2006. "Watchdogs or Attack Dogs? The Role of the Russian Courts and the Central Election Commission in the Resolution of Electoral Disputes." *Europe-Asia Studies* 58, no. 3: 391–414.

Pottie, David. 2002. "Party Strife and Political Impasse in Zanzibar's October 2000 Elections." *Representation* 38, no. 4: 340–50.

Powell, G. Bingham. 2000. *Elections as Instruments of Democracy: Majoritarian and Proportional Visions*. New Haven, CT: Yale University Press.

Pravda, Alex. 1978. "Elections in Communist Party States." In *Elections without Choice*, edited by Guy Hermet, Richard Rose, and Alain Rouquié, 169–95. London: Macmillan.

Quimpo, Nathan Gilbert. 2005. "Oligarchic Patrimonialism, Bossism, Electoral Clientelism, and Contested Democracy in the Philippines." *Comparative Politics* 37, no. 2: 229–50.

———. 2009. "The Philippines: Predatory Regime, Growing Authoritarian Features." *Pacific Review* 22, no. 3: 335–53.

Raleigh, C., A. Linke, H. Hegre, and J. Karlsen. 2010. "Introducing ACLED: An Armed Conflict Location and Event Dataset Special Data Feature." *Journal of Peace Research* 47, no. 5: 651–60.

Randrianja, Solofo. 2003. "'Be Not Afraid, Only Believe!': Madagascar 2002." *African Affairs* 102: 309–29.

Rauschenbach, Mascha, and Katrin Paula. 2019. "Intimidating Voters with Violence and Mobilizing Them with Clientelism." *Journal of Peace Research* 56, no. 5: 682–96. Published online ahead of print. doi:10.1177/0022343318822709.

Reeder, Bryce, and Edward Goldring. 2018. "Does Peacekeeping Lead to Peaceful Elections?: UN Peacekeeping and Election Violence." Working paper.

Reeder, Bryce W., and Merete Bech Seeberg. 2018. "Fighting Your Friends?: A Study of Intra-party Violence in Sub-Saharan Africa." *Democratization* 25, no. 6: 1033–51.

Reif, Megan. 2009. "Making Democracy Safe: Explaining the Causes, Rise, and Decline of Coercive Campaigning and Election Violence in Old and New Democracies." Paper presented at the Annual Meeting of the American Political Science Association, Toronto, September 3–6, 2009.

Reilly, Benjamin. 2001. *Democracy in Divided Societies: Electoral Engineering for Conflict Management*. Cambridge: Cambridge University Press.

———. 2011. "Understanding Elections in Conflict Situations." In *Elections in Dangerous Places: Democracy and the Paradoxes of Peacebuilding*, edited by David Gillies, 3–18. Montreal: McGill-Queen's University Press.

Reka, Armend. 2008. "The Ohrid Agreement: The Travails of Inter-ethnic Relations in Macedonia." *Human Rights Review* 9: 55–69.

Reno, William. 2011. *Warfare in Independent Africa*. Cambridge: Cambridge University Press.

Reuters. 2015. "Burundi's Nkurunziza Wins Presidential Vote Boycotted by Rivals." Reuters, July 24, 2015. https://www.reuters.com/article/us-burundi-election-results/burundis-nkurunziza-wins-presidential-vote-boycotted-by-rivals-idUSKCN0PY1TN20150724.

Riquelme, Marcial A. 1993. *Negotiating Democratic Corridors in Paraguay: The Report of the Latin American Studies Association Delegation to Observe the 1993 Paraguayan National Elections*. Pittsburgh, PA: Latin American Studies Association. https://www.lasaweb.org/uploads/reports/negotiatingparaguay.pdf.

Robinson, James A., and Ragnar Torvik. 2009. "The Real Swing Voter's Curse." *American Economic Review: Papers and Proceedings* 99, no. 2: 310–15.

Rodríguez, Marta, and Alfonso L. Congostrina. 2017. "La Generalitat cifra en 844 los atendidos por heridas y ataques de ansiedad." *El Pais*, October 2, 2017. https://elpais.com/ccaa/2017/10/01/catalunya/1506820036_546150.html.

Roessler, Philip G. 2005. "Donor-Induced Democratization and the Privatization of State Violence in Kenya and Rwanda." *Comparative Politics* 37, no. 2: 207–27.

Rose-Ackerman, Susan. 1999. *Corruption and Government: Causes, Consequences and Reform*. Cambridge: Cambridge University Press.

Rosenzweig, Steven C. 2016. "Dangerous Disconnect: Voter Backlash, Elite Misperception, and the Costs of Violence as an Electoral Tactic." Working paper.

Ross, Cameron. 2011. "Regional Elections and Electoral Authoritarianism in Russia." *Europe-Asia Studies* 63, no. 4: 641–61.

Rothstein, Bo. 2011. *The Quality of Government: Corruption, Social Trust, and Inequality in International Perspective.* Chicago: University of Chicago Press.

Rothstein, Bo, and Eric Uslaner. 2005. "All for All: Equality, Corruption and Social Trust." *World Politics* 58: 41–72.

Rothstein, Bo, and Aiysha Varraich. 2017. *Making Sense of Corruption.* Cambridge: Cambridge University Press.

Rouquié, Alain. 1978. "Clientelist Control and Authoritarian Contexts." In *Elections without Choice,* edited by G. Hermet, R. Rose, and A. Rouquié, 9–35. London: Macmillan.

Ruiz-Rufino, Rubén, and Sarah Birch. 2020. "The Effect of Alternation in Power on Electoral Intimidation in Democratising Regimes." *Journal of Peace Research* 57, no. 1: 126–139.

Saguier, Rubén Bareiro. 1979. "Paraguay: Culture of Fear." *Index on Censorship* 8, no. 1: 26–32.

Salehyan, Idean, Cullen S. Hendrix, Jesse Hamner, Christina Case, Christopher Linebarger, Emily Stull, and Jennifer Williams. 2012. "Social Conflict in Africa: A New Database." *International Interactions: Empirical and Theoretical Research in International Relations* 38, no. 4: 503–11.

Salehyan, Idean, and Christopher Linebarger. 2015. "Elections and Social Conflict in Africa, 1990–2009." *Studies in Comparative International Development* 50: 23–49.

Samoff, Joel. 1987. "Single-Party Competitive Elections in Tanzania." In *Elections in Independent Africa,* edited by Fred M. Hayward, 149–86. Boulder, CO: Westview.

Sampford, Charles, Arthur Shacklock, Carmel Connors, and Fredrik Galtung, eds. 2006. *Measuring Corruption.* Aldershot, UK: Ashgate.

SAS (Small Arms Survey). 2012. "Political Conflict and Vulnerabilities: Firearms and Electoral Violence in Kenya." *Small Arms Survey Issue Brief* 2 (December 2012). http://www.smallarmssurvey.org/fileadmin/docs/G-Issue-briefs/SAS-AV-IB2-electoral-violence-kenya.pdf.

Scarnecchia, Timothy. 2006. "The 'Fascist Cycle' in Zimbabwe, 2000–2005." *Journal of Southern African Studies* 32, no. 2: 221–37.

Schaffer, Frederic Charles, ed. 2007. *Elections for Sale: The Causes and Consequences of Vote Buying.* Boulder, CO: Lynne Rienner.

Schedler, Andreas. 2002a. "Elections without Democracy: The Menu of Manipulation." *Journal of Democracy* 13, no. 2: 36–50.

———. 2002b. "The Nested Game of Democratization by Elections." *International Political Science Review* 23, no. 1: 103–22.

———. 2006. "The Logic of Electoral Authoritarianism." In *Electoral Authoritarianism: The Dynamics of Unfree Competition,* edited by Schedler, 1–23. Boulder, CO: Lynne Rienner.

———. 2013. *The Politics of Uncertainty: Sustaining and Subverting Electoral Authoritarianism.* Oxford: Oxford University Press.

Schmitz, Afra. 2018. "'Once They All Pick Their Guns You Can Have Your Way': Campaigning and Talking about Violence in Northern Ghana." In *Violence in African Elections: Between Democracy and Big Man Politics,* edited by Mimmi Söderberg Kovacs and Jesper Bjarnesen, 233–49. Uppsala: Nordic Africa Institute.

Scott, J. C. 1969. "Corruption, Machine Politics and Political Change." *American Political Science Review* 63, no. 4: 1142–58.

Seeberg, Merete Bech, Michael Wahman, and Svend-Erik Skaaning. 2018. "Candidate Nomination, Intra-party Democracy, and Election Violence in Africa." *Democratization* 25, no. 6: 959–77.

Siddiqui, Niloufer Aamina. 2017. *Under the Gun: Political Parties and Violence in Pakistan.* PhD dissertation, Yale University.

Simpser, Alberto. 2013. *Why Governments and Parties Manipulate Elections: Theory, Practice, and Implications.* Cambridge: Cambridge University Press.

Sisk, Timothy. 2012. "Evaluating Election-Related Violence: Nigeria and Sudan in Comparative Perspective." In *Voting in Fear: Electoral Violence in Sub-Saharan Africa*, edited by Dorina A. Bekoe, 39–74. Washington, DC: United States Institute of Peace.

Sives, Amanda. 2010. *Elections, Violence and the Democratic Process in Jamaica 1944–2007*. Kingston, Jamaica: Ian Randle.

Sjögren, Anders. 2018. "Wielding the Stick Again: The Rise and Fall and Rise of State Violence During Presidential Elections in Uganda." In *Violence in African Elections: Between Democracy and Big Man Politics*, edited by Mimmi Söderberg Kovacs and Jesper Bjarnesen, 47–66. Uppsala: Nordic Africa Institute.

Smidt, Hannah. 2016. "From a Perpetrator's Perspective: International Election Observers and Post-electoral Violence." *Journal of Peace Research* 53, no. 2: 226–41.

———. 2020. "UN Peacekeeping, Informal Institutions and Intercommunal Election Violence: A Quantitative Case Study of Côte d'Ivoire." *Journal of Peace Research* 57, no. 1: 199–216.

Snyder, Jack. 2000. *From Voting to Violence: Democratization and Nationalist Conflict*. New York: W. W. Norton.

Snyder, Richard. 1992. "Explaining Transitions from Neopatrimonial Dictatorships." *Comparative Politics* 24, no. 4: 379–99.

Söderberg Kovacs, Mimmi. 2018. "Introduction: The Everyday Politics of Electoral Violence in Africa." In *Violence in African Elections: Between Democracy and Big Man Politics*, edited by Söderberg Kovacs and Jesper Bjarnesen, 1–25. Uppsala: Nordic Africa Institute.

Söderström, Johanna. 2017. "Fear of Electoral Violence and Its Impact on Political Knowledge in Sub-Saharan Africa." *Political Studies* 66, no. 4: 869–86. Published online ahead of print. doi:10.1177/0032321717742835.

Solijonov, Abdurashid. 2016. *Electoral Justice Regulations around the World: Key Findings from International IDEA's Global Research on Electoral Dispute-Resolution Systems*. Stockholm: International IDEA.

Soroka, Stuart N., and Christopher Wlezien. 2010. *Degrees of Democracy: Politics, Public Opinion, and Policy*. Cambridge: Cambridge University Press.

Staino, Sara. 2011. "Preventing and Mitigating Election-Related Conflict and Violence: The Role of Electoral Justice." In *Elections in Dangerous Places: Democracy and the Paradoxes of Peacebuilding*, edited by David Gillies, 171–89. Montreal: McGill-Queens University Press.

Staniland, Paul. 2014. "Review Article: Violence and Democracy." *Comparative Politics* 47, no. 1: 99–118.

———. 2015. "Armed Groups and Militarized Elections". *International Studies Quarterly* 59: 694–705.

Staveley, E. S. 1972. *Greek and Roman Voting and Elections*. London: Thames and Hudson.

Steele, Abbey. 2011. "Electing Displacement: Political Cleansing in Apartado, Colombia." *Journal of Conflict Resolution* 55, no. 3: 423–45.

Steele, Abbey, and Livia I. Schubiger. 2018. "Democracy and Civil War: The Case of Colombia." *Conflict Management and Peace Science* 35, no. 6: 587–600.

Stockemer, Daniel, Bernadette LaMontagne, and Lyle Scruggs. 2013. "Bribes and Ballots: The Impact of Corruption on Voter Turnout in Democracies." *International Political Science Review* 34, no. 1: 74–90.

Stokes, Susan C. 2005. "Perverse Accountability: A Formal Model of Machine Politics with Evidence from Argentina." *American Political Science Review* 99, no. 3: 315–25.

Stokes, Susan, Thad Dunning, Marcela Nazareno, and Valeria Brusco. 2013. *Brokers, Voters and Clientelism: The Puzzle of Distributing Politics*. Cambridge: Cambridge University Press.

Straus, Scott. 2011. "Briefing: 'It's Sheer Horror Here': Patterns of Violence during the First Four Months of Cote d'Ivoire's Post-Electoral Crisis." *African Affairs* 110, no. 440: 481–89.

Straus, Scott, and Charlie Taylor. 2009. "Democratization and Electoral Violence in Sub-Saharan Africa, 1990–2007." Paper delivered at the Annual Meeting of the American Political Science Association, September 3–6, 2009.

———. 2012. "Democratization and Electoral Violence in Sub-Saharan Africa, 1990–2008." In *Voting in Fear: Electoral Violence in Sub-Saharan Africa*, edited by Dorina A. Bekoe, 15–38. Washington, DC: United States Institute of Peace.

Sundström, Aksel. 2016. "Violence and the Costs of Honesty: Rethinking Bureaucrats' Choices to Take Bribes." *Public Administration* 94: 593–608.

Svolik, Milan W., and Svitlana Chernyk. 2012. "Third-Party Actors and the Success of Democracy: How Electoral Commissions, Courts and Observers Shape Incentives for Election Manipulation and Post-Electoral Protest." *Journal of Politics* 77, no. 2: 407–20.

Szajkowski, Bogdan. 1999. "Elections and Electoral Politics in Macedonia." *Transitions* 1/2: 55–82.

Taylor, Charles Fernandes, Jon C. W. Pevehouse, and Scott Straus. 2017. "Perils of Pluralism: Electoral Violence and Incumbency in Sub-Saharan Africa." *Journal of Peace Research* 54, no. 3: 397–411.

Taylor, Steven L. 2009. *Voting amid Violence: Electoral Democracy in Colombia*. Boston: Northeastern University Press.

Teorell, Jan, Stefan Dahlberg, Sören Holmberg, Bo Rothstein, Anna Khomenko, and Richard Svensson. 2017. *The QOG Standard Dataset 2017: Codebook*. The Quality of Government Standard Dataset, version Jan17. Gothenburg: University of Gothenburg, The Quality of Government Institute (http://www.qog.pol.gu.se). doi:10.18157/QoGStdJan17.

Thompson, Mark R. 1998. "The Marcos Regime in the Philippines." In *Sultanistic Regimes*, edited by H. E. Chehabi and Juan J. Linz, 206–29. Baltimore: Johns Hopkins University Press.

Thompson, Mark R., and Philipp Kuntz. 2004. "Stolen Elections: The Case of the Serbian October." *Journal of Democracy* 15, no. 4: 159–72.

———. 2006. "After Defeat?: When Do Rulers Steal Elections?" In *Electoral Authoritarianism: The Dynamics of Unfree Competition*, edited by A. Schedler, 113–28. Boulder, CO: Lynne Rienner.

Tilly, Charles. 1978. *From Mobilization to Revolution*. Reading, MA: Addison-Wesley.

———. 2004. *Contention and Democracy in Europe, 1650–2000*. Cambridge: Cambridge University Press.

Toros, Emre, and Sarah Birch. 2019. "Who Are the Targets of Familial Electoral Coercion?: Evidence from Turkey." *Democratization*. Published online ahead of print. doi:10.1080/13510347.2019.1639151.

Transparency International. 2017. "Corruption Perceptions Index 2017: Technical Methodology Note." Accessed October 18, 2019. https://www.transparency.org/news/feature/corruption_perceptions_index_2017.

Treisman, Daniel. 2000. "The Causes of Corruption: A Cross-National Study." *Journal of Public Economics* 76: 399–457.

Tronvoll, Kjetil, and Tobias Hagmann. 2012. "Introduction: Traditional Authorities and Multiparty Elections in Ethiopia." In *Contested Power in Ethiopia: Traditional Authorities and Multi-Party Elections*, edited by Tronvoll and Hagmann, 1–29. Leiden: Brill.

Tucker, Joshua A. 2007. "Enough!: Electoral Fraud, Collective Action Problems, and Post-Communist Colored Revolutions." *Perspectives on Politics* 5, no. 3: 535–51.

Tversky, Amos, and Daniel Kahneman. 2000. "Advances in Prospect Theory: Cumulative Representation of Uncertainty." In *Choices, Values and Frames*, edited by Kahneman and Tversky, 44–65. Cambridge: Russell Sage Foundation and Cambridge University Press.

Ulloa, Felix. 2001. "Haiti." In *Elections in the Americas: A Data Handbook*, vol. 1, *North America, Central America and the Caribbean*, edited by Dieter Nohlen, 373–98. Oxford: Oxford University Press.

UNDP (United Nations Development Program). 2009. *Elections and Conflict Prevention: A Guide to Planning and Programming*. New York: UNDP Democratic Governance Group, Bureau for Development Policy.

Vanderhill, Rachel. 2012. *Promoting Authoritarianism Abroad*. Boulder, CO: Lynne Rienner.

Van de Walle, Nicholas. 2006. "Tipping Games? When Do Opposition Parties Coalesce?" In *Electoral Authoritarianism: The Dynamics of Unfree Competition*, edited by Andreas Schedler, 77–94. Boulder, CO: Lynne Rienner.

Van Ham, Carolien, and Staffan I. Lindberg. 2015. "From Sticks to Carrots: Electoral Manipulation in Africa, 1986–2012." *Government and Opposition* 5, no. 3: 521–48.

Wahman, Michael, and Edward Goldring. 2020. "Pre-electoral Violence and Territorial Control: Political Dominance and Subnational Election Violence in Africa." *Journal of Peace Research* 57, no. 1: 93–110.

Wanyama, Fredrick O., and Jørgen Elklit. 2018. "Electoral Violence during Party Primaries in Kenya." *Democratization* 25, no. 6: 1016–32.

Weeden, Lisa. 1998. "Acting 'as if': Symbolic Politics and Social Control in Syria." *Comparative Studies in Society and History* 40, no. 3: 503–23.

Weidmann, Nils, and Michael Callen. 2013. "Violence and Election Fraud: Evidence from Afghanistan." *British Journal of Political Science* 43, no. 1: 53–75.

Wilkinson, Steven I. 2000. "Democratic Consolidation and Failure: Lessons from Bangladesh and Pakistan." *Democratization* 7, no. 3: 203–26.

———. 2004. *Votes and Violence: Electoral Competition and Ethnic Riots in India*. Cambridge: Cambridge University Press.

Wilkinson, Steven I., and Christopher J. Haid. 2009. "Ethnic Violence as Campaign Expenditure: Riots, Competition, and Vote Swings in India." Working paper.

Willemsen, Heinz. 2006. "Former Yugoslav Republic of Macedonia: Persisting Structural Constraints to Democratic Consolidation." *Southeast European and Black Sea Studies* 6, no. 1: 83–101.

Williams, Richard A. L. 2017. "Catalonia Referendum: Firefighters Attacked by Spanish Police as They Form Human Shield to Protect Voters." *Independent*, 1 October, 2017. https://www.independent.co.uk/news/world/europe/catalonia-referendum-firefighters-spanish-police-beaten-attacked-independence-human-shield-barcelona-a7976766.html.

Wilson, A. 2005a. *Ukraine's Orange Revolution*. New Haven, CT: Yale University Press.

———. 2005b. *Virtual Politics: Faking Democracy in the Post-Soviet World*. New Haven, CT: Yale University Press.

Wintrobe, Ronald. 1998. *The Political Economy of Dictatorship*. Cambridge: Cambridge University Press.

Young, Lauren E. 2017. "Mobilization under Threat: Emotional Appeals and Dissent in Autocracy." Working paper. Accessed October 18, 2019. http://www.laurenelyssayoung.com/wp-content/uploads/2016/05/party_experiment_20150826.pdf.

———. 2020. "Who Dissents?: Self-Efficacy and Opposition Action after State-Sponsored Election Violence." *Journal of Peace Research* 57, no. 1: 62–76.

Zorbas, Eugenia, and Vincent Tohbi. 2011. "Election-Related Conflict Resolution Mechanisms: The 2006 Elections in the Democratic Republic of Congo." In *Elections in Dangerous Places: Democracy and the Paradoxes of Peacebuilding*, edited by David Gillies, 90–104. Montreal: McGill-Queens University Press.

Zvobgo, Tafadzwa. 2018. "Female Perpetrators of Electoral Violence in Zimbabwe." Paper presented at the Electoral Violence Workshop, University of Amsterdam, February 15–16, 2018.

INDEX

Page numbers in italics refer to figures and tables in the text.

A NOTE ON THE TYPE

This book has been composed in Adobe Text and Gotham.
Adobe Text, designed by Robert Slimbach for Adobe,
bridges the gap between fifteenth- and sixteenth-century
calligraphic and eighteenth-century Modern styles.
Gotham, inspired by New York street signs, was designed
by Tobias Frere-Jones for Hoefler & Co.

GPSR Authorized Representative: Easy Access System Europe - Mustamäe tee
50, 10621 Tallinn, Estonia, gpsr.requests@easproject.com